In loving memory of Robert H. Hoge. "As long as our stories live, we live." Let your legacy continue for generations to come.

Robert Hatcher Hoge's Autobiography: A Renaissance Man
Copyright ©2022 by Hayfield Farm, LLC.

All Rights Reserved. No part of this book may be used or reproduced in any
way without written permission except in the case except in the case of
brief quotations embodied in critical articles or reviews.

ISBN:

978-1-7372677-7-5 (paperback)
978-1-7372677-8-2 (hardcover)

For information contact:
madeline@belle-hampton.com
Belle-Hampton: www.belle-hampton.com

Robert Hunter Hoge's Autobiography
A Renaissance Man

Written by Robert H. Hoge
Compiled by Madeline S. Hoge

Forward
by Thomas Hunter Hoge

Grandpa Hoge was bigger than life to a kid that was too young to truly appreciate the worldly impact he made on those around him. For those that never had the opportunity to cross his path, he was a man of admirable strength, artistic creativity, and substantial intellectual depth, who always relished the opportunity to share his breadth of opinions with anyone willing to engage. Known to me more as a highly respected artist within the Carmel California art circles, it was not until after he passed that I learned in more detail of his extensive business success during the industrial revolution. As a family, we are blessed to have his writings to draw a bit of wisdom, family history, and a perspective on living as well as loving life that we all can benefit from. This compilation of life lessons and thoughts is valuable to anyone willing to take some time to read as a reference manual for risking getting out of one's comfort zone, an affirmation of core values that have sustained multiple generations, and a reminder of a life lived by a true "Renaissance Man."

I have, from time to time, worked on my autobiography. It now looks like I might actually get such a document written. At least, I am far enough along to carry out my intention to include some, or maybe all, of these writings, in serial form, in issues of This and That. The first chapter begins below.

CHAPTER I

CHARLESTON

I was once a little boy three years old. I know this for a fact because I can remember some important circumstances during the third year of my life. My father was a Baptist minister, and, as Southern Baptist ministers do, he was moving to a new location where the Lord had called him. We, his family of five, were arriving in Charleston, S.C. coming from Onancock, Virginia.

I, of course, do not remember all the details of the move. I was told about many of the circumstances later in life, but I do vividly remember approaching our new home in a horse and buggy conveyance down a narrow red brick street. The houses on either side seemed so close. The excitement of the event taking place must have been built up by the total experience of moving. I recall an urgent sense of importance to the simple fact of our arrival at our new place, the parsonage, located on Church Street close to Battery Park. The park was built beside the Ashley and Cooper rivers where they joined and flowed into the sea.

The front door of our new home opened onto a porch that faced a side yard. The end of the porch next to the street was walled in, and a door through the wall opened directly onto the sidewalk. The porch ran the entire length of the house. The yard beside the porch was a narrow strip that included an entrance driveway bordered with flowers. The driveway led to a larger enclosed area behind the house. The driveway was also separated from the street by a high wooden fence at its end. The fence was embellished with some modest floral designs, and through it was an arched gateway to the street; there was an ornamental double wooden gate that closed across the arch. The back of our neighbor's house was along the driveway, but it presented only a single wall without windows. There was complete privacy in the yard and on our long porch.

The porch served two purposes: it was a front porch and a back porch. Tall green shutter blinds, built as double swinging doors, separated the front from the back about half way along the full length. This kind of blinds was familiar to me even at three years old, because they were a common sight on tall windows on the Eastern Shore of Virginia, from which we had just arrived. My surprise was in seeing what I knew as window blinds being used as doors swinging on hinges in two directions. I swung upon the doors in fascinated joy.

I ran all over the house and yard investigating everything. There were fireplaces in every room upstairs and down. These attracted my special attention; I leaned in or climbed in each fireplace, and looked up the chimney where daylight could be seen above.

Through double doors, from the front section of the porch, one entered the house through an adequate entrance hall. Directly ahead in the hall were steps leading to the upstairs. These steps were composed of two flights; the the first flight lifted one to a landing half way up the ascent, The second flight continued from the landing, in a reverse direction, and reached an upstairs hall. Two bedrooms and an upstairs long porch, that ran atop the lower one the full length of the house, were joined to this hall.

To one's right on entering the hall downstairs was a parlor later furnished with antiques, some of which had gone beyond that stage. A few of my mother's prized parlor chairs were of questionable safety for a heavy person. This parlor became a room that was kept spotless and was used only for very special visitors.

To one's left on entering the hall was a large room that became our family room. Across the room from the entering door was a large fireplace. This became a place of remembrances of evenings spent around the fire with my father, being the good father, telling his son interesting stories of his childhood in Virginia.

To the right of the fireplace was a door that opened into a room that became our dining room. This room was the same dimension across the house as the living room but not so deep in the other direction. The effect was to form a long room across the house that perfectly accommodated an extensive dining room table. The same chimney that vented the family room fireplace served a similar fireplace in the dining room; the fireplaces were built back to back in the wall between the rooms.

Across the dining room, on the same end of the room as the door joining the living room, was an entrance to a butler's pantry; this small area was followed by the kitchen and, on beyond, connecting sheds for storing canned and other nonperishable foods. There were still more sheds for garden tools, wood and coal. These sheds were obviously later additions to the finished house: they were one story high with sheet metal roofs; they gave the house, when viewed from the side yard, an appearance of tapering down and away -- very slender on the terminal end.

Beyond these sheds was a fair sized yard that spread out from the driveway, and continued behind the house. From the far end of the sheds, and joined to them, was a fence that ran diagonally across the yard to join, at its other end, a large barn. The yard behind the fence was to be the paddock for our horse. The barn contained plenty of room for our horse and buggy which was our means of transportation in 1907. All the otherwise open sides of our property, as were the other properties in the neighborhood, were enclosed by high, wide board, fences that gave a great sense of privacy, even though the lots were not large, and house followed house along the entire length of Church street.

In spite of the fact that segregation of the races was practiced in those days, our next door neighbors, on one side, were Negroes. The children in the family were among my playmates. Their neighborliness, long before our laws demanded an end to discrimination, demonstrated the unfairness and foolishness of the Jim Crow laws that preceded this human rights legislation. The property had been in their family for generations, and as fashionable upper middle class whites developed the area the blacks on that lot were not to be dispossessed. Therefore there is no great lesson in fairness represented in the presence of this one black family in an otherwise totally white neighborhood in the deep south. There is, though, a credit to both sides that they lived in peace and friendship. This was the home we came to on Church street.

Church street began at Battery Park, which was several city blocks from our home, and continued past our home to a marketing area about the same distance in the other direction. Along the way in this direction, one would pass a church resembling a Grecian temple, with tall Doric columns supporting a gable roof above a stone floored porch two steps above ground level. This was the church at which my father was to be the pastor, the First Baptist Church of Charleston, South Carolina.

I was to accumulate many fond memories of this edifice. Among these are memories of companionship with my father as he took me with him about the church on errands connected with the duties of his profession. Dad seemed to even feel responsible that the windows were properly closed. Either that or he wanted an excuse to visit the church after hours or an excuse to take his son for a walk. Whatever the reason, we often strolled down Church Street in the early evening, and stopped in at the church to see how things were. I particularly remember my father checking out the large windows. While I do not remember their exact construction, I recall that they combined beautiful stained glass sections with lower sections that opened for ventilation.

I too learned to love the church. This was at a time when I had no theological concepts, and the church was just a beautiful building in which I had had, and was having, happy experiences. Not only did my father let me hang about him, I think he encouraged it.

The Church services to me were music, singing and my father talking in the pulpit. I could also see that he was honored by his congregation, and that made me proud. My Sunday school teachers were loving mothers doing their bit by teaching or taking kids on picnics. The Bible stories were just good stories. I even now remember this church as one remembers a house that's been a happy home. We, my playmates and I, played among the tombstones in the burial ground. Combined with some adjacent lots containing private homes and the grounds of St. Michael's famous Episcopal Church, on Meeting street, the grounds of the Baptist Church became a regular short cut to school and to our downtown area around the post office.

It is difficult to believe that, in four years from 3 to 7, a young boy could learn to love a neighborhood so that it became a life long pleasure to recall, but the fact is I did. The section of Charleston in which this part of my story lies is called the historic section, or just Old Charleston. It includes Charleston's famous battery park with Civil War cannon on display. A long sea wall protected two sides of the park from the arm of the ocean formed by the two rivers that join there. The wall also flanked East Battery Street and Murray Blvd. that contained several blocks of antebellum homes. These homes are still kept in repair, recalling the great days of Charleston before the Civil War. At the end of the wall on East Battery, there was a yacht club. By a kindly caretaker, I was allowed to play about the grounds.

Meeting street was paved with cobblestones. Both sides of the street, beginning at St.Michael's on one corner and the Post Office on the other for many city blocks, was lined with imposing homes of a bygone era. The street ended at the water front.

After several years our horse and buggy days ended. My father bought a one cylinder Reo automobile. The motor that drove the automobile was located under the single seat of the contraption. A large flywheel, necessary to smooth out the impulses of a one cylinder engine, was encased between the spaces provided for two occupants of the seat. Since the engine was positioned across the car, the person starting it stood on the right side of the vehicle and used a hand crank. The rear wheels were driven by two chains, like very large bicycle chains, that were driven by and drove sprockets, one on each end of the motor shaft and one on each rear wheel. The tires were designed after old fashioned buggy tires of solid rubber. They bounced and bumped over the cobblestones of many Charleston streets.

There must have been a top for the automobile, but my memory contains only pictures of my father and I riding under clear skies and, I suppose, a hot sun at times. I remember particularly rides down Meeting Street: There was a steady rhythm of bumps over the cobblestone pavement. My father in all the dignity of his ministry would frequently tip his hat from the car as he passed lady parishioners upon the sidewalk.

The seat upon which we sat was perfectly flat with a long stuffed removable cushion. The steering wheel came up completely vertical from the floor. To steer, one sat erect. I can see my father now making a slight bow to the ladies, and removing his derby hat with pride and graciousness.

Our family life in Charleston covered a four year period. My memory is not continuous, it is made up of instances that for one reason or another were impressed upon it. To recall these instances should bring to light the story as it was seen by one small boy and may reveal influences that have continued through his life.

Our family of five consisted of, in addition to mother and father, me, a brother two years older and a sister sixteen years older. She, at the time of our arrival in Charleston, was nineteen and was actually not in the buggy that came down Church street. She was away at college, Cox College, in Roanoke, Virginia. Because of the large difference in our ages and her school attendance, I remember very little about my sister during this period, and that on occasions when she was home for her holidays from school.

The memories are all pleasant except one, and that occasion only proved she was a young girl that might tease little brother. It seems I must have done a bit of whining, at times, to get what I wanted. At least, this time Anne was calling me "Whine Box," and I would whine all the more trying to get her to stop it. She would go to the telephone, crank it, and pretend she was talking to museums or the police dept. asking them if they would like to come over and pick up a whine box. This caused me what is referred to in the courts as pain and suffering, and left me with a permanent memory of the instance, but I cannot recall whining since.

My brother, James Fulton, was only two and a half years my senior, but still I remember very little about him. He was given a goat and a wagon, and Jim rode all over historic Charleston in style. He would not let me drive his steed, and I remember few rides in his wagon. There is a dim remembrance of disappointment in this connection but nothing that seems to have made a significant difference to the pleasure of our days.

When one is a child, the days are endless and full of wonderful things to do. I assume that, at our ages then, two and a half years made a big difference, and that my brother lived in his world, and I in mine. He comes in and out of the pictures, in my memory of these times, as a person I contacted briefly and occasionally without any significant connection to the events of the passing days during our sojourn in Charleston.

My mother took me one night for a walk along the Battery wall. The moon was full on this balmy South Carolina night. There was a bright star very close to the moon, bright enough to be seen in the glow of the moon. My mother was moved by the night and our association. She talked to me in words of great warmth, not all of which I can recall. I do recall her saying," I am like that moon and you are the small bright star so close beside me,"

That night made on me a tremendous impression. I was aware of nothing specific, but somehow I could tell that my mother was troubled about something, and I had been chosen for her companion on a walk to clear her feelings. What troubled her I never knew, probably something of the passing moment, but I was given a sense of importance that has never left me. It was my first experience of being conscious of a special filial affection and of being a lady's support in time of need.

Another source of pride, at that time of my life, was associated with a Gospel wagon. I certainly had no theological views at that age, and the drama that was enacted in and from the back of the wagon, and my father's part in the performance, mattered greatly without any interference from theological opinion. The wagon was pulled by two horses that, with feed bags on their heads, were willing to wait any length of time.

I believe the driver of the wagon and the sexton of the church were the same person. The wagon was specially built for the service: There were two seats, one on each side of its body, that ran the entire length of the wagon, except for the spaces occupied by the driver's seat and a special platform extending from the rear end. On this platform was a podium and ample space for the minister to stand while he preached to the people who, it was hoped, would fill the area behind the wagon.

I am sure that the places to park and hold services were chosen in advance to assure audience space, and to attract an audience considered most in need of the gospel that would be preached. The expressed purpose, of these services, was to save souls by bringing sinners to "the acceptance of Christ as their personal savior."

The attack was well arranged. Lining both sides of the wagon, good members of the church sat upon the provided seats, and passionately sang the old hymns in volume and well articulated words that would bear their message. These people were the choir for the service and, in all likelihood, were the regular choir members of the Church doing extra duty. There were more women than men.

One specific time I recall an outdoor service, It was at the intersection of Water street and Church street. These streets do not meet at right angles. Church street is offset and Water street widens at the intersection so as to provide a spacious plaza. It is reported that during pre-Civil War days slave auctions were held regularly in this plaza. Possibly, there was some sort of special appropriateness in Gospel services being conducted beside the old slave market.

I remember so well standing on the sidewalk on Water street, toward the Battery end, looking up at my father standing behind the podium on the back of the wagon, preaching in a loud voice, to all and sundry. Passion showed in his flashing eyes, and conviction in his deliberate assertions of what he believed to be the truth. I was simply fascinated; I had never seen a show so good. I was proud; It was my father who was the center of the interested crowd.

I surely did not understand what was being said, but I believed it was being well said. When the preaching stopped the choir sang with gusto to the music of a small organ. I knew this was a very special moment: They sang resoundingly, "Oh Lamb of God I come," and other old hymns, calculated to bring the sinners up to the back of the wagon to shake hands with my father and, symbolically, make a declaration of repentance and acceptance.

And people did come up in noticeable numbers. Spontaneous cries of amen! and praise the Lord! were to be heard on every hand. To a small boy the whole thing was a wonder to behold. A child sees the drama and feels the excitement. He does not reason about, or debate the credibility of, what the preacher is saying. Christ made the point when He said, "Unless you come as a little child..."

Vehicle traffic was almost nonexistent at that time on Church Street in Charleston. The street in front of our house was, to me, an extended play area. I remember one day being very busy out there with a toy wagon that I used to haul, about the area, whatever was the the current project. My father, noticeably solicitous, came up to me with a strange man. It surprises me the degree to which children sense the feelings of adults who are significant to their lives. I recall the very special consideration being shown me on this occasion. The strange man was a surgeon, and I was about to have an operation; my father was the concerned parent preparing his son for the ordeal. However, for me it was to be no ordeal: I trusted my father and, by transference, the surgeon who was going to operate.

For some weeks there had been a swelling on the side of my neck, just below the right jaw. I do not know what the medical diagnosis was, but the decision was to have it out. We went into the parlor of our house, and I was asked to lie down on a davenport, with a pillow under my head. As I recall the instance, I rather enjoyed so much unusual attention. My face was covered with a cloth, and a cool liquid was poured onto the cloth. I know now that it was chloroform.

I do not recall any unpleasantness connected with the event. In fact, the experience stands out in my mind as a special occasion that, at the time, gave me a sense of importance. I remember coming out of a deep sleep with a bandage about my neck, and with my father and his friend, still being the souls of kindness, showing me great consideration. My memory ends at that point, but I assume I healed soon and well, because all I have as a reminder of the experience is a very small scar on my neck.

How soon does a child become conscious of the opposite sex? Someone younger than I was at that time would have to be asked. I was getting along in life, probably 5 or 6 years old. There lived, across the street from us, a girl who, to me, was pretty and sweet. I do not know that I used any words to describe my feelings, but I used every opportunity to be around her, and to make some type of physical contact, even if only to touch her hand.

There was another girl in the neighborhood, older than I, a playmate of my brother Jim's. I also remember her with fond recall, but she spurned my advances. Being a bit over eight years old, she could not take one so young seriously.

For the scientific value of reporting accurately, I remember comprehending some undefined significance to what was going on in these contacts, and I definitely felt drives to repeat each warm and friendly encounter. Even though I had this ongoing interest I did not develop into a six year old Casanova.

During the fall of 1985 Halley's Comet was of exciting interest in the news: there was scarcely a publication that did not have something to say about the comet and its history. One of the things I remember vividly about our life in Charleston was the advent of the same Halley's Comet in 1910. There was pronounced excitement then, frequent conversations at meal time, and explanations in Sunday school and church.

Many people believed the end of the world was at hand. My father preached sermons to quiet the fears of some of his congregation. During the period, when the comet was predicted to be at its nearest point to the earth, some of the Charlestonians left the city and pitched tents in the countryside. Outdoor prayer services were held at times around the clock; this was particularly an expression of concern among the black population, but they were not alone in their superstitious fears.

One night when the viewing was expected to be good my father took me up on the roof of our house, and we saw the comet with the naked eye. It was certainly bright enough to leave an impression, but I could not testify to its technical magnitude. I remember it only as a light object in the sky with an extension on one side described to me as its tail. The tail was not the dramatic thing I later saw in painted pictures, and it was not quite what I had expected from the advance talk, but the comet as a whole left a special memory that became more special after its 1985 return to our skies.

I do not know the date, but at approximately the time of the comet another event left an indelible impression: There was a hurricane. Reports at the time stated that the storm was the worst on record for that area. I have a clear memory of the experience expanded by what my parents said at the time and for years after, as they recounted, to new acquaintances and old friends, what happened on that alarming night.

The wind came up early in the afternoon and by evening it was a gale. The official reports mentioned sustained velocities of 125 miles per hour and gusts above that. The tide came in and stayed in: It was held to a high level by the force of the wind that carried huge waves over the the battery wall into the streets and eventually into the homes along the water front.

The section of Church Street where our home was located was higher ground than the surrounding streets and all of Battery Park. We were spared water in our living area.

Nevertheless, in the early evening, the street was a running river on which floated all manner of home utilities. In numbers, garbage cans, washtubs, chairs, tables, children's toys, and even pieces of picket fences composed a water parade that I watched, in fascination, through our parlor window.

The water eventually covered our high long porch, which was several feet above ground level, and began to seep under our front door into the front hall. It spread, and we had some water damage on the first floor. I do not know its extent. The fortunate fact is that we did not get water above the first floor.

In homes along Water Street, just one block from our home, on a lower level, some people spent the night upstairs on tables to keep above the water that had inundated their lower floors, and risen to about table height on the second floor. The roofs of many of these houses were blown off early in the evening, and people upstairs, on their table tops, were drenched with rain throughout the night.

Slate roofs were ripped off, rows of slate at a time. The individual slates were sent zip-zip-zip across the street into the the siding of the houses there. They penetrated with force, and some slates became anchored in the siding like little black shelves irregularly spaced.

Trees could be heard falling, roofs crashing as they were torn from homes. Our own home cracked, creaked and swayed at random with the wind. In those days I slept in a trundle bed that rolled under my parents bed for storage. It was pulled out this night; my parents wanted me to go to bed, storm or no storm. I did so for a few minutes, but soon got up because my bed was rolling back and forth across the floor as the house swayed in the wind.

I do not recall that my parents were very alarmed. I think that, as the storm settled into a steady pounding, they began to realize that their house was well built and was going to hold.

The drama of the storm was witnessed again after dawn when the wind died down, and we took to the streets to see the damage, and hear the stories of other experiences in the Charleston area.

Diagonally across from our house, on the corner where Church street intersected a short street leading to the battery, was a vacant lot. An old tree, not too vigorous, but proud, stood in the corner of the lot leaning slightly against a substantial house. I had discovered some limbs on the tree that joined each other in crotches. These joints offered ideal support for a tree house. Over a period of time I had appropriated enough lumber and nails to build a platform supported by these limbs, and had erected sides to form a house. The roof was a canvas tarpaulin.

My first investigation was to determine if my tree house was still there. The tree was still standing, stripped of most of its leaves and some of its branches, but not its main limbs, and my house was intact minus its roof. I was very proud and pleased. All about the area trees were down, fences and indescribable debris were in the middle of the street, and roofs of houses were in various stages of destruction.

Along the water front, behind the battery wall, were severely damaged boats, of all description, that had been floated over the wall on waves reputed to be as high as small houses. These waves had also crashed into the palatial and historic homes apposing the Battery wall. Large windows, reaching from the floor to the ceiling, were broken out by small craft that still rested in the window frames, as though the frames were their berths. Front porches, or piazzas as they are called in Charleston, were crushed by falling trees. The whole area looked like the disaster scenes that appear on television too frequently.

I was too young to take all this in specifically, but the general impression of wonder and surprise is still vivid in my mind, and I have some specifics that were described, time and again, by my elders for a long time after the storm: They insisted that cotton seed blown from local cotton patches were buried, by the force of the wind, like rifle shots in the bark of trees in many places throughout the city. The nearby Charleston Navy Yard reported that a very heavy sheet of steel, used to back up targets during gun practice, was lifted by the wind, and carried over the city like a kite. It was deposited on a farm forty miles from its starting point.

Radio and television did not exist at that time, and communication was relatively slow and inefficient. The early accounts of the hurricane in newspapers from New York, Chicago and other large cities exaggerated the disaster. One paper reported that the only people who survived the hurricane and flood clung to the tops of church steeples. It was not that bad, but it was a storm to remember, and its impression upon me as a child is still vivid.

It seems strange to me that when I was only three years old strong impressions were made in my memory about our move to Charleston, but I remembered nothing about leaving Charleston and arriving in Richmond Va., when I was seven, in a move we made to that city..

The Lord's Prayer is a masterpiece of simplicity, while at the same time being fully comprehensive. In a few words one says all that is needed in divine supplication and worship. The poem below is intended only to point with reverence to these facts.

Amen

Our Father who in Heaven art,
Are also in one's mind and heart,
Hallowed thy name, love finds you there.
May Thy will be done everywhere.

"Give us this day our daily bread."
A small request, the way its said,
But trespasses are so much more.
Forgive us these we do implore.

Lead us through temptation's luring,
Deliver us from evil erring.
Thine is the Kingdom held in store,
And the glory for evermore.

From The Lords Prayer
R. H. Hoge

CHAPTER II

RICHMOND 1911-1912

Richmond, Virginia is an interesting city with its present beauty and noble history, but it must not have seemed that way to a seven year old critic who was comparing it to the city he had just left behind. My memory of Richmond, during the two years that we lived there, is made up of instances that lack sequence and consistent relationships. I simply did not develop the affection for Richmond that I had for Charleston. In memory I just find myself in Richmond: I do not remember any special experience of arriving and discovering with excitement our new home, as had been the case when we arrived in Charleston.

My first recollection is the memory of a small scenario concerning my being admitted to school. My father and I were in conference with a man who I assume was the school principal. The discussion concerned to which grade I would be assigned. A test was being made of my education: The principal said, "Son how do you spell all right?" I knew how to spell "all," and I knew how to spell "right;" so, I spelled the two words in sequence, got 100, and was promptly put in the second grade instead of the first. I, of course, had been credited with knowing that, at that time, "alright" was improper; even today Webster shows it as substandard usage. Actually, I did not know anything about the correct usage, but the appearance that I did made the right impression on the academic nature of my interlocutor, and probably saved me a year of schooling time.

From the principal's office I was escorted to a classroom, given a desk, a pad of brown paper and a pencil, and told to write. I do not remember the subject of my writing. I do remember the year in the date that I wrote at the top of the page, 1911, which establishes the time of our move to Richmond.

I also remember another introduction to our new community. The weather was cold, real cold, not at all like the balmy climate of Charleston, S.C.. On the way home from school, which seemed a very long distance in the circumstances: the wind blew and my nose ran, and what came out froze below my nose. I cried a bit, and the moisture produced on my chin also froze. I arrived home uncomfortable and very unhappy, crying as I tried to make the situation clear to my parents.

Another introduction to the colder climate of Virginia, as compared to South Carolina, was a sled ride down a long hill well known to people who have driven along Broad street in

Incidentally

In This and That issue #24 I explained that I was beginning an autobiography, and started with a few pages of life in Charleston, S.C.. For several issues it will be my intention to entitle each biographical section by the city in which we are living at the time. This can be done for some issues because, as a Minister, my father, through some periods, moved every several years to a new church.

Issue #25 includes details from our sojourn in Richmond, Va. and consequently the several pages are entitled "Richmond."

I have made the above comments primarily because there are some new individuals on my mailing list who otherwise might wonder how Richmond got into "Thoughts On This and That." That's how, and special greetings to newcomers.

R. H. Hoge

Richmond. The hill is a classic in that city, and goes by the obvious name, Broad Street Hill. The street we lived on parallelled that main thoroughfare; we had the same long hill without the distinctive name. I was glad to join new playmates. We took lengthy sled rides that gathered momentum on the down hill course, accomplishing frightening but pleasantly exciting speeds.

On the icy and snow covered sidewalks foot traffic was nil. We confined our rides to the side walk, and block after block we crossed intersecting streets. With the street traffic today, crossing street intersections bellybusting on a sled could easily be fatal; even in 1911 it was dangerous. On one down hill ride the danger became all too real: about halfway down the long run, traveling at a breathtaking speed, I approached an intersection with my head down; I looked up and was startled, almost to panic, to see a wagon slowly crossing and completely blocking my path. The mind works fast at such times: I swung slightly to my right, and passed between the front and rear wheels. Under the wagon, I straightened slightly to the left, and came out safely between the wheels on the downhill side, and continued at high speed the rest of my journey to the bottom of the hill.

A minister's home is usually provided in the neighborhood of the church, but when we first arrived in Richmond the parsonage was not ready, and temporary quarters were provided quite far from the church building. As I remember the setup, we lived for a short interval in one half of a duplex. The property had a large, fence enclosed, back yard. This play area was supplemented by two alleys that intersected at right angles behind our place. These were wonderful places to play games like hide and seek, to catch baseball, or to just mess around. I do not remember much in detail about our temporary home except the alleyways in which the children of the neighborhood spent much of their time.

A project, participated in only by my brother and me, had as its purpose the creation of a small steam engine. Using a discarded syrup can, we punctured two small holes in the sides of the can, near the top, exactly opposite to each other. We then prepared a straight round stick approximately 3/16" in diameter and a couple of inches longer than the diameter of the can. A lengthwise slit, about one and one-half inches long, was made in the middle of the stick measured from end to end. A rectangular piece of tin was cut to fit tightly in the slit and extend about an inch on either side of the stick.

The assembly procedure for the whole machine was: first, slide the stick through the two holes in the sides of the can, with equal amounts of the excess length extending from each side; then, reach in the can, and push the sliver of tin into the prepared slit and completely through the center of the stick. The extended ends of tin on each side of the stick were to function as turbine blades for our steam engine.

After assembly the can was partially filled with water. A small hole was punctured in the center of the metal lid, and the lid was then pressed firmly into the grooves that secured it to the can. A couple of bricks constituted a furnace. The can was placed in a lying down position supported by a brick on each side. There was space for a small fire between the bricks and under the can. The concept was that when the water commenced to boil off the steam rushing out of the small hole would create rapid directed motion near the hole inside the can. This motion acting upon our turbine blades would rotate the stick, and so a steam engine.

It worked, but with almost tragic consequences: the can overheated, and the lid commenced to move to release the steam. With my brother behind and me in front we tried, with long sticks, to hold the lid in against the pressure. Nevertheless, it came out with a bang; the can left its base with violence, spun in the air, and drenched my face with boiling water.

The doctor came; he salved my face, and, with eyes, mouth and nose only exposed, bandaged my head. We were all assured that after a slow recovery there would be no scars. My principle memory is of surprise how, after the first shock of the water hitting my face, it felt so cool; yes cool. It must have been a quick reaction caused by cool air and accelerated evaporation immediately following the splash of hot water on my face. The doctor was right in his prognosis: except for some days of discomfort wearing bandages over my entire head there were no negative consequences from the scalding.

In the other half of our duplex home there lived an older boy who noticeably was a boy scout: he strutted in his uniform. I envied his fine accouterments. They looked so important. He liked to tease me by insisting that he was a real soldier, and might at any time have to go to war. I didn't quite believe him, but there was enough credibility in his story to arouse my jealousy and, at the same time, my admiration. Some years later, when I was old enough to become a Scout, I understood this neighbor better. I also felt proud of my uniform, almost to the point of treating it as a fetish. It always had a meaning for me beyond just an article of clothing. Maybe I strutted too.

Traveling for a short distance down the alley that ran beside our house, and then to the right along an intersecting alley, I could arrive at a street that remained unfamiliar to me except for a house on the corner where the alley intersected the street: in that house lived a cousin whom we, nevertheless, called Aunt Annie. She was beautiful, and I was in love with her. She was probably 35 years old, and I seven or eight. I spent as much of my time as possible in her home, glad to run errands for her or pretend errands from our place.

My father and her husband were close friends and the two families active relatives. He continued to think well of me, as he proved some years later, without the slightest sign of jealousy over my youthful infatuation with his beautiful wife. When we lived in Norfolk Virginia he, as a member of the governor's staff, was able to pull the right strings to get me a birth for one month on a pilot boat in the Norfolk harbor, and that he did. That was a great experience which belongs in the eventual chapter on Norfolk.

I have mentioned earlier the very long hill that runs through Richmond in the direction of Broad Street and many parallel streets. While exploring our neighborhood, I found that many of the streets crossing these parallel streets at right angles eventually led to dead end barriers beyond which the land fell abruptly away. One was left standing on the hill top with a precipitous cliff just beyond the barrier.

As a child, it was thrilling to view such a large section of Richmond. It aroused in me some inner sense of importance, almost like being "Lord of all I surveyed". This experience was repeated as often as possible, and it left an impression on me that made me fond of high places with lookouts upon natural or man made scenery. My sense of perspective on a vista point is often associated with these early incidental experiences.

During the couple months that we lived in the temporary parsonage I am sure we attended all church services as becomes a minister's family, but, strangely, I do not recall even having seen the the building until we moved to permanent quarters located on the same street with the church. Again I made comparisons: The plain brick church expressed the rectangular architecture, with the inevitable corner tower, that I was later to recognize as Southern Baptist or maybe Methodist. It had none of the charm that I loved in the Greek temple design represented in the First Baptist Church of Charleston. The houses along the street were just as plain and repetitious, being, block on block, obviously built from the same blueprints. One of these houses was the parsonage.

In fact the houses were so alike that one night, after a young peoples meeting, I came home and went directly toward what I thought to be my room on the second floor. I was met at the door by a strange man who plainly understood the situation. He informed me that I lived next door, and in a kindly manner escorted me back down stairs and onto his front porch from which I quickly went home.

The street on which we lived also ended abruptly at a precipitous cliff from which one could view a sizable section of Richmond, but this section was not all beautiful: it emphasized the fact that segregation was practiced in Richmond and probably that district deserved to be called a black ghetto. Sometimes, the snobbish and disrespectful name of "Nigger Town" could be heard. The white children never ventured down the hill and the black ones never came up. At the time I knew nothing different, and the situation was accepted. In looking back, I have a feeling of sadness, and am caused to think with regret about the racial struggles and tragedies that have confronted both races.

Ironically if one turned right on a cross street, very close to the dead end referred to above, where one looked down on a segregated black neighborhood, he could walk several blocks to the revered home of Jefferson Davis, the president of the Confederacy during the Civil War. It was an attractive colonial style home with an elegance that became the President's status.

So here in this neighborhood, close together, were two stark symbols: one very much alive, and the other a relic of a national problem that had been a focal point of a bloody civil war. The problem had changed its face, but it was still with us in this year of our Lord 1912 when Beverly Lacy Hoge moved into the parsonage on the street with his church.

As I said earlier, it has always surprised me that at seven and eight years old I remembered less about Richmond than I did about Charleston where we lived from the time I was three until I was seven. I can only conclude that the charm of the old section of Charleston had its effect even on a small child. Until this day, scenes of Charleston spontaneously pass through my mind more frequently than do scenes of places we lived after I was in my early teens. I can list some disconnected events in Richmond and be done with that part of my story except for one instance that deserves some detail:

The Southern Baptists are evangelical. Every service ends with an appeal to the congregation for individuals to come forward and signify their acceptance of Jesus Christ as a personal Savior. I had witnessed the ceremony repeatedly in services going back to my earliest recollection. These appeals got to me. I do not recall if I considered myself a terrible sinner at age eight, actually nearly nine, but I do recall that I felt sincerely convinced that I should come forward and be saved, as the action is designated in the Baptist Church.

I expressed my intention to my parents. There followed a family discussion as to whether or not I was old enough to understand what I was doing. I will not attempt any theological opinion, even at this time, because I have none. I do remember that it was a serious experience with me, and, to the best of my childish understanding, the step that I took had significance which I still appreciate in the sense that one feels he has reached for the best he saw at the time. Probably it does not matter which window you look through so long as you look with sincere appreciation.

My youngest sister was born in Richmond. I must have been really busy with my own things, I recall no instances connected with that happy event for my parents. Actually it was over a year before events connected with my sister Nettie remained in memory.

I had enjoyable playmates in the neighborhood but none that I recall as a special buddy. My brother Jim's two and one-half years advanced age must have caused us both to cultivate a completely different set of pals. I have no recollection of him being in my picture, or I in his, throughout the entire time after we moved to the parsonage. Our contacts must have been of a type that made no permanent impression. As I reflect upon these facts I am persuaded that a happy eight year old finds his days and interests quite sufficient and his spirit independent. Apparently he enjoys everyone but attaches himself to no one in particular.

Some of the kids in the area were not entirely benign. We had a few scraps with kids from other streets and there was some rock throwing down the hill. Fortunately the distance to the homes was too far, and no damage was done.

Traffic on the streets of Richmond in 1912 was not particularly hazardous but there were automobiles and delivery trucks. The greatest sport for the kids on our block was roller skating, and the highlight of skating sessions was getting a tow behind a delivery truck at speeds that seemed fantastic. Looking back, I am inclined to think now that the drivers knew well that we were hanging on, and regulated their speeds accordingly, but, at the time, the rides seemed like real adventure. We felt like heroes taking these daring trips for many blocks, hanging on for dear life, as our skates quivered from the high speed, and the wind blew through our hair and clothing. I confess I loved it.

One activity that I still recall with pleasure seems to have been a little advanced for a eight year old. Street cars operated on the street parallel to the one on which we lived but one block over. The ladies styles included what was known as a hobble skirt that did just that: it hobbled the wearer. What did this fact have to do with the street cars? The car steps were high and ladies alighting were hobbled to such an extent that their skirts slipped up their lower limbs as they stepped up. Some attractive legs were revealed. This phenomenon, which I accepted with appreciation, was surely a deliberate product of the fashion designers. I always paused in passing and was amused at the the show. At the time, I made no attempt to define the fascination. "Beauty is truth, and truth beauty--that is all ye know on earth, and all ye need to know."

The time came when I needed my tonsils removed or so the doctor said. I have been told since that tonsils were removed at that time as a matter of course. I do not recall any discomfort; the whole process seemed routine. My dad took me in an automobile to the hospital, and talked the while about how it was a simple operation with nothing to fear. My ignorance and my trust were such that it had not occurred to me to be the least bit alarmed about the coming operation. There was certainly no shock, and we were out of the hospital the same day. What I remember most vividly about that experience is the ice cream I was fed for several days as part of my convalescence.

Memories of Oysters, an abundance of large oysters, stays with me. Our friends in Onancock, Virginia sent them by the barrel, and we ate all we could, and shared them with the neighborhood. How many oysters a young boy can eat at a setting is not known, it is certainly over a dozen. A happy memory.

Some of the rougher kids from another section would occasionally come through our street, and fights would occur that were more frightening than harmful. However I did dramatize the fights to a realistic scenario in a dream about getting shot. In my dream the shot seemed so authentic that I could feel the penetration; I can now on recall.

As I reviewed this chapter, it seemed obvious that I missed Charleston, and did not fully open up to Richmond. Spotted and sparse memory has left that impression.

I recall few outstanding things with my family in Richmond. There were the oysters from the Eastern shore, my mother sticking a crocheting needle in her stomach, and me pulling it out, a fireplace from which coal popped out with a threatening noise, and me being with dad at my entrance to school and the hospital. I remember being about the house but have no recollection of anyone being unpleasant to me, ever, or much else done there with the others. I can only conclude it was a kindly place, and that I had a penchant for amusing myself.

The instance of pulling a crocheting needle out of my mother's stomach lets me recall her as a brave woman: Mother while holding her crochet work in her hand lifted the lid of a trunk in her room to obtain more material. She lost her hold on the lid, it dropped closed, struck the end of the needle on the way down, and drove the needle through her clothing and inches into her stomach. A crochet needle has a small hook on its end that surely must have torn flesh as I removed it. A doctor should have been in the act, but mother steeled herself and said simply, "Pull it out" which I did with one quick jerk in order not to prolong the pain. There was probably some internal bleeding, but the operation was successful; the instance was forgotten.

My last specific occasion to record about memories of Richmond takes me back to the church and its choir. The church auditorium was dominated by a stage or platform, 4 or 5 feet above its floor. The front of the stage was oval, and the ministers pulpit was near its edge in the center of the oval. As a child I felt I was looking up at majesty enthroned: On the side of the stage to the minister's left sat and sang the choir. It was always a treat to me to attend service and hear the singing. There was one woman in the choir who often sang way above the rest in a voice that possessed an inherently comical sound. Looking around the congregation I could see people smiling. I had heard gossip about this good soul singing off key in a loud voice, and it made me feel as one with the grown-ups to share the amusement of her high pitched voice every Sunday.

Without much ado my father announced one day at lunch, or dinner as we called the noon meal, that, within the week, we were moving to Norfolk Virginia where he had a call to a church in a suburb named Brambleton.

CHAPTER III

NORFOLK VIRGINIA 1913-1917

As I reflect upon our time in Norfolk Virginia I want to use the word sojourn because as a minister my father seemed to periodically heed the call to a new church. Four years is the longest I remember living at home in one place, and two years the shortest time.

As I look back on our sojourn in Norfolk I am aware of a distinct period of growth in myself that was probably the norm for boys or girls of my age. During our very early years the question of right and wrong is not an independent factor, it concerns us acutely for the moment when mother says bad boy or girl. One is not given, by such remonstrances, so much a sense of guilt as a knowledge of temporary estrangement from the parent. Later on, long before the early teens, a consciousness of right and wrong commences to take an active part in decision making, and guilt over ones actions can be felt without anyone's criticism.

I remember Norfolk as a city of many experiences new to me as a growing boy. I remember being proud of my part in many of these and, for the first time in my life, not so sure or maybe a bit ashamed of others. The matter-of-fact objectivity of very early childhood was being replaced by introspective and personal identification with what was happening. Playmates and older persons, for that matter, became more definitely people that I liked or disliked. Playmates in Charleston or Richmond have no names or faces today; they were just kids like me. Many of my playmates in Norfolk are recalled by name and the uniqueness of their personalities. Some left a lasting impression on my life.

I never knew the district limits of Brambleton, the suburb in which we lived. To me it was a certain number of streets running at right angles and a small central area formed by the intersection of Brambleton Ave., the main street of the community, with Park Ave. Each corner of this intersection contained commercial establishments. On one corner was the inevitable hardware store and a few incidental shops. Across the street was a drugstore on one corner, and a Chinese laundry and a sweet shop on the other. These were the establishments that interested me, I do not remember what the few other buildings contained.

I spent a good bit of time in the Chinese laundry. I liked the Chinese man that operated the laundry and he seemed to like me. On occasion some of the kids on the block would band together and shout in his doorway, "Ching ching Chinaman eat dead rat." With eyes that seemed to be popping from his face, he would chase us in his shuffling slippers, brandishing a very large butcher knife, shouting and making horrendous faces the while. The game was that he never caught us or had any intention of doing so. I knew even then that he enjoyed the sport as well as we.

This Chinese man, who was probably a good Buddhist, seemed to have a real affection for my father, a very good Baptist, and from time to time presented him with a box of delicious Chinese litchi nuts. For anyone not familiar with these nuts, they have a very edible, sweet, raisin-like, pulp that surrounds a single large seed all enclosed in a rough, brown, papery shell. Dad passed on to me a generous share of these nuts which I am sure increased my affection for the Chinese.

The sweet shop was popular when money was available for ice cream or candy. There was also a great moral battle about the Tutti Frutti ice cream available. The Baptist of Norfolk were Temperance people. I do not know why they used the word temperance, because they were firmly opposed to a single drop of liquor. The point of objection was that Tutti Frutti ice cream was reputed to contain a touch of brandy or wine. I was taught that there was probably no crime worse than eating this iniquitous ice cream. My mother was emphatic that no child of her's was to be taken down the primrose path on Tutti Frutti. There was a tremendous sense of enjoying the forbidden as I ate the very rich pink ice cream that was delicious in its own right.

We lived on Windsor Ave. one block over from Park, and parallel to Park. My father's church was across the street from the parsonage about four residential lots to the left, as you faced Windsor Avenue from the front of our property, toward Brambleton Ave. The block between Brambleton Ave. on our left, and the street to our right, nameless to me now, became an extension to our very ample front yard as a place to play. It was more than that, it was a playground for all the neighborhood kids, and in this block we played the rough game of roller skate hockey. We also just skated, rode bicycles, caught baseball and played several different games of marbles. In the latter we again ran into Church doctrine:

Our favorite game of marbles was called roly holey. A hole about three inches in diameter and about five inches deep was dug usually in the strip of ground between the paved sidewalk and the curbing. A line was agreed upon and drawn a number of feet back from the hole. To qualify each player was required to ante up a certain number of marbles. In play he would kneel at the line, and roll all the antes (this meant a handful of marbles) at once for the hole. With proper skill and English he might with a single thrust roll all the marbles in the hole. That was seldom the case.

Usually, a number of marbles would be scattered around the hole at various distances from it. The roller would then take his tar, knuckle down, and try to shoot the remaining marbles into the hole. The tar, as all will likely remember, is the special marble that a player uses, like a pool player uses a cue-ball, to strike the other marbles. The tars were interesting agates or large steel ball bearings; they came in many sizes. They were prized by their owners for real or imagined properties, and were treated with a respect that some religious people pay a sacrament. I do not recall all the fine details of the game, but with the rolling distance, the size of the hole and the circle from which the Knuckle shooting took place, skill was essential. Each player took his turn and each kept the marbles he got in the hole.

The fact that players could win marbles brought the Church into the game with firm opposition to playing marbles for keeps. In Sunday School and in the Church Services speeches were made against the games which were considered iniquitous gambling. I do not recall that my father personally ever spoke out against playing marbles for keeps, and I always suspected that he did not consider the matter that serious. However, when playing this marble game I always felt a spiritual struggle, a dilemma between the love of the game and the desire to be on the right side where the church and its threats of damnation were concerned.

On our side of Windsor Avenue there lived, in three houses in a row, six boys of approximately the same age. My brother and I were two of these, the Chief of Police of Norfolk, Virginia had three sons; they lived two doors from us, and in between lived "Boogley" Trowel who really occupied a double house. His Aunt lived in one half the double and his immediate family in the other half. He was in and out of both these half houses so much that one associated him with both halves.

Again I found myself blessed with alleys to play in: the blocks formed by Windsor and Park Avenues, other parallel streets and their cross streets were quartered by alleys running at right angles to each other and intersecting in the middle of the blocks. Quite far behind our homes, on the next street back, was a large lumber yard which will bear more discussion. We kids found ways to pile lumber over separated stacks, and build secret rooms that were well concealed by appearing, from the outside, to be lumber stacked on a bias. We formed clubs, and the secret rooms created in the lumber piles were our meeting places. It increased the fun of our exploits that we had to enter the back of the lumber yard, and proceed to our rooms surreptitiously.

One of the organizations we formed was the Little Bridge Sharks. The organization got its name from an actual narrow bridge that crossed a small inlet from the Chesapeake Bay. In its entirety, the bridge crossed a marsh land on one side of a railroad bridge going in the same direction. It proceeded until it crossed the inlet and then turned right to pass under the railroad bridge. When it was clear of the railroad bridge it turned left, and continued over marsh land until firm ground was reached. It was a pedestrian bridge only, and little used except by the young boys of Brambleton. The title "Little Bridge" was probably unofficial but it was universal.

Passing, as it did, primarily through marsh land overgrown with tall reeds, the bridge had a built in secretiveness about it. With few people passing through it was an ideal place to meet your pals well away from adults in the neighborhood.

There was an odor about the little bridge that was a combination of salt spray, rotten fish and sea weed that was pleasing to smell, and gives me nostalgia now to reflect upon. We would go to the bridge on the slightest provocation and carve our names on the railings, fish and crab. Crabbing was by far our principle occupation. We used the direct method of tying a piece of old meat to a heavy string dangling in the water, and, when the crabs were eating peacefully, pulling the string up slowly until the crabs could be plainly seen. With a net on the end of a pole we could scoop up from one to three, or occasionally more, crabs at one pass.

When the tide was out there would be large open areas of mud, called flats, among the seaweed. With our pants rolled well up we could slowly walk across the flats searching for soft-shelled crabs. We wore no shoes in the summer which left us ready for crabbing the flats at all times.

To locate a soft shell crab you searched for a very slight sink in the otherwise level surface of the flat. At some risk of getting bitten by a crab that had not yet shed his hard shell, you would start in a few inches back from the center of the sink that had caught your attention, and, with your palm up, plunge your hand down in the mud, and then under the hoped for crab in the sink hole. On a good day, keeping at this activity for a little more than an hour would yield enough soft-shelled crabs to feast a family of five.

There are few dishes that can give a lasting satisfied taste comparable to soft-shelled crabs deep-fried in a proper batter. Some called that comforting food. You eat the whole thing, shell and all. Each morsel has a unique taste that can become addictive. These crabs rank high among the sea food dishes around the Chesapeake Bay.

From the little bridge area I could supply our table with gourmet food in fish and crabs.

For bigger fish, and also for hard shell crabs, the Little Bridge Sharks extended their territory by taking to boats. Some member of the club always had an available row boat in his family. The Elizabeth River flows through the Brambleton area of Norfolk on its way into the Chesapeake Bay. We spent much of our spare time on the mouth of the river fishing and crabbing from a boat.

On occasion we would go exploring up the river where it wound in and out behind industrial plants and eventually some open fields. I am sure the plants must have polluted the river, but it was not considered a problem at the time we lived in Norfolk. The fishing was good, and we swam at any location, where fancy struck, without a thought of the sewage or the chemicals that were probably there. Maybe they fertilized our personal growth.

I remember one occasion when several of us left Little Bridge in the early morning for an exploration up the river. The inlets had their fascination, the fishing and crabbing was good, and by afternoon we had a washtub nearly full of fish and hard shell blue crabs to be divided among us. It was a hot southern summer day; we frequently dove into the water for a swim, and dried off while we fished. Working slowly back down river we arrived at the bridge at dusk, a late arrival on a summer day. Several fathers were on the bridge terribly agitated with genuine concern for our safety. In our excitement and pleasure we had completely forgotten time, and were long overdue at home.

The other end of the little bridge, opposite to Brambleton, was one entrance to Chesterfield Heights, a residential community probably a notch above Brambleton in modern homes and the income of its residents. I developed friendships in this community with two boys my age. I was nine years old when the family moved to Norfolk and thirteen when we left.

The two boys with whom I became friends in Chesterfield Heights brought out the the worst or the best in me, depending on your point of view. Both the boys were more refined or, as my friends in Brambleton saw it, sissy. They were harassed on occasion when they passed through Brambleton, and I became their defender. I cannot recall that I was really any braver facing up to some of the bullies in our district than they were, but I could put on a better show of belligerence, and took the chance. I would defy their tormentors with threats and occasionally actions that kept the wolves at bay.

I knew in my heart that I was frightened of the, so called, toughs, but being the hero in the eyes of these two unstreet wise kids filled a need in my life that made me risk a beating to acquire. My posing and acting as a hard guy gave me a reputation of being one. For several years I risked my neck to live up to what was expected. Even in sports I had to swim farther, dive higher, run faster, be superior at marbles, and catch more crabs or fish than anyone around. Somehow I got by with this, and, as I look back, I must recognize that these two timid souls made me bold beyond my nature, and caused me to develop a life time habit of trying to excel.

Norfolk as a city had its unique characteristics which probably are still easy to recognize. Sea food is the thing I remember most. Daily a wagon pulled through Windsor Ave with the driver crying, "Fresh Fish" over and over. On occasion when I was not fishing, Mother would send me out to the wagon for a specified purchase. Across the back of the open ended covered wagon was a wooden step the full width of the vehicle. At one end of the step was a shelf that served as a cleaning table for fish. It was fascinating to watch the driver clean your order. With a very sharp knife he made short work of dividing the fish into three pieces. One piece was compounded of the head, still attached to the skins from the two sides, and the vertebrae; the fillets comprised the other two pieces.

On the wagon were wonderful crabs and fine fish. All this food was picked up from the fishermen's boats early in the morning and brought to your table by the man on the wagon. Others enjoyed this system too: behind the wagon was a parade of cats that were favored with a fish head from time to time.

Other deliveries were made also. Electric refrigerators were for the future; ice preserved food and the iceman came frequently to make deliveries right into your icebox. On his back he wore a leather apron that reached from his shoulders to below his waste. Using an ice pick, with the skill of an artist, he would divide 300 pound blocks of ice into smaller blocks that properly fit your icebox. He would hoist your piece, with his ice tongs, onto his back, and carry it to your kitchen.

With similar convenience, milk was brought into your kitchen and placed in your icebox. Unless you left a note for a special order the milkman decided your requirements on the spot. These methods seem primitive but they had advantages that some older people miss as they shop at the supermarket.

On our block great games of hockey were played on roller skates. The field was the entire block on which we lived and it was an unusually long block. The hockey sticks were made by the players by an ingenious procedure. During the summer months the kids from the block would go for hikes in the woods. We knew wooded areas where sturdy saplings were growing. The sapling was tested at about waist height to determine a shaft size that would, when cut, afford a good hand grip like the grip of a good golf club.

When the right size sapling had been chosen it was caught at the top and bent over until the top branches were tight on the ground. A forked stick, previously cut for the purpose, was straddled over the upper end of the main stalk of the sapling and driven tightly into the ground. With the sapling securely held in this bent position, a controlled fire was built directly under the bend in the stalk. With careful watching, the point was determined when the sap had dried out of the sapling at the bend, and before the wood was burnt. At this point the fire was extinguished. The dried out section of the sapling maintained a permanent set with a curve that matched well the bend in an official hockey stick.

The process completed, the small tree was sawed off at the ground, the little limbs were trimmed from the stalk, the bark peeled off, and the stalk cut to a proper length for your height. You were then the proud possessor of a good hockey stick. With a little practice one could style a well shaped and balanced stick. In time you made several of these; as they aged and seasoned you found your favorite, and played with that one until it was worn out in service.

The hockey puck was usually a tin can that received a terrible beating before the game was done. The rules of the game permitted blows to your opponent's shins, if he moved over to your side of the puck. Such blows were accompanied by shouts of "shinny on your own side!." The games got rough and fast, and were the medium for some fancy skating. There were injuries from falls on the asphalt, and from the follows through of the hockey sticks. The deliberate blows to the shins did little damage. The players wore improvised leggings made of carpet or several wrappings of heavy canvass, when that could be found. No helmets were worn, and head injuries were the most serious. Nevertheless, I knew of no permanent injury that resulted from these frequent and exciting games.

A Ministers son among the parishioners receives honor and reproach, depending on the circumstances, beyond what is deserved. He is part of the minister's family which is expected to be composed of role models. Behavior considered as pranks among average kids is shamed in the minister's son who is expected to be a bit more Holy. Likewise, he is often applauded for simple decency.

In turn, I accepted a certain amount of special status, and felt a proprietary interest in the church itself. The Sunday school assembly hall and class rooms were built integral with church and located behind the main part of the building. The chancel of the church was elevated 4 or 5 feet above the nave and included the preacher's pulpit, the choir and the Baptistery. The choir was to the left of the congregation. Steps were located behind the choir that led from the Sunday school area to the chancel. The steps could not be seen from the nave and provided a smooth entrance to the choir and the balance of the chancel. The choir was seated on benches that were open below the seat. The legs of anyone seated on these benches were exposed from the rear. The Sunday school level at the foot of the access steps was an unintended viewing platform.

I often joined the choir; I hope there was a minor contribution in my presence. I found as I entered up the steps from the Sunday school area that the already seated singer's legs, viewed from the rear, looked like a seated chorus line. There was always a delayed reaction of struggle coming up the steps: should a minister's son look or turn away? In retrospect I recall these viewing demands somewhat as I recall the beautiful Rockettes of Radio Center Music Hall kicking in unison. There was not as many legs, and not the rhythm but there was a pleasant interest which comes back in memory as I write. I guess I decided that even a minister's son should not turn away.

CHAPTER IV

More Norfolk 1913--1917

The Norfolk Southern Railroad had a dominant affect upon Brambleton; it's tracks ran through the neighborhood on a diagonal, crossing no streets at a right angle. As you walked across the tracks at intersections, you could see buildings sitting at odd angles to avoid the railroad right-of-way. The yards feeding the freight station in the center of the community, immediately behind the business district, completely absorbed several blocks to provide multiple tracks that afforded unloading facility and temporary storage of freight cars.

There was walking space beside the railroad tracks used by many. The kids of the Brambleton area used this space as an artery, a private road to the center of Norfolk. The boys from our neighborhood, were primary wayfarers. We walked the track right-of-way on most of our errands and used it as a shortcut to the downtown movies. From the Brambleton ave. intersection we could progress diagonally through our entire district, and come out at the railroad passenger station at the end of Granby Street, the main thoroughfare of Norfolk.

Walking along a couple city blocks on Granby, after leaving the Railroad Station, one found the movie houses, entrance fare 5 cents! We made the journey often, via the tracks, to see the war between the States fought over and over from the point of view of southerners: The strong, clean, decent Confederates were always the victors over the conniving, cruel Yankees. We cheered our side on, and sat through the show a second time to recapture the thrills of virtue victorious. Sometimes I fell asleep. I was more than once brought out of a trance by my father shaking me and saying, "lets go home son."

With some impatience he would explain that it was after super time, and he had been required to drop some important matter to come after me. I was always sorry but it would happen again.

Granby street ran from the Railroad Depot along a water front. At one point you could turn into a ferry station and take a ferry to Portsmouth. After several blocks Granby made a right turn, but kept its name and function as the main thoroughfare of the city. I was always impressed at this corner by the very modern water front buildings and docks.

There were other interesting things to do on Granby and in the environs after it made this turn. The kids of Brambleton made their way to this section by turning off the R.R. tracks, before reaching the main R.R.station, discussed above, and walking through residential and commercial areas of continuously changing character. These trips were adventures in themselves.

Of particular interest was a very old church and its cemetery grounds. Stories were told, the details of which I have forgotten, of the famous people buried in these grounds and of historic events associated with the church. One I do recall is how the Yankees fired from the harbor into Norfolk and damaged the church. One of the cannon balls was, at the time of our trips, and I assume still is, cemented into the side of the church. We would look at this ball and do much talking about the war.

As we turned a corner by the church property we proceeded into another and contrasting district of the city: within several city blocks behind the church you entered the red light district of Norfolk, which, being located in a naval harbor, in those days, was of considerable size. I did not know the depth of the district behind the street we always traversed, but the street was long, and it presented quite a show to the minds and imagination of curious youngsters. In the doorways, and at most windows, girls in kimonos were soliciting with coquetry and rashness. Most of their prospects seemed to be sailors on shore leave in the harbor. They stopped and bantered with the girls at different doors before entering at some.

The range of ages of the boys on our jaunts to the city varied, and from the older boys we learned about what was going on behind the doors and curtains. Sometimes an older boy would see a familiar face at a doorway or window, and believe he had recognized a girl from his neighborhood. This would create much excitement and conversation. These were educational trips, and the conversations in our crowd were classics in juvenile eroticism as we made our way across the district into the more respectable areas of the city.

Just before reaching Granby street, we came out of the red light district into a square that contained more moving picture houses and many shops. The square was large and when we arrived we took time to do, what we called, some "messing around". Sometimes we would go to a movie, which cost ten cents in this higher class section of the city, and, after the movie, would visit Child's Restaurant.

It was a recurring high point in my life whenever we visited Child's. I felt grownup and important to have the money and the freedom to go to the counter, or sit at a table, and order the dish I might, at the time, crave; usually a hamburger. And to be waited on, that was real special. I can today recapture the warmth of being a guest at Child's.

At the end of the Norfolk Southern R.R. system, near where we lived, the tracks crossed Brambleton, Ave., on its customary diagonal just around the corner from the end of Windsor Ave., our street. At this intersection, the neighborhood fell off from its residential status into a commercial area on both sides of the tracks.

On the far side was a grocery store, the name of which I have forgotten, and a barber shop. On the near side was another Grocery store owned and operated by Mr. Jarvis, a Deacon in my father's church. I worked at this store as a delivery boy on Saturdays. My bicycle was equipped with a large basket on the handle bars and another over the rear wheel. I arrived at work at seven o'clock in the morning, and quit when deliveries were complete in the evening. During the day I pedaled all over Brambleton and Chesterfield Heights, and finished my day after dark cleaning up the last miscellaneous orders. For this I received seventy five cents.

I did feel my hours were quite long, and the pay low, but I enjoyed the work and equalized things a bit by eating cookies when I passed the cookie boxes. The cookie I adored was a round biscuit covered with marshmallow and chocolate, topped off with a pecan. I could throw one of these whole into my mouth with a quick pass that anyone could miss seeing, if he were not looking carefully. I would try self control but would sometimes lose count.

About the cookies, I did feel some guilt, but, from his attitude, I felt Mr. Jarvis knew what was going on and was amused. He was a kind and generous man, and probably felt he had a good deal in his 75 cent delivery boy.

The barber shop across the tracks from the Jarvis grocery was a real joy. You felt grown up just having your hair cut where older men came for their daily shave. Above the mirrors, behind the barber chairs, was a long shelf containing a line of customers' shaving mugs and individual brushes. The brushes and mugs were personalized by the customers' names along the edge of the shelf.

This barber shop was also the only place where I ever saw a Police Gazette with its scantily clad women in provocative poses. Anything like Playboy magazine could not even be imagined in those days, and, at 11 or 12 years, the Police Gazette was surprising and titillating. As I waited for my turn in the chair, I absorbed the pictures and the low grade literature, and listened to the grownup man-talk which included some risque words and stories.

On each visit I heard the Barber crack his classic joke about having his cat around to pick up the pieces, if he nipped off part of an ear while shaving a customer. Each visit to the shop was a learning experience.

It would be impossible to grow up as a minister's son in a Southern Baptist church of the early nineteen hundreds, and not have been caused to think, for years, about the theology and dogmas of the church: On one occasion. which was not an uncommon practice as a minister, my father was calling with condolence on a family of his parish. The husband and father had died. The family lived only a couple blocks from our home, and we were walking to their home, and we were talking about the deceased. It was mentioned, in our discussion, that the man had been associated with the beer industry; questions were raised whether or not, with him being on the wrong side, he could make it into Heaven. Considering the militant attitude of our church about demon rum, I guess I accepted the logic of the doubts, but felt personally frightened by the severity of the doctrine.

Opposition to alcohol was a passion that, when considering some areas of the drinking fraternity, was understandable, but to a Southern Baptist it seemed to mean that a drop or a barrel was the same; it was all the work of the Devil. Their fight against demon rum was active. There were occasions when all the children of the church were dressed in their Sunday best, and loaded into wagons. With a band of several pieces playing, our wagons rolled through Norfolk streets while the children all sang enthusiastically a song that had as a concluding refrain, "The big brewers horses shan't run over me".

Next door to the Church lived a family that desecrated Holy Ground from the point of view of the Faithful. The man of the house owned and operated a brewery, and had on his covered back porch logos of the several brands he brewed. At an angle these logos could be seen by church members on their way to services. Much was said about the impudence of these displays. It seemed to be regarded as a sin for him to live there in the first place. Be that as it may, it was certainly awkward.

The Brewer's family included a son who probably attened private school: he only occasionally appeared in the games with his contemporaries on the block. Since he was the son of that sinful brewer, I always expected him to be different in some strange way. But it never happened; he went right on being a normal kid. I remember enjoying his company whenever he was around.

In circa 1916 people did not go to hospitals or other institutions as readily as they do today. There were numerous chronic and acute illnesses being nursed at home by families who were members of my father's church.

I can recall, on our street, a man with audible suffering. Over a period of probably months, the man could at intervals, be heard moaning up through an occasional crescendo to a scream from his pain.

There were a couple families who had, living in a third floor room, some helpless relative. Caring for the sick at home was more the norm of the period than it is today. Going to the hospital was unusual. I remember several homes where daily living encountered significant limitations because of helpless relatives to care for.

Belonging to the Little Bridge Sharks, holding meetings surreptitiously in a wood yard, left an impression on me, that we were pretty macho boys. However, as I now reflect on our robust behavior, I recall our hockey games, skating, bicycling, Y.M.C.A. swimming and Gym classes, trips to Virginia Beach and Ocean View, boating on the Elizabeth River, and much much more. I simply see some pretty good kids having fun, and staying out of trouble. The families in the neighborhood were almost entirely what were called, "good church people." Were the values exemplified in the homes remembered in the alleys, the streets and the playing grounds? I think so.

And then there was the "other school." This was the name it went by among all the kids in our district of Brambleton. Of course, between two schools in neighboring communities the other school was the one we were exposed to but did not attend. Both of the schools were middle schools, containing no grade higher than the seventh, which, at the time, graduated its students into high school. Here the equality ended. The physical differences were conspicuous. As kids, we were not concerned about whether or not there was a difference in the quality of education.

Our school was located on a street corner in a residential community. Two sides of the school came right up to the sidewalks on the intersecting streets. The other two sides were bordered with a playground that formed an L. The playground was enclosed by a high board fence that certainly did not leave the impression of the playing fields of Eden. The surface on which we played our games was dirt, not greensward. On rainy days we took our recess indoors, and waited out a drying period before we returned to the yard.

The other school was completely surrounded by spacious grounds, landscaped and planted. There were special areas set aside for baseball, horseshoes, hopscotch or whatnot. Around the grounds was an ornamental iron fence. The place was really fancy in our youthful view, but I do not recall envy on a personal level, only admiration.

Our real thrill was when we were included in activities at the other school. There would be group musical lessons for kids from either school. I took violin and learned to play, in one session, one refrain from "My Country 'Tis of Thee." I felt like a child prodigy, but, of course, there was no big deal: to stimulate interest at the beginning of the class, the instructor taught some of us, by rote, the finger positions in sequence. I loved my violin and the status of studying at the other school. But alas the group study plan did not survive, nor did my ambition to become a great violinist.

My fondest memory is taking part in a play that called for many practice performances at the other school, and eventually the main performances that ran for several nights. The music of the Anvil Chorus was an integral part of the play, and I was assigned to the task of making the anvil sounds at proper places. I struck a metal bar against some large triangles to produce the anvil sound. This seemed extremely important, and I put my soul into the timing and striking the proper blow.

Charlie Ford, the police chief's son who lived on our block sang; he had a fine voice. His songs were Sweet Lilani and one about "Jerousy Jane" being," of all the pretty girls 'round about the town," the sweetest. His tenor voice really filled the room, and made me proud to be his friend and a part of such a fine performance. The applause was frequent and loud.

The affect on Charlie was profound; as the time went by he seriously tried his hand at acting. Many years later, after Charlie had given up his ambitions to be an actor, and had become the successful owner of a furniture store, he visited me in New York. We went for dinner in a night club where I successfully got the manager to let Charlie sing Sweet Lalani. He rose to the challenge: you could feel in his manner the realization of a dream; the song has never been sung better. He brought the house down in rounds of applause, and we were all proud of him, and, by reflected glory from this instant celebrity, of ourselves.

On our way back to his hotel, we reflected upon the influence upon our lives of the Other School, and were thankful that it had been there to give us a taste of the arts and sports that more than supplemented the three R's we got in our school.

We acquired something else at our school, a very unusual teacher named McWhorter. He was one of these people that seem to just happen and give of themselves far beyond the call of duty. McWhorter was not only a good teacher, he was a good man and a busy one in good works. He was a dedicated Boy Scout master. In our area, under his leadership, we had the finest hikes and camping trips in a full program of scouting. Due to his insistence upon excellence, our scouts were always working for that next merit badge, and, as a result, we had a record number of Eagle Scouts in our troop. For anyone not familiar with scouting 21 merit badges were required for an Eagle Scout rating. Such a rating represented a lot of work for the scout, and much encouragement and leadership from the Scout Master.

As I recall it, we would march, like Christian soldiers, clear across Norfolk and on to Jamestown, where in 1907 an exposition was held. Our marching would have been in 1916 and 1917. In 1907 elegant buildings had been constructed, for the duration of the Exposition only, without regard for further durability. Outside finishes, including Grecian columns, were made of plaster of Paris. In the few years, that had followed the Exposition, the exterior finishes of many of the buildings had seriously deteriorated, but the basic structures remained safe for occupancy. Permission to use a buildings for troop encampment was easy to obtain. On our visits to Jamestown the ambience, among the empty buildings and the decaying grandeur of the place, was a bit like "a banquet hall deserted."

These encampments lasted several days, games were played, marches were taken, and merit badge tests were passed or flunked. What I recall as the greatest pleasure was simply the thrill of being part of the troop, wearing the uniform, and marching through the city to an occasional applause from the sidewalks.

To me my scout uniform was a target for my pride. With its warm tan color and design it looked like a real soldier's uniform, and borrowed more distinction as the First World War developed in Europe. In those critical years soldiers were more and more in evidence on the streets, in Church and other public places, and increasingly were the objects of private and public praise.

I even had a sensual feeling for the texture of the durable cloth from which the uniform was made. The crowning glory was to be just as eligible to wear a scout uniform as was that boy in Richmond, a few years before, who had put on such a show of his status in our building.

McWhorter lives in my mind as a stern but sincere friend, with a bit of the father image coming from his relationship as Scout Master and Teacher. On one occasion for some unacceptable behavior, on my part during some group activity in the classroom, he gave me a single sharp crack with a switch that surely got my attention. On other occasions he would put on his roller skates, and join the boys, and sometimes me alone, in the streets for a skating session. I am caused to think of a quote put in the mouth of Napoleon, by Emerson picturing Napoleon watching a farmer plowing his field, "Nor knowest thou what argument---Thy life to thy neighbor's creed has lent."

There was a special experience that argued well with me to support a creed of gratitude for the earth and its wonders: The main thrust of Norfolk is that it seems to be in and of the Ocean and one of its inlets to the land, the Chesapeake Bay. The climate of the sea coast, the smells, the products of the sea, the traditions of a water front town dominate its ambience.

As stated in the chapter on Richmond, a John William Williams, my father"s cousin, was on the Governor of Virginia's staff. The position was honorary, but certain perquisites went with the job. One of these gave him the right to arrange a birth for his young cousin, me, on a Pilot Boat that plied the waters along the edge of the three mile limit, opposite the mouth of the Chesapeake Bay.

The boat served as a floating station for professional pilots who went aboard foreign vessels, and piloted them into Norfolk Harbor. Like a gift from the heart of nature, I was informed, by an official document, that a motor launch would pick me up at a dock near Ocean View, and deliver me on board the Pilot Boat for a ten day visit to their ship on the open sea.

Just being on board the pilot boat was an experience in self enlargement. I was daily among the sailors that made the ship a viable home for the pilots. The trip over to the ship, at the bow of the small transport vessel, as I watched the bow cut the swells, and felt our roll over waves and the hammer blow of the boat dropping from the crest of the larger ones, introduced me to the sea as I had never known it. I was wet with the blown spume, blinded by the suns glare on the water, alive to the taste of salt, and eager for what was ahead. Then on the larger ship with the crew scurrying about, and orders being shouted, it seemed to me, a drama was about to begin.

The wooden decks were white from repeated scrubbing. I was sensitive to these in a tactile way, they looked so absolutely clean. I was to learn that that was the way it was with all things on board. The bunks were steel compartments built to the sides of the ship. They were a white gray color, and seemed always to have been just freshly painted. The mess table was made of simple thick wooden boards firmly fastened to steel supports. It too showed the affects of frequent scrubbing, and presented a dry white surface that seemed a symbol of sanitation. I liked the environment, and commenced to move about the ship with eager curiosity. I was encouraged by the captain to make myself at home, but to be careful in the engine room.

Surprise and pleasure seem to be the words that describe my general attitude as I took in the surroundings and the inhabitants. I was certainly pleased to find myself on board, and soon began to find many surprising details about the properties of the ship and the sea-going characteristics of the personnel that manned it. Compared to the ocean going liners, that I would some day cross the ocean on, it was a small ship, but, to me at 12 years old, the sea worthy craft on which we resided was large and magnificent, and it was beautiful to behold as we cut through the waves off Cape Henry and Cape Charles. I was soon seduced and felt an instinctive love for the open sea, overwhelmed by its magnitude, and stimulated, through the eyes, by the sparkling light on the waves, and, through the lungs, by the clean fresh air that enveloped me. This was to be love at first sight that would never leave.

I was adopted and treated as a mascot, bossed around, but favored as a young brother by the seamen. Out of protective consideration, I was given a lower bunk. The movement of the ship in rough water is less noticeable that much closer to the center of gravity of the ship, compared to an upper bunk. Nevertheless, at night I felt the side to side swing of our craft, and sensed its rise and fall with the waves. It was to me a good feeling, secure and confident in my bunk, and proud of myself for being a sea worthy salt. It was somewhat like the relaxed feeling of sleeping dry and warm under a good roof while the rain outside beats down upon it.

Our routine was varied and our activities many. but several will have to suffice to give the flavor. When morning came a shower was mandatory; the mechanics were unique in my experience. I was told to run out on deck naked and was directed to a place to stand near the railing. As I faced a small group of sailors, one tossed fresh cold sea water from a five gallon bucket onto my naked front. I was instructed to turn and the process was repeated on my rear. Others in their turn took their showers as I had done. Men with ropes tied to the five gallon buckets kept the water coming by dipping the buckets in the sea and hauling them up to the deck. A person wakes up fast in such a shower, and, if he lends himself to the exercises that follow, he feels invigorated through the morning as his reward.

We also went deep-sea fishing from the motor launch or a life boat. Various sailors would be off duty at different times, and several seemed to want to take the "kid" fishing. I experienced a lot of that sport during my visit to the ship. It's pleasant to recall the camaraderie that developed tossing around in a dinghy, always with the expectancy that the one big fish was about to be caught. One that I recall was a large flounder that I hooked in the side, and brought on board without much credit from the sailors. A side hook is an accident, not a demonstration of skill.

Even though these were long and lazy days they went by too fast, and the time came for me to take the motor launch back to Ocean View and home to Brambleton. I was leaving a place and a taste of a life style that would have been fun to continue, but the vacation was over, and I stepped aboard the launch for one more thrilling ride on the ocean and across the Bay.

Not apropos of what follows, but purely for the proper sequence, shortly after my visit on the sea, there was talk in our home of moving from Norfolk to a place with the strange name of Waycross Georgia. There will be more on this later, but first there is more of Norfolk.

The justly famous movie, Citizen Kane, used an explanatory device that had a particular appeal to me. It was shown that an emotional attachment to a sled, named Rose Bud, could stay, for a life time, in Citizen Kane's subconscious. The picture revealed delicate nuances that showed sensitive psychological insight on the part of the author and the director. The point being made was that his love for simply a prized toy, one that had served him in youth with exhilarating physical experiences and joy, made the toy a real companion that he missed severely when the experiences of his later complicated existence began to crush. After the death of Kane, and the drama had played out, the audience got a glimpse of the sled being trashed. They saw plainly the name "Rosebud" embossed on the riding platform, and they understood. This simple device, said more about the real man, than the complex surface events of his grown up life.

Until I had seen this picture, certain experiences in my life, similar to his attachment to "Rosebud", had seemed unique, and I did not expect anyone to understand them. I certainly did not talk about them because I did not know how to explain my feelings; even now I will use this movie as an analogue to do so. My roller skates and my bicycle were my "Rosebuds." I had an affection for these two companions, toys, tools and friends that was beyond a simple pride of ownership. I was aware of all the details of their construction, and worked on them with TLC almost before repairs were needed.

Some things you just see, other things seem to penetrate your consciousness in a tactile manner that gives you a permanent memory of the object and associated emotional experiences. Today, in this manner, I recall my roller skates and my bicycle. Probably our first important extensions of ourselves have a meaning deeper than what we feel for similar events later in life.

Our house in Norfolk was a two story construction. There were three porches, a small front porch, a 2 story side porch that, on the lower level, formed a side entrance to the dining room, and on the upper level extended the usefulness of the master bedroom, and a low back porch that ran along the side of the kitchen and butlers pantry, and provided entrance to each area.

Growing just off the edge of the back porch, was a very old cherry tree that leaned toward the house, and, at the roof level, spread its limbs over the roof. The entire back third of the roof was well shaded by the limbs of this tree. In season, these limbs were loaded with delicious black-heart cherries. The situation was ideal: I spent many wonderful hours, on hot days, lying on the roof, in the shade, meditating and eating cherries almost beyond capacity. From time to time I was put under orders to cease and desist, but I do not recall that the restrictions lasted long enough to create any great sense of deprivation.

The front of our house was approximately centered on a large lot. The front entrance was close to the sidewalk. A white picket fence ran the full width of the lot. On one's extreme right, facing the house, there was a wide gate through the fence for vehicle entrance, and, in the center of the fence, a small gate for people. One entering the yard through the vehicle gate could follow a sand clay driveway back to a barn. The barn was actually in a second yard behind a second fence that separated the front yard from the back area. The fence was high, and was also controlled by a gate that, when closed, gave complete privacy to an enormous back yard.

This back yard was a wonderful space for the young and old in the family. It was wide and deep. On the opposite side, away from the large gate mentioned, there was another fence, joined to the house, that extended to the property line. This fence is well remembered because at frequent intervals it required my services: Unslaked lime was put in a wash tub, water was added,and a violent reaction, giving off much heat, was allowed to take place. When the mixture was again quiet we had, of course, white wash which I applied to the fence with a wide brush on a long handle. There must have been a personnel gate through this fence, but, in my memory, it seems that I always climbed the fence to go from the front yard to the back on that side of the house,

On this same side of the back yard was an abundant vegetable garden that extended several hundred feet to the rear property line. Both my mother and father had been raised on farms; cultivating vegetables came naturally, and their produce was a credit to their culture and a great addition to our table.

The garden, however, took only half the space available as a back yard; there was the large barn with space to spare in front of it and a smaller yard behind. Very ample chicken houses were located in this smaller yard. All these areas and buildings served a double purpose: they were also play places for my brother and me. The family owned a model T Ford that was hardly noticeable in the immense barn. The barn was two stories high with a tower.

This barn was a center for our activities which spilled over into the adjacent yards. My brother Jim was two and one half years my senior. He was into body building. On the second floor of the barn he installed a punching bag hanging inside a metal ring that gave a rapid rebound to the bag. On one occasion he took a mighty swing at the vibrating bag which wasn't there to meet his timing. In some odd way, his fist came around and connected with his jaw for a bit more than a technical knockout. We sort of dated things from the time Jim knocked himself out.

I have nothing so colorful to report of personal accidents, but one potentially more dangerous. A great deal of my activity, at this time of life, was on roofs, the roof of our home in search of cherries, or on the roof of the barn in various exploits. The two storied barn was covered by a gable roof with rather steep sides. On its left side the barn merged into a lower building occupied by general utilities and chicken roosts. This building was covered by a less steep inclined roof sloping down from the gable roof.

On one occasion I lost my footing, fell and rolled down part of the gable roof onto the lower incline, and from there completed a fall to the ground. Fortunately, I landed in dirt that had been plowed for planting which adequately broke the fall. No permanent harm was done. (Of course, some of my friends may believe there could be a hangover affect from the blow to my head.)

Before I end the description of the yard and its contents, two special trees have great significance: At the edge of the vegetable garden, on the property line of that side, stood an old but healthy paper-shell Pecan tree, with long and drooping limbs that covered a large area of our back yard and that of our neighbor's. The tree was prolific, the pecans fell to the ground like rain in season, and you could hurry the process by using a long stick or a bit of climbing. I experienced the feeling of greed: I resented the pecans that fell on the other side of the fence. Since the tree got its nourishment from its roots in our yard, it was difficult to reconcile our neighbor's equal rights to the nuts.

The other tree was decorative standing tall beside the entrance drive in our front yard. It was a southern magnolia that produced lovely white blooms as large as a man's two hands in a praying posture. I loved the looks and the sweet smell of these blooms, but I was less affectionate concerning its penchant for constantly shedding large leaves that gave me a weekly job of raking, hauling and disposing. The tree had other features that were of interest, it was very tall and, with its many limbs, easy to climb. Very frequently I could be found in the top of this tree keeping careful tab on the neighborhood. From my vantage point at tree top level I could see the entire block. There was also a spiritual elevation that accompanied the physical height.

Opisite the white washed fence, at the head of our vegetable garden, in the front yard on that side of the house was the only lawn we maintained, and, according to modern standards, we did not do that very well. But, according to my standards at the time, there were some special features that I recall with pleasure. We let the grass get quite long before cutting, and even the cut grass was left longer than is allowed for fine lawns. On hot days the grass was a cushion to lie on, or in, and look up at the cumulus clouds go by. I spent what spare time I could at this congenial pursuit, and laid in the grass, and meditated upon the clouds: How far was it up to the clouds? Would one get wet passing through them? What really was the blue between? Was the Heaven I heard about in church anywhere in range of what I was observing? Today it might be difficult to explain so much fascination; at the time it seemed the natural way to be.

Chickens have, as do some other birds, a sack-like enlargement of their gullet that is known as their craw or crop. Most people know this fact, but I did not know it when my mother said she wanted me to help her operate on a rooster's craw. The thick muscular walls of the craw are used to soften food to make it more digestible. Chickens improve on the process by picking up bits of gravel that does some grinding in the craw. It can happen that gravel pieces will block the outlet to the craw, food cannot pass through, and an enormous swelling develops in front at the base of the neck. Unaided the bird will starve to death. These were the circumstances confronting our rooster, and we were to be the surgeons attempting to save his life, or rather I was to be the surgeon while my mother held the rooster.

As painlessly as possible, we removed the feathers from the bird's neck, sterilized the neck and all tools with alcohol, and proceeded with the operation. A razor blade was my scalpel. I made a vertical incision in the center of the swelling, and easily removed the impacted food and gravel from the craw. With a needle and fine silk thread I sewed up the incision. All the while the rooster seemed to suffer little. He was almost cooperative.

For many days the patient seemed to be in good health eating and associating with the chickens, but, sad to say, one day we found him dead. I do not recall whether his craw had swelled again or not, but no matter how successful the operation was the patient died.

Jutting into the back yard, and connected to the kitchen by a short and narrow breezeway, was a wood shed that served also as a storage place for garden tools. It was not a large building. In fact, with a gable roof and white windows with green blinds, it gave the impression of an oversize doll house attached to the main house.

I have a special memory of this building: My pockets were usually full of pecans gathered from our wonderful tree. My customary way of cracking nuts was with my teeth. Looking back on the matter, I can believe that my father reached a point of being unable to stand hearing one more crushing sound from his son's teeth. He had told me over and over, "Son don't crack nuts with your teeth." I could quickly forget the admonition and CRASH! CRASH! would go my teeth again.

It was the only licking my father ever gave me, and I deserved it. When the limit of his endurance had been passed on one occasion, he said," Come with me to the woodshed." With the dignity of his profession, and the methodical approach of a master craftsman, he went about his task. While I waited he cut and trimmed several switches from the pecan tree. I was asked to lean over a low bench, and the operation on my rear began. It was not a cruel whipping, but it was thorough, and I never forgot the emphasis that it provided. To this day, I have not cracked nuts with my teeth.

While being a minister in a fundamentalist type of church that I now associate with intolerance of other faiths, I never found my father, in practice, to possess that characteristic. With his children he was a kind and loving father, and showed, all through my growing years, an ability to understand and tolerate many transgressions of rigid rules. He also had a sense of humor. In a sermon, He would say to his congregation, "I don't mind if you look at your watch while I am preaching, so long as you don't hold it up to your ear to hear if its running".

Even though I would disagree today with many of the theological specifics that were important basics in his

outlook on life, I learned from him an attitude of faith
that is still a fundamental part of my life.

The front porch of our house in Norfolk was very close to
the street. A short cement walk led from the sidewalk
through the gate in the picket fence to two steps rising to
the porch. Double doors opened into a vestibule, and a
second set into an entrance hall that, on one's left,
presented a flight of steps rising to the upstairs area. One
door on the right side of the hall opened into a parlor, a
second into a living room. A door to the dining room was at
the end of the hall. The parlor and the living room were
truncated by the entrance hall but the dinning room occupied
the full width of the house.

Across the complete end of the dining room there was a food
storage pantry, walk-in constructed with shelving to the
ceiling over the entirety of one side wall and the two end
walls. There was a narrow walk space in front of the shelves
that still allowed enough room for boxes to be stored here
and there on the floor.

Some detail on this special pantry is pertinent because it
served a special purpose in our lives: In those days in that
part of the country the minister's family were frequently
recipients of complimentary food. Some years ago a book was
written entitled, "Chicken Every Sunday". The author was a
minister's son who remembered the southern custom of church
members inviting their pastor and his family for midday
dinner Sundays after the Service. I can testify that that
custom was highly respected. I remember wonderful chicken
dinners eaten all around shores of the Chesapeake Bay, close
to Brambleton, at the homes of parishioners. But what has
that to do with the pantry?"

There was a kindred custom, honored more when the minister
was new; A shower would be announced for the new Minister,
and people would bring all manner of food to the church, as
a staging point. There would be Hams, chickens, and produce,
fresh and canned, along with all the kinds of jellies and
jams that women with rural backgrounds could produce. My
mother would then be busy for days canning the surplus fresh
vegetables and fruits. The pantry would almost swell with
food packed on its shelves, and, at times, on the floor.

As if to make certain that no space in that pantry was
unoccupied, my father would, on occasion, buy at the Farmers
Market a whole pig's carcass, bring it home, and butcher it
in the kitchen on a handy long table. Dad had been raised on
a farm, and knew all the technicalities of "putting down"
meat in salt and other preservatives. He properly butchered
the standard cuts and hams to be cured. Our pantry was, in
practice, a complete store room, including boxes of salted
meat on the floor, and hams hanging from the ceiling.

A special bonus at this time came from the necessity to use the fresh pork before it spoiled: we had feasts of pork loin and other special cuts before we were through with the carcass of the pig. I remember these periods with glutinous pleasure; they fit the style of pagan Rome more appropriately than the grave facade of the Southern Baptists.

While Norfolk Virginia can have some quite cold days, it is a comment on the times and the mild climate that we heated our sizable house with a few stoves. A large cast iron pot-bellied stove stood in the living room, which room was center to the commonly used rooms of the house. This stove was supported by lion-footed legs that came up in graceful curves to the body of the stove. The door to the stove had transparent mica windows. When a good fire was going, the warm glow and the flicker of the flames, at these windows, was reassuring and cheerful. The art design of the stove, with its many embellishing scrolls, was baroque.

The ornamented top of the stove rotated horizontally to expose the utilitarian top of an ordinary cooking stove. This lid was removable with a fitted lever. On this lid always sat and simmered a copper tea kettle, discharging just enough steam to maintain good humidity. During the mild winters the dampers were set to let the fire coast during the day. It was usually lively in the evening, but was banked with ashes at bed time. When morning came the ashes were raked aside, the dampers opened, and the fire would soon be glowing brightly again.

With French doors between the rooms opened, this central stove kept the dinning room and the parlor warm enough for comfort, while the living room, occasionally, was a little too warm. The kitchen and butlers pantry were warmed by the kitchen stove.

The metal smokestack pipe from the living room stove went through the ceiling, and vertically through a room upstairs, and then through its ceiling to an outside chimney. This room was my father's study, and it was well heated by radiation from this stove pipe. There was, on the floor, a low metal fence around the entrance of pipe, to enforce a safe distance from its hot surface.

In the master bedroom was a small wood-burning stove that was fired at rising, and again, for a while, before retiring. There were two additional unheated bedrooms.

Among miscellaneous things that come to mind, of my life in Norfolk as a boy, is a church supper that must have featured bananas. The day after the party, a large surplus of the fruit was found in a Sunday School room by a few of us boys just exploring. There were also some bottles of grape juice. I can testify that an excess of bananas and grape juice can make one very sick. We had been playing baseball and our appetites were enormous. We ate bananas without restraint, and drank grape juice in the same intemperate way. There was a clandestine flavor to the operation. I do not know what happened to Charlie, but I surely paid for my transgression. It is the only time in my life that I recall being delirious. At the time the diagnosis was acute indigestion.

On another occasion Charlie Ford and I were returning, down our path by the railroad, from the movies on Granby Street. As we entered the Brambleton area, one of our mutual friends, very excited, ran up with the alarming news that Captain Ford, Charlie's Father, in the performance of some police work, had been shot through his left shoulder. The bullet, internally, glanced from a bone, and followed a main nerve down the Captain's upper arm. Painful months were to go by, and several operations were to be performed before the arm returned to normal.

Publicity of the shooting left a gruesome and lasting impression. The alleged criminal held an extended shoot-out with the police. Several were either killed or wounded. Apparently he was a powerful man: It took many shots to bring him down. There were pictures of his body at the police station that showed the many bullet holes. I cannot say just what was my reaction to the gruesome scene and the event it symbolized; dumfounded and sad come to mind.

However, most of my days in Norfolk were certainly not marked by melancholy or tragic events. On the contrary, the vast majority were filled with benign to happy experiences.

As a closing example, there were the wonderful open trolleys that took us to the ocean for a day of fun in the surf, games on the beach, or just grabbing for the brass ring, while you swung out from the platform of the merry-go-round at Ocean View or Virginia Beach. From a trick of pleasant memory, I recall so vividly riding clickidy clack through the sand dunes on the open trolleys in anticipation of the day ahead. One could smell the ocean in the distance and feel the mist in the warm summer air of coastal Virginia and sort of dream of the lazy but active day ahead. This meditation was at least half the joy of a day projected for fun in the sea, the surf and the sand.

CHAPTER V

Interim

There was much more that could have been recalled about our life in Norfolk but the story seemed complete at a time that coincided with the time my father felt (or heard) a call to another community, Waycross, Ga. We were to learn that Waycross was a small town in the southern part of Georgia. Except for some agriculture, Waycross had one reason for being, it was the home of a large railroad repair shop. The shop belonged to the Atlantic Coast Line R.R.. It seemed that everyone in town either worked for the R.R. or served the people that did. People in the town formed strata of society that corresponded closely to the status of their jobs at the shop.

At the time of moving to Waycross the family owned a Ford Model A. At the factory, the brass radiator of the Model T had been replaced by a formed steel outer covering that on our car was painted black. My parents had decided to drive the car to Georgia. In that day, without numbered or paved highways or accommodations, that was a courageous decision, an adventure. Throughout the family, for a couple months, the coming trip was a principal item of conversation. My father discussed the trip with anyone who had ventured out of the state in an automobile, books on traveling by motor car were acquired, the "Blue Book" was assiduously studied and notes extracted. I remember the plans as being, for a long period, the most exciting topic of discussion our family had ever experienced.

As the day approached the excitement mounted in family discussions of the final plans for the safari through Virginia, North Carolina, South Carolina and into Georgia. I do not know the date but the season was definitely summer. The morning drive, until noon, was clear and hot. We would have preferred it to stay that way, but we were not to be so lucky. We navigated by the guide used by all motor car travelers of the period, the "blue Book". We drove over sand-clay roads that wound through small villages and followed the property lines of adjoining farms. Our instructions in the Blue Book were accompanied by sketches of intersecting roads and notations of special landmarks such as watering troughs for horses, rural churches and, in one case, a welcome hand pump to supply the human traveler with drinking water.

My brother, being two and one half years older than me was the one that exchanged driving sessions with my father. I was a passenger, footman and general flunky. At the outset we moved at a leisurely pace, compared to modern travel, without a suspicion that the whole trip, by motor car, was destined to be a short one.

By leaving home before dawn we were able in one day to cover the southern part of Virginia and be well into North Carolina in the early afternoon. Our destination was to be Selma, N.C. where the home of my married sister Annie was to provide the first night's shelter and probably a visit of several days.

First the sun disappeared behind gathering clouds and cool breezes blew through the open car. Soon a few drops of rain showed on the windshield and, as it increased, the hand lever, inside the car on the windshield, that controlled the windshield wiper on the outside had to be constantly manipulated to maintain visibility. And then it came, the real storm: Lightning and rolling thunder orchestrated the beating rain upon the windshield and the top of the car.

There was a scramble to put up side curtains; Dad and we boys were drenched before the task was done. For a while we still made progress through the storm, the unpaved roads turned to mud, we slipped from side to side, stalled with spinning wheels and required digging and pushing to move ahead at all. Just short of our goal, on the outskirts of some small North Carolina town, we came to a forced stop in a mud hole much longer than the car and deeper than half the wheel diameters.

After the wheels had spun in a vain attempt to free themselves from the grip of the relentless mud, we saw a man in a slicker and boots just waiting beside the road with a team of horses. It was plain he had waited with confident expectations of a business deal and he got it. My father hired him to harness up to our car and we finished our proud trip pulled by a team of horses for miles of riding through small towns and open farm country on into Selma. It was, a not unpleasant, slow ride through rural neighborhoods, where a few people, in good nature, sent up cheers as we ignobly rode by.

It was nearly dark in the long summer twilight when we arrived at my sister Annie's home. We were tired and hungry but possessors of a sense of conquest and adventure to have made the trip at all. Members of the family, with some braggadocio, talked of the experience for a couple years if the occasion seemed a bit appropriate.

While we visited with my sister , Dad arranged to have the car sent on to Waycross by train. A few days later the family took the same more reliable alternative.

But before we go on to Waycross there was an element of our family life that belongs in the picture as an important factor in all our living arrangements. Through my, what is often called, formative years there was a Shangra-la, a retreat, a fresh sweet breeze that caressed and beckoned in dreams and in reality. Its name was Aunt Laura's.

My mother, when a very young girl, lost her mother and went to live with her father's sister, Laura. Aunt Laura was the only mother she ever knew, and Aunt Laura's farm in the valley of Virginia was her home until she went away to attend Cox College and shortly after marry Beverly Lacy Hoge when she was still in her seventeenth year. Before going on with my association with Aunt Laura there is important speculation about the psychological affect of this arrangement upon my mother and, through her, the family.

Mother's father married again and, in the close-by city of Roanoke, raised a family of two sons and a daughter by his new wife. Mother lived on at the farm and received visits from her father but was never included, except for short visits, as a member of her father's thriving new family living in the city.

I became convinced in later life, while trying to understand stresses in the relationships of mother to her family, that she, in her emotions, became a rejected child, cruelly isolated from her father by her living arrangements. Mother needed more than normal reassurance that her children and her husband loved her. She craved praise for her very real talents and services to other people. All the while she talked of her father as though he was a saint and endowed him with virtues beyond what, I was told, were a true picture of the man. He was a fine citizen and, according to his lights, a good father but mother displayed a worshiping attitude of one who has invented a father to fill the vacuum left by the absent real one.

On frequent and extended visits with my mother to her childhood home I knew nothing of conflicting emotions or historical relationships. Aunt Laura was to me what a good grandmother is to other youngsters that go home to grandmother's for a holiday. But her place was special to me beyond the average, and is still remembered with the glow of love and the joy of recalled scenes on mountain trails and brooks and long and lazy days, hunting, fishing and just plain fooling around in the woods, barefoot in streams and tireless in all manner of outdoor physical activity.

There was a brook that had its origin, I know not where, back up in the mountains behind Aunt laura's property. It flowed onto her land, across it, onto the county property and then beside a road that ran a couple miles to the junction with the railroad at which point was the flag stop for the area. At this same junction was a country store that supplied the snacks and sweets when we had the price.

About a half mile from the junction lived a farm boy that was a dead shot with a rock and a good companion in the woods. We would wander together along the railroad track and off into the woods and over to the Roanoke River at various special places where the swimming was good or the woods were deep and interesting. We ambled along throwing rocks at anything that made a good target and exulting over our prowess when we hit.

We climbed many trees and explored in detail the land along the river banks where the river cut through the deep woods. There would be great trees that had lost their root hold on the banks of the river and fallen across the river. The river was deep and narrow in this section and the fallen trees made bridges from bank to bank. These bridges made ideal vantage points for dives in the river for invigorating swims that might be taken from time to time on a single afternoon.

Our entire clothing on summer days was an over-the-shoulder strapped overall, no underwear, no shirt, no shoes or sox. To go swimming one simply had to slip off the overall and dive in. When the swim was over no towel was necessary, you put your scant clothing onto your wet body, let it absorb the moisture and then dry in the balmy breeze.

I remember one very exceptional day among these outdoor charms that included a minor drama. I went up into the mountains behind Aunt Laura's hoping to find the source of the brook that flowed across her land. I gave up on that objective after miles of hiking and climbing and started back walking, and climbing over boulders in the stream, and worked my way down to the valley and on across our property always staying in the brook. The water was clear and sweet, from time to time I got down on all fours and had a drink. I found crayfish in the water and saw many small fishes swimming among the rocks and an occasional one that made me wish for a line and tackle.

The hours went by and there seemed no end to the interesting things to see in the water and along the shore. I crossed all of Aunt Laura's land and out onto either county land or the property of a neighboring farm. The adventure continued for miles. I had no watch but from the sun I could tell it was well past noon, I had forgotten lunch and was determined to continue the few miles farther to the railroad junction.

In this mood I was walking in the cold mountain water, turning over rocks with my feet and surprising living creatures that darted out and away up or down the stream. I turned over one large rock and out into the stream came a grown water snake that I had been told was poisonous. My instincts were to kill it and I tried to accomplish this objective with a stone. The snake was crawling across a wide flat rock and I struck him a solid blow with a stone thrown at close quarters. The snake seemed stunned. I put my foot solidly on his head or just behind it and proceeded to sever the head with my pocket knife. The knife was not too sharp and it took a bit of sawing and a bit of talking to myself to hold down tight until the job was done

Aunt Laura had a husband even though it would seem she didn't in the constant reference to the property as Aunt Laura's. Her name was used to identify every thing about the place as though it were a single woman's property. Her husbands name was Charlie Chapman which used to amuse me as a youngster because of the similarity with the famous Charlie Chaplin. Chapman was never addressed as uncle and was always referred to by his double name in conversations where he was not present. I actually now realize that I have no memory of my mother addressing him at all. There may have been an occasional uncle thrown in of which I was not aware. I shall here call him Chapman.

Chapman was a pleasant man to be around and I was in that position often in the fields and the stables. He had a sense of humor. When he was milking the cows in the early morning the cats would hang about and beg in high pitched voices. Chapman had a dead eye aim with a cow's teat and the cats knew what to expect; they would open their mouths wide while chapman squirted milk directly from the cow into the gaping cavity. The cats would push and shove to assure their turn at the stream. It was quite a show of animal appetites and human plus animal dexterity.

Chapman was also a great tease where his wife was involved. Aunt Laura had an unusual reaction to face masks. It seemed that she almost believed there was a real monster behind a mask of one. Chapman would obtain these masks and dress me up to scare Aunt Laura. A lot of excitement would ensue. There was probably a lot of play acting all around, but the experiences were innocent fun that is pleasant to recall.

There were fences everywhere about the farm, some to delineate yards for the pigs, others for the horses and still others around the barn to provide an area that, with gates closed, could confine the cows being fed and waiting to be milked. In this barnyard was a very long deep watering trough available to all the animals passing through or assembled there for service. My fascination with the trough was two big catfish that swam endlessly back and forth and, from time to time, would be tame enough to take food from my hand.

This very large yard held fascination for me at all ages of growing up, and different experiences are associated with different visits to the farm. One year we were there in threshing season. Chapman did not, as was customary with all the private farms of the area, own a threshing machine, contractors provided the service at a price. The wheat was brought to the barnyard and the grain, after threshing, was fed directly into bins provided for the purpose in the immense barn.

It was fun to see the machine devour the sheaves of wheat, and quickly deliver chaff to one side, and maintain a steady stream of wheat grain pouring out of a large pipe on the front part of the machine. Kids from neighboring farms came over for these sessions and we spent the day studying all that was taking place and, I guess, getting in the way of the workers from time to time.

A well designed barn is not a plebeian arrangement of unsophisticated functions. If one studies the many ways devised by a good farmer to solve the many problems of handling animals and produce, he will discover ingenuity on every hand .

I do not know the actual numbers, but the farm had many pigs confined to an area that seemed too large to be called a pig sty. A field was fenced in just behind the back yard of the house. At the point where the field and the back yard met the fence was low enough to give ready access to the slopping troughs. There were wide boards running horizontal to protect the feeder from the splash of the enthusiastic pigs gorging their food. I particularly enjoyed feeding the pigs, they enjoyed, so much, the very act of eating.

From a wooden box I built a wagon that moved on skids. No wheels were available. With this wagon I could go to the apple orchards located on the opposite side of the farm from the pig sties, and drag back a good load of apples recovered from the ground. These apples had bad places in them and were bruised from their falls from the tree but the pigs did not mind these faults. I had located and trained special pigs that could catch a tossed apple in their mouths. Some, not so athletic, would hand feed with tender loving care, all the while being careful not to let my hand get caught in the act. If you've never heard a group of pigs attack a trough full of apples you've never heard the supreme essence of happy sound. The crunch, crunch, crunch of each pig blends with all the others in a rhythm of sloppy noise that blends with grunts and pants, into a crescendo of excitement that leaves no doubts about the sincerity of the orchestra. I spent many days hauling apples to the pigs and feeding them over the fence.

The back yard of the farm house was flat and level and some beautiful maple trees shaded most of the area. Chickens wandered about the yard without interference. Grain and other feed for the chickens was scattered from the back porch, which porch not only extended across the actual back of the main house, but also along the side of a one storied extension that included a large dinning room and kitchen. This extension housed the operations upon the supreme attraction at Aunt Laura's, food. Her table was a masterpiece of southern hospitality: At dinner several kinds of meat were served at once, two rather large tall stemmed glass dishes, loaded with honey still in the combs, were, one at each end of the table, always present, and all the fresh produce of the season was in abundance. In the big kitchen canning seemed always in progress, and delectable preserved foods graced the meals. Cured Virginia hams perpetually hung in the smoke house, which house had at one time been a slaves cabin. Aunt Laura bragged that a good ripe age for the hams she served was 12 years old. At most dinners a very good dandelion wine was drunk over the objection of my Temperance Society mother. It also seemed she felt she had done her duty with a statement of opposition. The wine drinking went on, without friction in a modest way.

As for the yard that extended behind the house, If you walked to the rear of the yard, on your left the yard ended abruptly against a hill that rose up at a very steep angle into the large mountains beyond. From the hill flowed pure clear water. It was said the spring had always been there, so far as any of the family knew, and was the source of water for the farm when the Chapman family settled the plantation in the early days of Virginia, even before its separation from England. The water came from the spring in the hill in a steady stream, and was accumulated in a double pool built of field stones. The pool was formed in two sections by being divided in the middle by a walkway supported by stone arches through which the water freely flowed. The whole area, where this main spring was located under large trees, was always cool and moist. Large edible Frogs populated the banks of the pool and jumped in with," plop,plop", whenever a human came on the scene.

Occasionally we captured several of the frogs, and had Aunt Laura pan fry the legs in batter, the dish was very much like southern fried chicken, only superior in taste and texture. This magic land under the great trees, by the clear cold perpetually running water, was a favorite retreat after a hot day in the hills hauling apples for the pigs or just exploring.

From the large pool at the spring a 2" pipe ran under ground, a couple hundred feet across the yard, to conduct water into the spring house built just off the left end of the back porch. The water flowed continuously, in a full stream and was the freshest, clearest water I have ever tasted.

A double series of rectangular cement troughs built into the floor of the spring house, were lined up in parallel and occupied the entire length of one side of the very ample building. The water from the 2" pipe flowed into the troughs which always contained a high level of good cold spring water held at that level by leveling holes at the opposite end of the troughs . Great crocks of buttermilk, sweet milk and butter sat in the water which was always cold enough to provide good refrigeration. Hanging from the wall where the pipe came in was a gourd dipper on a long cord that permitted the gourd to dangle always in the water. This arrangement kept it cold and clean. When one was hot or needed nourishment he could repair to the spring house and take his choice: a large gourd full of spring water, buttermilk or sweet milk. Whatever his choice, there could be no place where it could taste as good as it did in that cool spring house with the sweet smell of churning, that probably had just taken place, and the wholesome smell of open crocks of sweet milk, and the freshly churned butter and buttermilk.

On the other side of the back yard to one's right as he left the back porch was an indistinct walkway that led to the backhouse, a three holer. Members of the family sometimes used subterfuge when they took that path. There was a wood pile against the fence; some procured a few sticks of wood as they returned from a trip. The backhouse was in a second yard behind a fence covered with vines which yard was entered through a latched gate.

In this same yard but much farther back on the property were the bee hives, dozens of them; honey was a commercial product of the farm along with milk, butter, hams, beef and produce. Aunt Laura tended her bees dressed in a very large brimmed hat from which draped a netting to protect her face and neck. She wore long gloves and at times beat on a pan as she approached. I understood little of this operation but knew much about its product.

And so the years went by, with Aunt Laura's a wonderfully consistent place, in the mountains, that possessed a wholeness for the spirit. I visited and experienced this place nearly every summer and carried it in my mind and heart through the other seasons. We moved our home frequently, as my father felt the call from new locations; we were required to leave our old friends every several years, and make new ones. But Aunt Laura's went on in its same happy way. It gave me a sense of continuity that otherwise would have been impossible. As I said above, this was my Shangra-la.

CHAPTER VI

WAYCROSS, GEORGIA 1917-1921

What characterized Waycross was its down town area that was a bit citified by commercial buildings for retail stores and various services but at the same time primitive and open like towns in West Texas. The R.R. Station was dead center in the business section of the city. One walked from the station through a double doorway right onto the side walk that ran at right angles to Main Street. Across the street from the railroad station was a triangular park no bigger than a medium sized front yard of a middle class home. This park was formed by small pieces of main street and Railroad street on two sides and another, nameless to me, street on the other. This latter street completed a right angle triangle with the other two, the right angle being at the intersection of main and Railroad streets. The other two angles were approximately 60 degrees and thirty degrees with the smaller angle at the railroad street intersection.

This small park was a major object of attention to a newcomer to the town because of a very tall water tank that dominated it and all the immediate area of the town. The tank was a vertical cylinder the same size all the way from the ground to its towering top; not one of the more familiar tanks supported by steel structured legs. It was, and probably still is, a storage tank for the city water supply. The tank was painted green but was always rusty. Across the street from the railroad station several park benches were arranged along the edge of the sidewalk that ran beside the tank.

People were always resting on these benches and on occasion they received a real surprise. Suddenly in the bright sunlight one would seem caught in the rain as a deluge of water splashed upon them. Excitedly looking heavenward they would discover that the tank was running over. The water department would be filling the tank. Those in the know would realize that the level control had failed to function again to shut the pumps down. If the wind were blowing, one watching would see a large sheet of water spread out from the top of the tank and form a hard shower on the unsuspecting occupants of the benches; simultaneously water would pour down the sides of the tank. This was always exciting and wetting but no major flood ever resulted. There must have been an additional automatic emergency shut off that came into action once over flow began because an "all clear" could have been sounded within minutes after the storm. To a newcomer to the city, the wetting of the people was a surprising, amusing and, sometimes, an irritating experience.

When we arrived at the station in Waycross the tank did not overflow but the town just outside the doors presented a unique picture: The immense tank dominated a portion of mid-city; main street seemed to have only one side, the street ran straight out from the station door; along the right hand sidewalk there were the usual store fronts that are expected in the business section of any small city but the other side of main street bordered on a large open area that was planted with a few trees and some poorly tended grass. In spite of the fact that there was no real park development it was, in the center of town, a pleasant green area of a full city block. The tranquility of the park was at times sacrificed to the pleasure of the young: a skating rink occupied a section of the park farthest removed from main street.

On the north side of this larger park area was the towns only hotel. I have wondered what the hotel guests thought of skating rink noises when sleep was interrupted.

Other essentials that revealed the character of Waycross could be taken in with a short trip covering a dozen city blocks. There were the railroad tracks through the center of the city that within two blocks joined feeder tracks that led into a large freight yard. In addition to being a railroad repair shop town Waycross was also a junction of railroads and a staging area where freight trains were made up of freight cars with destinations in the same direction. This freight yard later became a personal matter with me. I had a job there which will be explained later. Sprawling to the left as one entered the freight yard from the town was the shop; at the time the Atlantic Coast Line's largest shop on their system. The railroad dominated the town with one whole side devoted to the freight yard and the shop. In the downtown area, just across the tracks from the railroad station, was the Railroad Y.M.C.A., and only a few blocks beyond the Railroad Hospital.

The Baptist Church, the one that called my father was not a railroad church but it was physically only separated from the railroad property by a small park that functioned as a buffer state between the Church lot and the main line railroad tracks. There was a fence along the right of way that gave some privacy. My father's parishioners were shop people or those that supplied essential services to the railroad or its employees.

There were three residential sections in Waycross. West of the city center was the Negro community on the north side of the freight yard and shop complex. On the south side of this same complex was the fashionable neighborhoods. Lying to the Northeast, East and Southeast, generally surrounding the balance of town were all white shop people, store keepers, civil servants and the general population.

The railroad tracks coming from the east entered the city at about down town street level but in a cut through ground higher than the western part of the town. The trains could be heard and the smoke could be seen above the crest of the cut but from the porches of the houses along the streets paralleling the railroad right of way no tracks could be seen. We lived to the east of the city center on the street along the south side of this railroad cut. There was no right or wrong side of the tracks in this area. It was a middle class neighborhood. I remember that two doors down from our house was Colonel Spence, a lawyer; lawyers carried that title in Georgia in 1918. Two boys were in the family, A. B. and Clyde. I never knew what the initials A. B. stood for he was addressed always as" Abee".

We lived next door to a large family all of who's male members worked for the railroad as shop mechanics. A journeyman mechanic for the railroad was, in most of Waycross society, a successful person of considerable status. I was often advised by older members of the community that a college education was not necessary or even desirable. " Look at me, I am doing all right and I never did nothing beyond grammar school" (or sometimes high school), was a common remark.

Some of the in-laws in the Owens family were bronze foundry men. They told me of the short life they expected from the noxious affects of bronze fumes. There seemed to be a sense of heroism in their dangerous work. They were braggadocio in their anecdotes. I doubt if the workers really believed their own stories of the hazards of their occupation but they hoped their listeners did in admiration for their courage. Others in the family were carpenters and painters.

If there is or was any such thing as a characteristic shop wife the women of the Owens family were typical, and each took pride in the standing of her husband in the trade. A machinist considered his trade tops, the carpenter his and so each to his own. I served an apprentice Blacksmith's trade and until this day feel that that trade is superior in its basic nature. Steel and iron are a basic of our civilization. The materials themselves are hard and strong and resist the worker. He must, almost literally go through fire to render steel responsive to his will and the images of his mind.

The character of all trades have changed over the years as specialized tools and procedures have been developed. The acetylene gas cutting torches, controlled by patterns, acting through panographs burn out forms that used to be forged. Die casting replaces skilled hammer work. Also materials easier to form, with properties better suited to particular uses, have replaced metals. But surely some of the same pride remains within the new specialized skills that have branched from the basic trades.

The church was a central influence in the lives of the shop people and a focal point of much of their social activity. As families, I knew only church people well; Baptist church people. My father was the preacher at the Baptist church. As individuals, I knew people from other churches, and some that were not of any persuasion. Some were free wheelers and even bootlegged a bit of corn whiskey into the shops. More about my time in the Railroad Shop will be narrated in another chapter.

Arriving in Waycross from Norfolk must have been routine: I actually have no recollection of the experience of arriving. I just found myself living along the Railroad tracks in eastern Waycross only about one block from the beginning of the down town area. To go downtown You went West one block to a corner, turned right, crossed the railroad tracks, and then turned left onto a very long street. This street in, in our neighborhood, began with several blocks, of small commercial establishments, some mama and papa type. These shops grew in size as you moved toward the business center of the town. When one reached that destination he found the hardware stores, restaurants, department stores and all the usual expected for a modest metropolitan center supplying even smaller settlements in proximity. The railroad tracks paralleled this lead-in street, and eventually arrived at the station at the end of Main street. This railroad track cut the entire city in half like a black pencil line drawn deliberately on a map.

Walking in the other direction, down the railroad track east from our home for two miles, would lead one to a swamp, a river and a swimming hole. The river flowed under a railroad bridge. We would leave the railroad track at the bridge, descend by a sandy steep path down the supporting embankment. We would hike along the river bank for several hundred feet, into the seclusion of the woods and then to a small open area on the river bank. A fallen tree across the river reminded me of a similar setup at Aunt Laura's. The swimming hole was beneath the log. The log was the diving location and a bridge to the other bank of the river. Water swirled among the branches of the dead tree that reached below the water's level. We went to the swimming hole in small groups. The place was never crowded . In fact I do not recall ever finding anyone at the hole when our group of from two to four went there for an afternoon swim.

We also went coon hunting in the associated swamp, or rather I recall vividly one such hunt. Some of the older boys had well trained hunting dogs. We went at night and stayed late; into the early morning hours. We walked to keep warm and listened for the sound of the dogs when they caught the

scent of a coon or opossum. And soon they did with a far
away lonely belling bark that was real communication to
their masters. It said, "We are on the trail of an animal";
each owner could distinguish the voice of his own dog and
seemed to believe his dog sounded a bit more appropriate to
the occasion than the dogs of his companions. In your
mind's eye you could see the dogs running through the swamp
growth and in and out of water and mud as they sought their
prey, and pursued it until it was finally treed at some
distance from where we followed. The excited sounds of the
dogs bellowing their impatience reached a crescendo.

When we arrived at the site of the confrontation, the dogs
leaped and pointed as though pleading for some one to knock
the coon from the tree to the ground below and the fight
that would follow. They were charging up the tree trunk, as
though they meant to climb, and then falling back for
symbolical leaps directly at the high limb on which the
raccoon was ensconced.

The boys in the know (I was a newcomer to this sport) by
climbing and using polls dislodged the coon from his perch.
As he hit the ground five dogs were upon him and the fight
was chilling. The coon seemed at first to be almost a match
for the vicious dogs but his fate was sealed, and I almost
prayed for him to win. It was pitiful to see dogs tear at
his throat and strip flesh from his legs. The handlers soon
called off the dogs and shot the wounded coon.

This has not been an experience that I have sought to
repeat. I will say, I do remember well the enchantment of
the deep woods at night, with the lamentations of the dogs
in the distance breaking the silence that was otherwise
complete, except for and occasional bird call and the
periodically repeated proclamation of a lonely owl.

Important to almost everything that follows in my
orientation to Waycross was the high school. The building
sat in midtown on a square lot bounded on four sides by
uptown business blocks; a few residences were thrown in
between stores and offices on the two streets behind the
school. The the portion of the lot left for recreation and
other outdoor school events, after the space occupied by the
school building, was far from adequate. All grass that might
have been cultivated in the area was trampled down. Except
for a few scattered small trees, I can recall no other
growing things in the area. There was no beauty about the
place. Whether or not I was sensitively aware of this as a
thirteen year old boy, I do not know, but in looking back I
see a gray dusty lot. Plain buildings that housed a greasy-
spoon restaurant, a billiard pool hall, and a movie theater
filled one business corner just across the street from the
school grounds.

My introduction to the school may have included some benign features but the event that sticks in my memory occurred on the school lot during a recess period. Mostly the older boys formed in small active groups or sat upon one of the benches that were scattered about the place. The girls seemed given more to walking about arm in arm or forming groups assembled just for laughter. The sound of girlish laughter was pervasive. I was new; a fact that was apparent to all the other pupils. I moved about the grounds trying here and there to join the play or other activities. Actually, at the critical moment, my attention was attracted by an odd tree root that was above ground. I stood there certainly minding my own business, or the tree's business, when a boy in his late teens walked up and spoke to me. I thought his tone was unfriendly but I responded with a smile and a,"How do you do?" He said,"This is how I do," and with that remark he swung his fist to my jaw and flattened me on the ground.

It is an understatement to say I was surprised; I was devastated: hurt physically and in spirit, and challenged to a response I could not rise to make or consider making in this strange land with that strange giant hovering over me. Some professor saved the day by ushering both of us into the building with some admonishments not to fight on the school grounds. Actually in hindsight the blow descended so irrelevantly that, so far as present personal emotions are concerned, it could have been a brick that fell loose from a building by pure accident. It no longer seems like a personal confrontation but, at the time, it taught me quickly that some of the boys from the swamps of southern Georgia were rustic, rough and ruthless. I learned soon to recognize the type and keep my guard up when they came around. I would like to have been able to end that story with how I challenged the bully on his home turf and, after an exhaustive struggle, with blood about and broken teeth, I made him cry uncle. But alas, I was still on the ground when the professor rescued me; the only cry I remember was,"that'll teach you; you damn Yankee!" I had come south all the way from Virginia to pay for the sins of people who came years before from above the Mason Dixon Line.

I do remember one thing pleasant about that school; a most unlikely recollection; my brief course in Latin. Not until I was much older, a man with a family toward the end of my business career and interested in travel, did I display any interest in foreign languages yet I remember no other course in that school. I can still recall the Latin conjugations learned in this interesting class. It was a surprise to me that there had been such a language; that people had walked the earth and talked like that. I cannot adequately tell how this intrigued me with actual emotional sensations that abide until now.

It is remarkable how little I remember about this school. I do know that high school classes were there because I entered my first year in Waycross. It was about this time that schools in the South changed from seven to eight preparatory years before High School. I came under the ending seven year rule. Junior high and even grade school classes were surely conducted on the premises. There were many pupils in a wide range of age groups around the place. If there was any other school in the city I have no knowledge of it; maybe that was the school for everyone. I was thirteen years old during my truncated first year High.

The people in Waycross habitually indulged in shop talk, literally, a large part of their time. Their relative positions in society were determined by their status at the shop. The shop buildings dominated the western skyline and, when the wind was right, the smoke blew across the city. There was usually a, not totally unpleasant, stench from the fumes. In fact one could find himself feeling at home in the smell when returning from an absence in a completely clear air community. The freight yards to the west were active and dramatic. Busy shifting engines moved freight cars hither and yon making up trains for specific destinations; there were frequent train whistles and puffing noises all characteristic of the area. All these things seemed designed to enchant a young boy. At least, they got to me. I became restless at school. I wished to leave and become part of the activities I saw about me.

CHAPTER VII

ADVENTURE ?

I seemed to become obsessed with the desire to quit school and go to work in the shop. I talked to my friends about running away from home. There was no logic in this because that act would take me away from the shops; I was just unhappy and ignorant of such things as human moods and compulsions. How many seemingly disconnected events impinging upon a young mind are necessary to build a persuasion that a certain direction to go is the all important imperative to its host?

In review it seems that in free time I covered a good part of Waycross on foot talking over my problems with friends or acquaintances. I remember one man much older than me who very nearly changed the course of my life. In conversation he always brought the conversation back to the practical consideration of, " Where are you going to get the three meals a day that you now get at home." I liked to eat and my mother was a good cook; purely for reasons of the stomach, not for any virtuous thought, I almost decided not to run away.

At thirteen the focus of attention can often be primarily on self. One's parents are a factor in ones life, sometimes a variable to be manipulated into approval or assistance. It is later in life when we really begin to understand that a parent is just another person in a one on one relationship with you. They may have some justifiable complaints about your behavior in the interchange.

One person sympathetic to my contemplated escape was the chief of police's son named Sy Colly. He was a character, wise in street psychology; one of the reasons I never forgot his name was its seeming derivation from the description of his characteristic wisdom for pure survival, entrepreneurial scheming and confident behavior among the rougher members of waycross youth. He not only approved of my intentions but proposed that we go together to Jacksonville Florida.

Sy explained that he could get the schedule of some freight trains composed of empty refrigerator cars leaving the staging yard for Florida fruit groves. There was an exit track from the yard that joined the main line South about three miles from our home. We planned that Sy would be on board a chosen train at that junction and I would catch it at that point before the engineer opened his throttle for the established speed for his trip South. With the schedule, all the timing could be worked out in advance and I could follow the track from my home to the rendezvous.

When the twentieth century was also still in its teens refrigerator cars were actually rolling iceboxes. There was a compartment at either end of the cars which compartments were probably three feet long in the direction of the train and as wide and deep as the car. Access to these compartments was through the top. Each compartment could be entered, or ice could be put in, through an opening in the top. A hinged cover with a lever type lock covered the opening. It was planned that such an empty ice box would be our private compartment on the ride to Jacksonville. Sy was to stake out a claim for our private quarters by climbing in and propping the lid open perceptibly. I was to locate him by walking the top of the moving train until I came to a car with the compartment lid ajar. After a confirming call, I was to open the lid and climb in. That was the plan.

The time finally came. The freight train had been picked, the time that it would cross the junction for our rendezvous was known and I had firmly committed myself to meeting Sy at that junction. I can recall my unhappiness at the time but without any definition of causes. The atmosphere in my home was strict but chiefly upon religious matters. I certainly recall no deliberate cruelty. My parents seemed to me, particularly my mother, remote and impenetrable on the personal level. Somehow, in my mother's presence I sometimes became convinced of my sinful nature. In fact the regular church services, with an occasional series of revival meetings thrown in produced a background radiation of morbidity. That is the only word I can find to describe the feeling that even lives in memory about the impressions made upon my mind by the, so called, four square Gospels as preached by many evangelists . All I recall clearly is my resolution to make my break for freedom.

The train schedule made our meeting time fall in late afternoon. On the chosen day as the time for my departure approached, my parents were weeding their vegetable garden, with me bound in as their general helper. I had hid an extra jacket in the railroad cut in front of our house to be picked up on the way. My escape path was easy: if I could get away from the house; it was to cross the street, follow the descending path into the cut and then, completely shielded by the banks of the cut, proceed down the tracks, in security, to the meeting. But time went on and on; I was becoming desperate for an excuse to leave the garden. As if by fate, my father gave me a bucket and said, "Son go over to the railroad cut and get some of that good top soil from the upper part of the bank". This was my chance.

I took the bucket with a haste that must have surprised my parents and nearly ran out of our back-yard, around the side of our house into the front yard, across the street and down the path into the railroad cut. I dropped my pail beside the path, picked up my jacket and started on a run to the junction for our rendezvous. It was a long run, surely a couple miles at top speed, from our residential neighborhood, through the center of town and on out to the vicinity of the freight yards. It was unbelievable, as I approached, the train I sought was moving slowly across the junction but picking up speed. I jumped the train catching the iron ladder of the last freight car before the caboose. This was too close for secrecy, the brakeman saw me and yelled for me to get off. I climbed to the top of the car and ran along the wooden catwalks, jumping from one car to the other as I reached them in sequence. About half way down the length of the train I saw what I was looking for: the cover of one of the ice boxes was propped open in a very conspicuous manner. I headed for that cover, got down on my knees and shouted as loud as I could, "Sy!"--"Sy!"-- . The call came back, "yeah man!" We had made connection and were on our way to Jacksonville. As I look back I am not so sure but at the time it seemed like a, not so minor, victory and a promise of adventure.

Unfortunately as I swung onto the iron ladder steps of the last boxcar before the caboose the brakeman was standing on the little forward platform of this control car of every freight train. He saw me come aboard. I could not hear his shouted words above the noise of the car wheels clanging as they crossed the intersecting tracks of the junction. There were only the two final cars left to complete the crossing but the noise was with us to the end.

When the crossing was complete the train gained speed with purpose; we could feel the power impulses as the engineer open his throttle in deliberate steps to establish his cruising speed for the one hundred mile trip to Jacksonville. We had climbed out of the refrigerator car and were standing on the end of the open bed of a flat car well loaded with lumber. The lumber was cut in long boards that were not all of the same length. The disparate lengths produced cavities or small rooms at the end of the lumber pile: several boards overhead, if you chose your place well, would extend four to five feet beyond the lower boards in the pile and form a ceiling. Lower down a few boards would extend out one or two feet and provide a seat. Other long boards on the sides seemed almost intentionally provided in the way they afforded the security of walls if not the complete protection from air currents. Our spot was cozy and we settled down to enjoy the anticipated several hours ride through the Georgia swamps on this warm summer night

But we had underestimated the diligence of the train crew who were already engaged in a car to car search. A Negro brakeman came across the pile of lumber and dropped down at our end practically in the center of our private room. He probably maintained his sense of security in the knowledge that other crew members were close behind. This same knowledge was the source of our desperation. Sy Collie had been there before and knew what to do: as if by reflex action he offered a bribe which was accepted and honored, at least for the duration of the encounter; the brakeman accepted five dollars and went on down the train without raising an alarm for his associates.

The silence of the brakeman gave us time to climb off the lumber flat car, up to the walkway along the top of the refrigerator cars. We opened the cover and descended into first ice box. These iceboxes were by no means air tight. They were separated from the perishable food storage area by slats only. When light was available one could see through the slats into the main compartment. Nevertheless we feared asphyxiation and propped the lid open with its own opening handle. That act plus the fact that, in our excitement, we chose the car next in line to the lumber car made our discovery imminent; soon it happened. A couple brakemen opened the cover door and hollered, "we know you are in there, come on out". In my innocence I was ready to obey the command and take the consequences, which I imagined to be severe, but my companion was not so disposed. He was street wise or, in this case, train wise and understood the psychology of the situation. He whispered to me, "They have no idea who are in here or how dangerous we might be. They have no light (it was dusk when I caught the train and it was now dark) and they would not dare stick their heads in here in the dark. Sit tight and say nothing." I obeyed.

The brakeman left after assuring us they would be back and "take care of us". But after waiting for the men to have time to reach the caboose, we assumed they were going for a light and would stay together, we climbed out of our ice box and purposely moved only to the icebox on the other end of the same car. My mentor reasoned that they would not expect us to do something that stupid but would go to a car far removed unless we were willing to confront them in our first abode. This time we closed the cover door after us and settled down to await developments.

We did not have long to wait; the men returned with a strong light that we could see plainly from our private cubby hole. The slats from our ice box opened as described into the main body of the car. The compartment we had just left was at the other end of the same car and was separated from the storage area by slats also. The men lowered their light in to our erstwhile abode and through the slats lighted the main interior. Light from there made us visible to each other but apparently not to our pursuers. No one climbed into the other ice box. The men evidently had a good view from above and saw that it was empty. We held our breath that the next move would be an inspection of our end; it didn't happen. I can only believe that our strategy, of trusting they would rule out our going to the other end of the same car as being a chance we would not take, paid off. we heard the men depart along the top of the car we occupied. We hoped the search was over.

That was not to be. We did have a respite, that seemed to be of about one hour's duration, at the end of which the train began to slow down. We ventured out of our hiding place and from the top of the car could see in the distance a railroad station with a small town adjacent. The lights were intense in the contrast of the dark night. We guessed that they might stop at the town and make a complete search for the hobos they were sure were on board. The lighting along the tracks at the station would help their cause but the lighting was on the station side of the tracks only. Our protective move seemed obvious: climb down the ladder on the dark side and hug the side of the car. From this vantage point for, what seemed like, an interminable time we felt the train stop and heard main car doors open and then close as car interiors were inspected. We saw the feet of men pass over head along the top of the cars as the ice boxes were opened and closed. We hung on and kept quiet. No one came along the ground on the dark side of the train and for sure no one spotted us from above as we clung wrapped in our blanket of darkness.

The train began to move and then in jerks reach new levels of speed until it became obvious we were on our way again at the cruising speed for the trip. We climbed back to the cat walk along the car tops and chose another icebox as a stateroom. Our excitement and acute insecurity subsided slowly. I became conscious of the rhythm of the rail noises. After a while we opened our trap door to the warm night air. The stars were out; It was surprising how soon after our escape from the hunters we dropped into the mood of a summer evening when one is riding along under the stars in his private coach. Evidently the enemy had surrendered: we rode on for hours undesturbed and made plans for what we would do when we reached the vacinity of Jacksonville.

We decided that we had no real knowledge of the train's destination. Probably the train would slow down for crossings on the outskirts of the city. If it did, that would be our real chance to disembark in proximity of our destination without being carried through the city or caught getting off in some freight terminal area. I remember the point of departure, Kings Road crossing; here the train slowed almost to a safe jumping speed. We took a chance on the margin. Sy climbed down the steps of one end of our car; I took the other end. The time was very early morning; the dawn had broken and our landing was clearly visible. The rhythm was: as sy's steps reached kings road he put a foot down, turned lose and ran at maximum speed in order to dissipate his forward motion; when my steps reached the road I did the same. The speed needed for balance was too great;

we both fell forward after a noble run and I, coming from behind, piled on top of sy. Except for a few scratches no one was hurt. We had arrived and had before us about a four mile walk into the city.

We got to our feet just as the caboose crossed King's Road. The temptation was too great; we jumped and shouted to two brakemen that were out on the rear porch of the caboose and waved frantically to convey our feeling that we had won over them the contest for our freedom and a free ride to the city. Only one waved back; he was the Negro we had bribed into temporary silence.

I remember that early morning walk into town that eventually led through a large Negro district called, in those days, nigger town. The streets and sidewalks were there but unpaved. By nature and not design the surfaces of both were reasonably good because of the off-white sand clay that, when it rains, drains well and becomes compacted into what might be mistaken for a low grade cement. Due to the early hour we saw relatively few people but with some frequency we would pass on the sidewalk women and men hurrying to their jobs, probably in a white neighborhood. The atmosphere was friendly; from and occasional horse and wagon or automobile someone would send a mild salute or wave. I recall the personal relationship between the whites and blacks of 1917 as one of detached friendliness. It included none of the open hostility that has in recent years come to the surface. I say it has surfaced recalling that Negros were segregated in the extreme at that time and there were instances of outrage and discrimination that surely must have caused the Negro to harbor strong resentment beneath the surface but in all contacts, on a one to one basis, I remember their friendliness and my reciprocal feeling.

I remember little about Jacksonville as a city. There were of course shops and store fronts and more imposing business buildings, and traffic that gave me the feeling, as a young teenager, that I was in the "Big" city but greater detail escapes me. We found our way to what could only be called a flop house. The rent for a bed was fifty cents per night. I do not remember that we were mixed with and large number of other itinerants and probably the place was quite clean on a practical basis. We seemed to have had a divided off area that represented a room for two.

My total wealth was five dollars; I do not know how much money Sy had. We promptly spent a small amount for a very adequate breakfast in, what we called, a greasy spoon. We bought one newspaper and started our search for a job.

When we arrived in Jacksonville I must have been in the hands of a guide that had been there before. I simply found myself, under Sy's guidance, in a place of beds, wash basins and toilets commonly called a flop house. The price was right: 50 cents per night. The fact that several others shared the same large room did not disturb me at thirteen years old. At that time I took for granted that people treated right by you would respond in kind. That belief was never contradicted in my contacts among some very doubtful looking people.

I would not be so naive today but, be it luck or faith, I will not, in this writing, have anything to report about having been taken in and abused by some street wise characters. My contacts with derelicts, dock workers and sailors on the streets and along the water front of Jacksonville are among my pleasant memories and are without any threatening encounters. It is almost a conspiracy, to confound the alarmist, that a young boy would go unprotected into the evil world of a water front city and have only friendly encounters to recall.

With sleeping quarters assured but with less than five dollars in my pocket a job was a first consideration. We searched the want add columns and zeroed in on, "man wanted to wash dishes." My mother had given me ample training to assure that I had the skills required for a dishwasher and the fact that meals were included was convincing: I was in line the next morning responding to the add. I was surprised that there was a line of applicants that overflowed through the restaurant door and down the sidewalk for many feet into the store front area of the adjacent building.

Sy had other plans but stayed with me to see if I got the job. My position was out on the sidewalk near the tail end of the line.

I was thoroughly discouraged, felt overwhelmed by the numbers in line ahead of me and was ready to quit before being interviewed. Sy was again my teacher. He said, "Take a look at the others. Do you believe you have no chance in this bunch." I looked and gained a certain confidence in myself. Probably that simple incidence taught me early on not to discount yourself. Realistic comparisons of one's self with others in a critical situation and objective appraisals are not conceit. I have remembered this experience, and its outcome, to my advantage on numerous occasions when job opportunities and related appraisals have been required. The outcome was sudden and convincing: the restaurant owner walked briskly down the line turned and walked back to my position, literally pulled me out of line and said to the others, "Thanks and sorry guys but that's all. I felt I had been chosen the queen of may. Dish washing was not a factor; I had become first among a line of contenders for a coveted place. That is an experience that always pleases. I have never since given up in despair when my merits were being weighed and, with some disappointments, have, more often than not, been rewarded for my self confidence. Doubtless I owe my street conscious friend a lot for making me stay in line to get a dish washing job.

I remember vividly one encounter on the water front with gratitude to the captain of a merchant ship loading for a trip to ports of call in the Orient. I had requested, of a seaman guarding the gang plank, permission to board and talk to the captain about a job. I was surprised at the ease with which the permission was granted. With no questions asked, the sailor guided me up the plank and ushered me into the captains quarters and the presence of a man whose hands caught my attention first. His hands, in blotches that were not covered with freckles, were impressively pink-white but the freckles were so numerous that they ran together to effect a general tan except for the intermittent white patches that caught my attention. The backs of the hands were covered with blond hair beginning to gray. With very fully modelled fingers the hands were unusually large. They were obviously the hands of a very strong man. The captain stood, shook my hand in a strong grip and a warm welcome and invited me to take a chair beside his desk. I was impressed to be made welcome in such austere quarters and was overwhelmed by the height and breadth of my host. Nevertheless I felt an immediate sense of security and talked freely to the captain about wanting a job on his ship. Probably he led me into talking freely about leaving home and wanting to get away from what seemed like an excessively restricted life.

In any event, the Captain was soon talking to me like a fond uncle and advising me to forget my plans to go to sea. I do not remember the details of our talk but; I do recall the feeling at the time that he was genuinely interested with concern for a boy that had stumbled into his orbit. His words came across not as opposition to my program, but as the expressions of a new found friend.

How often when we listen to the plans of others, sometimes very personal plans, do we realize that it is just possible they are in the mood to be greatly influenced. We should probably assume that all such conversations are critical. I know that I have among my memories several people that have said precisely the right thing at the right time and have made *the* difference.

Prior to the interview recounted above I had visited several ships along that Jacksonville water front but do not recall the particulars except that none had hired me or shanghaied me; I was ready to drop the project. There must not have been many exciting occurrences because I recall almost nothing. I learned to wash mountains of dishes and ate well at the restaurant. In off time I did a lot of window shopping and frequented the railroad station to see the trains come in. At a soda fountain, in the station one afternoon, between the lunch dish washing period and the dinner period, I was enjoying a chocolate ice cream soda when a policeman came over to the counter and said, "son could I have a word with you?" The word included asking me to let him see my left hand on which I have a distinctive scar.

The people in Jacksonville must practice a southern hospitality because all my encounters are somehow pleasant to recall. The policeman, in a very friendly manner, explained that he thought I was Robert Hoge, had run away from home and that my father was waiting for me at the police station and that I had better come along with him. And so I was given a ride across town in the little black wagon, known at that time as the black marria.

When I arrived at the station my father was waiting dressed in a cap. I had never seen him in any head covering but a derby or, on very special occasions, a high silk hat. I hardly knew him. Maybe he was playing detective and that was his disguise. Without formality I was turned over to his care and we departed in a taxi back to the railroad station. I have always remembered my dad's greeting and his handling of his rebellious son: he said, "let's go home son" and that is all he said then or forever after concerning my run away. His silence about any trouble I had caused him or my mother and his friendliness all the way home on the train may not have been fully appreciated then but over the years I have understood the psychology of letting events preach the sermon. I was being put on my honor to do the right thing and I could not fail the trust.

CHAPTER VIII

Off TO WORK

When we returned home from Jacksonville I expected to be severely disciplined; actually I was received with warm affection, my problems with the school and my desire to work in the shops were discussed with sympathetic understanding and a decision was reached that I could quit school and begin to search for a job. No job in the shop was immediately available and my age, 13 years, was below the allowable beginning age. I had been advised however that, in practice, physical size determined ones acceptance if the application testified to 17.

Actually, I was big enough, tall, and physically mature for my age, and would have no difficulty passing for 17 on that basis. I must have attended to the application detail because, after a period of waiting for an opening, I was accepted as an Apprentice Blacksmith, which was a trade that, in the teens of this century, still included forging a substantial part of all the essential metal parts of the locomotives and the cars that composed a train.

During the period of waiting for the above assignment there is a story of a peripatetic youth trying diverse jobs enthusiastically but with a reach that may have at times exceeded his grasp.

First it was the Coca Cola Bottling Works, washing bottles on a production line, that introduced me to the world of the employed worker. The building was a frame structure built on a cement slab; it could have been an oversized barn, rectangular with open rafters overhead, but about one half the floor area provided ample open space for the washing and bottling operation.

Except for persons setting up and attending the automatic machinery the washers performed the only manual operations: Each washer stood in one place and was fed bottles from a moving conveyor. Beside him was a rotating brush arranged on a metal stem that was functionally and extension of a vertical shaft that turned at high speed. The stem was hollow and performed as an open ended tube to supply water and detergent to the rotating brush built integral. The washer would grab a bottle from the approaching conveyor, upend it, place the neck over the rotating brush and push down. As the bottle descended on the brush it contacted, on its outside, a levered mechanism that turned on the pressurized flow of the liquid cleaning mixture. The rotating brush stirred up a storm inside the bottle, cleaned out the flies that often had perished in the residue they sought and otherwise returned the bottles to a condition that was clean and sanitary enough to pass the inspection of local health authorities. As the washer began to remove the bottle from the brush the bottle released the levered mechanism; the detergent was turned off and for a short time water only rinsed the bottle.

The washed bottle was placed in a second conveyor composed of a moving chain with built in metal compartments sized right to receive, snugly, the bottles, that were now ready for filling, and convey them to the bottling area. The compartmentalized conveyor held each bottle steady while a mixing nozzle descended and automatically filled it with the syrup and carbonated water and then moved it to the capping machine that applied the familiar crinkled edged cap that has been the seal on "pop" bottles for many years.

Almost immediately there were features about this Bottling Works job that made me unhappy with the arrangement. There were several much older boys that persistently made life uncomfortable for the younger and smaller workers. To maximize the negatives, the other half of the barn of the building, in which we worked, was occupied by a casket factory and, behind the building, we shared a common freight dock which was always loaded with caskets waiting for the freight cars in which they were to be shipped.

It was the custom to bring our lunch to work and, on clear days, to consume it in picnic style on the freight dock among the caskets. In fact there was always a casket or two, sitting one deep, that provided seats for the workers and a convenient place to spread their lunches. At first this seemed a unique custom but, very soon, picnic lunches on and among the caskets grew increasingly macabre. Some bottlers counted the boxes daily and philosophized about death and speculated on the destiny of this or that box. There was at every lunch a strong reminder of our own mortality amid conversation and wise cracks on the subject. In a short time I resolved to not stay on that job. The resolve grew to be a compulsion and one day I just didn't go to work. I had forgotten to bring my lunch box home the day before but, never mind, like Joseph leaving his coat in the hands of the Harlot and fleeing I left my lunch box. My mother pressed me frequently to recover the box but I just as frequently avoided a return trip to the Works, until the lunch box was forgotten. Apparently I had had it.

My next job had several factors which people often refer to as learning experiences; the first was biological or anatomical. The job was in a meat packing company making link sausages. Here I learned that the hog's intestines held the ground up meat. I worked beside a bench on which cleaned and prepared intestines were stretched out along its back edge. To my left was a meat grinding machine not unlike the one in my mother's kitchen except for its larger size and a special nozzle to deliver the ground meat. When turned on the machine ground rapidly and extruded a cylinder of meat about the size of the inflated intestine.

My job was to tie the right end of each intestine, then stretch the left end over the protruding nozzle and press a foot switch that caused meat to flow smoothly into the biological tube producing a single sausage about the length of my workbench. I then removed and tied the left end and began making links by holding the long sausage firmly in my left hand, pinching in the soft meat and rotating the right end until, by repeated similar operations, multiple short lengths were held permanently between the twisted positions in the intestine. The short lengths were gauged by white marks painted on my bench.

It was also part of my job to keep my immediate supervisor, who carved and mixed the meats and spices, supplied with meat from a refrigeration room adjoining our work area. Preliminary larger cuts were hung in here on "S" shaped snaring hooks, the room was quite cold, it felt good for a few minutes to run in from the hot work area and grab a few sides of meat for the boss. I had no reason to foresee danger in a refrigerator but danger was there.

I do not know what the voltage drop to ground was on the electric circuits that supplied power but I can testify that it packed an awful wallop. The insulation had deteriorated and fallen from a wire along the wall near the hooks that held the meat. My forearm fell against this wire. It gave me an electric shock to remember I felt that I had been possessed by a monster internally and shaken viciously from the inside out and then in some strange manner seized on the outside and thrown to the floor in a nearby corner. It must have all happen in a flash but I recall it in slow motion. Considering that the floor was wet with a semi-frozen slush and my feet were damp, the shock could have been fatal except that I was quickly knocked down and free from the exposed wire. This was my second learning experience,

Again the job was not for me, I had been on it only a couple days but I left in haste and alarm without my pay. In looking back it is quite possible that, for a few days, I suffered some sort of continuing shock with irrational behavior. Physically there were symptoms of strain and passing internal damage. For a couple days, I could not take a deep breath without acute pain in my sides and chest. This condition continued with decreasing severity for over a month.

Then I became the Railway Express Delivery Man. In hindsight that seems like a considerable responsibility for a thirteen year old but at the time I was confident and probably supplied the personnel office with the right age to record.

Delivery was by horse and wagon, a fine green and red wagon, with suitable logos, that I kept clean and neat. The team was also my charge.

Each morning I walked about a quarter of a mile to the Express Company's stable. After feeding the two horses I would harness them to the wagon and take off for the Railroad Station for an early check in. This, and even the driving, was all new experience for me. At times my enthusiasm would tempt me to let the horses out on an empty street, or give them a touch or two with the whip, and feel the exhilaration of speed. I felt like the chariot racers of old that I had seen in the movies. I did enough of this racing to cause some good citizen to report me for, what he called, overtaxing the horses. My boss, who was a kind and understanding man, gave me a reprimand and strick orders to maintain a dignified speed at all times. On this, in the future, I followed orders.

My first day with the horses I drove them home for lunch to surprise my family who did not know that I had a new job. Adjacent to our property was a vacant lot. I pulled the team onto the lot and tied the reins to a small tree, went in the house and waited for the comments. They came quickly and vigorously. My mother used her childrens' double names when remonstrating or otherwise wished to be emphatic. She exclaimed, "Robert Hatcher! where did you get those horses?" I quietly answered, "I am the new Express Man". Her look of surprise was profound and eloquent as she made a declaration, " you are no such thing!--you take those horses back where you got them this instant".

Working for the Express Co. became a routine of hitching the horses in the morning, making deliveries to ordinary people during the day and putting the horses to bed, as it were, in the evening but most of what took place was exciting to a boy probably too young to be on that kind of job. Some people were regular customers and we became friends. Two of these relationships developed a special significance, one not so friendly, from what may be called a common root:

Two of my regular customers purchased, at regular intervals, small packages of fancy meats from the same supplier, the meats were perishable, and the customers wanted home delivery on the day the meat arrived, even if this required me to work overtime. Neither party knew the other.

One of the meat buyers was a very attractive lady about my mothers age who fed me cookies and coco on each trip and insisted that I come into her living room for a rest while I consumed quantities of her offerings. She was also very flattering in speech and, in a restrained way,very affectionate. Sometimes her enthusiasm was a bit overwhelming and I was caused to wonder if that sort of thing went with the job of being an express man. I enjoyed the attention and the food and, at the time, gave no thought to anything except that she was a kind lady expressing her motherly instincts to a hard working boy. As I write this, even from the cynicism of age, I shall continue believing those were her intentions that I recall with gratitude.

The other customer for imported meats was a man of some foreign origin who spoke with an accent that I did not recognize. He would respond to my ring of his door bell by quickly opening his door, taking the package from my hands, saying "thanks" and just as hastily closing the door behind his retreat, as though the whole operation was one continuous movement. Through many deliveries there were no problems, But then, one day he called the office, stated that he would not be home that afternoon but for me to put the package of meat on the shed; he would recover it that evening.

Now in my family and among our friends the word shed described two specifics: One was a small building behind one's house such as the woodshed; the other was the roof of the front porch that shed the water when it rained. The man's request made sense to me: there was no question of my ability to climb a post that supported, what I will now call, the roof of his front porch and place a small package of special steaks up there safe from any dishonest passersby. At home if I came in late, or had forgotten my key and the folks were out for the evening, my way of getting in was to shinny up a post, cross the roof and enter through an upstairs window. I felt a certain kinship with my customer for the first time, thinking that he too used his upstairs windows in a sensible manner: he could step out on the roof and claim his package that had waited safely for his return.

There was one difficulty: he did not use the word shed as my neighbors did. "Shed" meant to him the front porch itself. He was astonished that anybody didn't know you walked across the shed to go in your front door not your upstairs windows. Actually his astonishment came many days after the delivery when his nose found the package on what he called the roof of his shed. Before the discovery he had called and, with some heat, demanded to know what had become of his meat. I insisted I had put it on the shed. From his tone and insinuations, I gathered that he suspected that I was the culprit who had enjoyed a good meal at his expense but only until he did actually go through an upstairs window and bring in a box of very badly spoiled meat.

The other driver spoke my language and called a shed a shed. Unfortunately my boss called neither the roof or the porch a shed. These differences led to a babel of languages as my fiasco was rehashed time and again about the office. Our head man was confused by the abusive language of the customer and, really, was not too complimentary about the way I had handled the matter. I am sure the occurrence did my rating as a driver no good but I soon found a chance to take a job with the Railroad Co. and my boss wished me well.

My first job with the Atlantic Coastline Railroad was not in the shop (I had my application in there) but was as a freight staging call boy. There were two of us on the night shift.

Our headquarters was in the switching room of the control tower high above the freight yard that stretched out below us. On my shift the yard was always loaded with puffing switching engines and, apparently, endless freight cars that rested or moved about upon the maze of tracks that provided the basic facility for making up entire trains from the cars parked or stored about the yard. A very impressive counter, containing a row of large levers, stretched along the side of the glass enclosure positioned so the operator, from his high position, had a wide view of the entire freight yard. It was his job and responsibility to throw the proper levers to change switches down on the tracks and thus combine sections of track into configurations needed by the switching engines moving freight cars from one position to another to make up trains of cars logically associated by destinations along a given route.

Along a back wall of the tower room, the only wall that was not glass, was a billboard that controlled our work. We were expected to keep close watch on the billboard for the names an addresses of crew members listed under our names. The men so listed were classified further by a reporting time for the makeup of a freight train, being put together by the shifting engines, that would depart at the posted hour. You would tear off your list of names for the call, man your bicycle and go out to wake up the crew and get them to the yard on time.

The crews were mostly Blacks and lived not too awfully far from the yard, they had no telephones and had to be advised of their assignment by messenger of which I was one. These were dark night rides over sand-clay paths that wound among the shacks that were the homes of laboring railroad personnel. There were also unpaved streets but the bicyle-foot paths among the houses were the shortcuts.

A bleeding heart liberal would not be required to describe the houses as "shacks": They were usually composed of one main room with a half room attachment that contained a kitchenette and a table with chairs. These latter furnishings and the balance of the small half room provided a combination dining and general living space that, in the homes I frequented on my calls, was cluttered with clothing, newspapers, and general bric-a-brac that sometimes included a bicycle and even a few garden tools.

Waking the the man on call was simple: you opened the door and walked into the main room which was a bed room plus more cluttered living area, the doors were never locked and no one seemed to worry about having the their privacy violated. The Negro men were never lonely there was always a girl in bed with the man when I called and, on the south Georgia hot nights, both parties were well exposed if not entirely naked. The man and his girl were usually sound asleep, when I arrived, but were well entangled in each other and the sparse bed linen. I soon learned to take the situation for granted and went to work shaking the man awake and persisting in conversation until I was assured he would not fall back asleep and miss his train. If one of my men did miss, I was chewed out for not doing my job right. These visits certainly had an ambivalent educational value to a boy just turning fourteen.

The other boy on my shift and I did not get along. I remember no specific instance of irritation; the reaction was general; there seemed to be a jealousy coupled with an arrogance that left me just not liking the fellow and not knowing why. I am sure he had the same high regard for me. We resorted to no violence but exchanged wise cracks in the control room that caused each other to alternately bristle. This young man in another place and time unknowingly played an important role in a small drama that had a large affect upon my manner of working, giving me confidence and resolution to all I undertook; but that belongs to a later chapter.

After a matter of months on the job, calling the crews for the night trains, I, one evening, found a letter addressed to me clipped to the bulletin board. My stomach turned over: "What had I done wrong?" "Was this a dismissal notice--the famous pink slip?" No it was not; it was a letter to advise me that I had been accepted for a job, in the Railroad Shop, that was the object of my aspirations. I was to be an Apprentice Blacksmith. As I look back upon the milieu of the shop town society in which I was pretty well immersed I can understand my excitement. My friends among the sons and daughters of shop men would be impressed with the career in which I was making a beginning.

CHAPTER IX
Career #1 - Blacksmith

The morning I reported for work at my new job of apprentice blacksmith remains in my memory as an experience of super awareness. I walked from my home to the shop down the tracks that ran through the cut that paralleled our street. After passing the railroad station I left the tracks, and walked a sand-clay road that ran beside them, and led to all the railroad property. Soon, on my right, the tracks began to multiply as they branched off into the freight yard located on the north side of the shop area, and others came from the freight yard and curved into the shop.

Engines or cars that were in the freight yard were often scheduled for repairs, and, with this arrangement of tracks, they could move straight from the yard into the shop. Other engines and cars that were on the main line tracks could be switched onto spurs that fed the shop directly. As I walked down the road the ubiquitous tracks somehow impressed me that I was entering a place where important activities took place: everything looked so precise, extensive, complex and well planned.

The shop area was completely fenced in. People going to work entered through a gateway for vehicle traffic. There were few vehicles. The road, in the early morning, was covered full width with men walking abreast, hurrying to reach their stations, and punch the time clock by starting time.

I soon learned that the official rule was, if you were 3 minutes late punching, you lost twenty minutes. You were free not to start work until the expiration of the twenty minutes but you lost that much time in your pay check. This device worked its purpose: when the time for starting became close the men running to reach their shop time clock gave the appearance of a marathon race.

But as I came in that first morning I was well ahead of time and saw no sprinters for the clocks. I was fascinated by the large area before me on the other side of the gate and the large roundhouse that was immediately inside the gate. Enormous doors opened from each side of the house and a double line of railroad tracks went through. The largest engines could be accommodated within diameter of the building with an abundance of shop room left over front and rear and all around. Locomotives or cars, in for repair, were accommodated on a power driven turntable that enabled the shop men to position them for convenient access or change their direction. Also engines that brought freight cars to the other shops for repair could be turned around here and sent on their way to other services. When I could, later on, I spent some goof off time in the roundhouse watching the repair processes and just admiring some of the majestic steam monsters that pulled our trains in the late teens of our century.This first morning, however, I just thrilled to being a part of the great show that was opening ahead of me. There were duplicate long buildings that housed the various trades: the bronze founders, the steel founders, the machinists, the carpenters, the painters, the plumbers and, of course, the blacksmiths. In our shop, the excitement of the place, with which I soon became familiar, was suggested that first morning, before the men began their days work, by multiple oil furnaces that had been lighted to preheat.

Each blacksmith had a specified area down the middle of the long and narrow shop. In his area was his forge and anvil. Along both sides of the shop, spaced by large doorways were the steam hammers, the trip hammers, bulldozers and drop forging hammers, an array of powerful tools for turning hot metal into the forms that kept the engines running and the cars in good repair. Any iron or steel part of a train could be made in this shop.

For many parts the decision of whether to repair an old part or make a new one was left to the blacksmith: Outside, beyond one of the large roll up doors, was "the pile", and a pile it was, composed of broken or worn parts of engines cars and even some stationary railroad property. From this pile any of the Smiths, lacking an assigned job at the time, could pick, in fact he was expected to pick, any piece from the pile and make the decision as to the efficiency and economy of repairing or making a duplicate.

When this shop was in full swing during the day it was a place of challenge that stimulated one with its virile masculine ambience. It possessed a beauty that would today be called psychedelic, with lined up oil furnaces belching flame, flashes of hot steel on the anvils located from one end to the other of the the long shop, and huge steam hammers at intervals striking large slabs of white hot steel that spit burning flux and sparks from overheated spots in the steel. These spots sparkled as the metal combined with oxygen and burned like a stick of wood.

The pounding of the steam hammers shook the unpaved earth in which the hammers were embedded in concrete slabs and, truly, there was an anvil chorus as the men and there Negro helpers pounded out shapes on their anvils. The chorus was accented, and at times, raised to a crescendo, by the rapid rat tat tat of the small trip hammers and the single but recurring sharp blows of the drop-forgers.

The shop itself and the men who worked in it were of a pattern: rustic and strong but decidedly of the age in which they lived and worked. I liked this place and dreamed, at the time, no higher than becoming like some of the master craftsmen that I soon came to admire.

Our foreman's name was Bill Clair and he had a real office that opened, on one side, into the work area and on the other into the open passageway and storage yard between two shop buildings.

In this open space were racks of steel, flats, rods and special forms of all useful dimensions. When material was needed the smith went into this storage yard, with his Negro helper carrying a cold chisel and a small sledge. He picked a piece of steel that was of the right dimensions for the job he contemplated. The chisel and hammer were used to nick a sliver of steel from the chosen stock in a manner that cut and finally tore the sliver from the main body. The torn place revealed the grain in the steel, essentially the finer the grain the harder the steel, which enabled the Smith, at a glance, to pick the grade required for the job ahead.

When I had progressed with my apprentice training to the point where I had my own anvil, my own Negro helper and a full set of blacksmith tools, most of which I had, by that time, made, I was expected to pick the steel from the bins and judge, as an expert by the chip method, the grade of steel I was choosing. I walked into the storage yard with a sense of deep satisfaction that I had arrived. Having arrived I was even allowed, and expected, to curse the helpers.

Yes cursing was a form of direct communication between a blacksmith and his helper. An apprentice picked up the habit as part of his on the job training. Except that apprentices were assigned as helpers for a short time in their training, all helpers were Negroes. No Negroes were blacksmiths. What is more significant, I believe no skilled jobs in the entire railroad shop were open to Blacks. That was segregation in south Georgia at that time. It was taken for granted that Blacks were meant to be helpers and fill other common labor jobs. I can't say, as an apprentice, that I protested the injustice, or reacted in any way other than accepting the discrimination as normal. In reflecting on the situation today I feel sad for some of the very good black men (some outstanding in character and ability), that I knew, who lived out their lives with no chance of rising above the arbitrary and rigid barriers, placed by the concept of white supremacy, upon the lives of these loyal citizens.

And loyal they were. Your helper was all the word means; you cared for him and he for you. He took the cursing, that flew with the sparks when the iron was hot and being beaten by his blows guided by a touch of your hand hammer between each strike of the sledge, as the language of the trade and you meant it as such without malice. Segregation and the customs that kept it in place were all most of the Blacks, or the whites, had ever known. At the time we are discussing there was no protesting, at least none around the shops.

But I am ahead of my story. My first job was to act as a helper myself on a three month assignment working with a blacksmith who was short in statue, inches shorter than I, but broad, stocky and powerful. He was a serious man who brooked no "horse play" but, when I attended to my job, was pleasant and conscientiously instructed me in the mysteries of good blacksmithing. His instruction to me included the customary swearing reserved for helpers.

I learned what it was like to be on the receiving end of expletives. A large part of every day I spent swinging a 16 pound sledge hammer that I, after a painful breaking in period, did learn to handle with ease and accuracy. The first day with the hammer left my muscles so sore I could hardly stand much less walk, and to even lie down was tortuous. The extreme soreness continued for about one week, began then to subside. Some pain persisted, to some degree before disappearing, as I recall it, in approximately a full month. But I was not suffering for the whole month. After the severe irritation subsided there remained only tolerable sore muscles, I began to feel proud of my expanding arms, legs and well conditioned body that was being built by daily labor.

The accommodations at the shop were ample to good: The wash rooms were really for washing. The toilets were separate but adjoined the wash rooms. Many men worked without an upper garment; a panel of their leather aprons covered their fronts nearly to the collarbone, protecting against sparks. They were very dirty after a day in contact with smoke and iron that had accumulated rust in the storage yard. Washing up was more than a hands and face job and facilities were provided for that purpose: There were very large circular cement basins, full circle, with the plumbing in the center that, in each basin, supplied as many as ten men at a time hot and cold water from his own individual tap and rinsing sprinkler. The basins were low, one could lean his entire upper body over them, and were large enough to supply ten men ample room around their rims, while they simultaneously scrubbed and rinsed from the waste up.

A locker room was integral with the wash room and each man had his locker. Because of the unusual amount of perspiration endemic to the job most blacksmiths did not wear their working clothes to and from the job. There was, at any shift change, a great washing and dressing scene around the multiple wash basins and the adjacent lockers. We had one man who frequently went through an astounding ritual. He did not like his associates, some of whom were habitual tobacco bummers, to bum his chewing tobacco; so, he performed an act for all to see, designed to discourage anyone inclined to say, "gimmie a chew." He would stand, stalk naked, on one of the dressing benches, shout to get attention and proceed with rubbing his plug of tobacco through his crotch and over his attachments. I believe it is safe to say no one bummed from the exhibited plug.

Incidentally virtually all blacksmiths chewed on the job and, with a relish, spit volumes of juice on the white hot iron to watch it run, at high speed, in a ball like mercury across the surface, or, if the iron had cooled to a dark red color, see the juice spit and fry. Yes, I soon "joined the club" both in the chewing and the on iron spitting.

In addition to their intended purpose the toilets were used for the clandestine act of buying and selling bootleg corn whiskey, and a bit of on the job drinking. To my knowledge, there was never any excess drinking during working hours. Whiskey was sold by entrepreneur shop men who bought at country stills, smuggled in filled pop bottles packaged and delivered to the toilets. The whiskey was for home consumption and a few coke bottles were often in the pockets of the men, on the way home. As they passed inspection at the gate no personal search for whiskey was ever made. The guards were really looking only for company property that might be on board. The-on-the-job drinking was a now-and-then shot to sample a new batch or exchange a drink with a friend.

I was surprised, shortly after I began my apprenticeship, to find that the other young man from the freight messenger job, the one with whom I held some reciprocal bad feelings, was again to parallel my undertakings. He too was an apprentice blacksmith, beginning the assignment only a few days after my arrival. He was assigned to the spring making department at the opposite end of our long building, we rarely saw each other, and I forgot his very existence and any unpleasantness associated with our previous contact.

I do not recall that during the first months after I had finished my helper period, which I had begun to call the sledge hammer assignment, that I thought of my progress as a budding blacksmith as very good, very bad or mediocre. Probably I gave that aspect no thought; I was spending my days busy at my anvil. I would sometimes pick from the pile and at other times work on an issued job. But apparently Bill Clair held an opinion that I was worthy of his special treatment for high level motivation of apprentices, which treatment consisted of generating competition between two likely candidates. Bill could not have known how well he chose my competitor when my turn came to be inspired.

Mr Clair, as I called him then to his face, came to my anvil one afternoon, which act in itself was unique and surprising, and said, "Hoge, lay that job on your forge and come with me." We took a long and vigorous walk, practically from one end of the extensive shop to the other. Bill Clair stared straight ahead as we passed, one after another, the blacksmiths at their labor who looked on quizzically and toward whom I smiled in embarrassment. Our champion toolmaker, who always laid his days work on the ground just off the central walking space, so that his peers could admire, raised his chin, as he caught my eye, winked and drew the side of his hand, as a symbolic knife, across his throat as a gesture of prognostication. We continued into the spring making department where, behold!, I saw my old antagonist, of the freight call days, leaning on his anvil with a smile of satisfaction on his face. Bill wanted me to see one very good job done by this apprentice.

Lying in front of his work area was a half dozen large locomotive leaf spring bands finished to perfection. Leaf springs were basically like early automobile springs only much more massive, essentially spring steel leaves piled up and bound. An engine spring band had to possess a perfection of square angles and exact dimensions; the inside dimensions of the band must be precisely the right amount smaller than the pile being bound: When a spring was assembled a specified number of curved spring steel leaves were brought together in a pile and held firmly in a large hydraulic press. While the spring assembly was thus held the band, heated to a cherry red heat, and with the help of some sledge hammer blows, would be slid into place on the assembled leaves. A splash of water from a bucket created an immediate shrinkage that bound the leaves permanently in vise like grip. As the band cooled further the grip became greater.

Therefore the work I was observing was, at once, not only a high level undertaking but also, apparently a well done job that was receiving recognition from the boss. Bill pointed to the work and said, "If you don't watch out that boy's going to leave you way behind".

He needed to say no more: The boy was not one that I intended to have surpass me. I could see that he had chosen from the pile a real challenge for a beginner, and was enjoying a moment of triumph. His triumph was my spur; after a temporary embarrassment I could feel the resolution: I would show them, and this, in time, I did with a passion and a new found self confidence that was more than of the instance, it was a birth of a new attitude that remained with my work through the years. I believe that people often find that a small occurrence at the right time, in a fortuitous setting, can have a large and lasting affect upon their approach to life. I have often thanked Bill Clair in memory for having picked that particular time, place and person for a training lesson.

The following day I went out to the pile of broken and worn pieces and sought an item that would give me a greater challenge than spring bands that seemed to have been set as a standard. It was there, a part known as a buffer that, in use, was a shock absorbing attachment to each end of all passenger cars. This is not the place for a tedious detail description of the assembly or its parts. One of the parts was a forging that, to reproduce, would require careful advance planning, accurate layout calculations and skillful execution of the operations under the steam hammer. This would be followed by good craftsmanship at the forge and anvil. I chose this part for my next project.

When an apprentice so obviously started venturing out on more complicated terrain the older smiths were interested. As the steps of my project developed I was flattered, but a bit self conscious, as they commenced to stop and watch my progress.

Part of the undertaking was carving hot steel at the anvil, drawing to dimensions under the steam hammer, folding drawn and shaped sections to precisely fit other sections, and then forge welding the whole in place, without losing overall construction form and dimensions. I took the work step at a time, never allowing impatience to get me ahead of myself in careless haste. As the work progressed, and I saw my creation maturing into an exhibition of good work, my euphoria was pronounced, but it soon settled into a quiet confidence that remained a characteristic of my approach to complex undertakings. Had I known the poetry at the time I would probably have said with Emerson,
"He builded better than he knew,
The conscious stone to beauty grew."

When the piece was finished I proudly laid it in the cooling space of my work area for all to see, and immediately started a repeat---two were required for each buffer. I felt vindicated and on my way to bigger things.

From that time on I chose from the pile projects that, in complexity and required skills, were up to my new found ability and confidence. I was gratified to see that the assignments that I received from Bill Clair were complimentary to my status as a blacksmith; they differed in no important respects from the jobs being passed out to the older smiths on the line.

The months that followed were for me, as a person and as a worker in relation to his job, a period of maturing. I enjoyed the experience of being accepted by the masters of my trade, if not as an equal, at least as one that was soon to be. I was entrusted with complex work without reservation.

This was not high society but there was hospitality, that was sincere and flattering, extended by the blacksmiths on a social basis: from time to time I drank from their bottles, joined their pool hall games, was invited to their homes and okayed for dates with their daughters.

I have dwelled on this connection of events that followed the spring band incident, because I recall it with gratitude that I found myself at such an early age, not in the work I would do for life, but as the person I could be in relation to any seriously undertaken task.

After six months on the job, I was not only eligible but was required to become a member of the union, the American Association of Blacksmiths, Boiler Makers and Helpers.

The initiation into the union was rough and, in conclusion, quite indelicate: the candidate was blindfolded, paddled and pushed around, as a hazing concept, while being indoctrinated with the precepts of loyalty to his own union and to the general cause of unionism. The piece de resistance, which was the indelicate part was designed to put down, I suppose, the arrogance of the upstart newcomer: While still blindfolded the candidate was told to kneel and kiss the book of the constitution and bylaws of the union. A member standing behind him guided his head so that his mouth would touch the "book" but when he kissed he realized the object of his affection was human skin. His blindfold was immediately removed and he saw in front of him the bare bottom of the fattest member of the fraternity.

With that dramatic(?) ending the novice was a fully christened member, but he had to wait until he saw an initiation, or someone told him the facts, before he found out that he had not kissed the fat man's behind but instead another man's bare arm that was placed in position and quickly withdrawn during the kissing process. My upbringing in a minister,s family did not make me an example of righteousness but it did cause me to think only naughty kids were "dirty." Consequently I was surprised, if not shocked, to discover that these older men, heads of families,were the producers of this earthy scenario. It was not long however before I learned that "What the preacher is likely to teach ya, aint necessarily so" and that in some repects we never grow up ----a fact for which I probably should be thankful.

World War 1 was in progress during the period of these acts but that did not prevent a Railroad strike. My father was not of the shop culture and was not sympathetic to many of the union mores, and he was particularly in opposition to the strike while the country was at war. I do not know what active opposition he expressed but he gave me a divided mind: My patriotism was aroused to oppose the strike but my pecuniary interest made me wish for a favorable settlement. One of the specific demands was that apprentice wages, having long been neglected, be this time substantially improved. My wages were 9 cents an hour for a ten hour day and a six day week. The resulting 90 cents per day and $5.40 per week did not seem too bad in 1918 but the 27 cents per hour being demanded by the union seemed like a promised bonanza that captured my sympathy for the cause

I became acquainted during the strike with a labor point of view that, in this confrontation with management, talked more violently than it acted. The men would spend their days in the one square block of public park which was in the center of town across the street from union headquarters.

The city appeared invaded by the numbers of men in working clothes that spent their days on main street and in the park. I joined the group daily and listened to threats that they would go to the shop, and beat up some scabs, hog tie them and haul them off the property in wheelbarrows. The talk was all very exciting and, to a degree frightening but I do not recall that anyone, for or against the union, got hurt. I also have no recollection of the duration of the strike or all the terms of settlement but I do remember that the apprentice wage for my time of service became 27 instead of 9 cents an hour.

That fact some how left a warm place in my heart for the union and made me realize that there was strength in union and that some inequities would not be corrected without united action. I was, in years to come, to frequently confront this management labor dilemma from the other side of the question and to find ample reason to both confirm and deny much that I learned in Waycross.

Many intangible things come to mind that represented life in the shops. In the society of shop people a man walked more proudly, and had a stronger voice in union meetings, and even church meetings, somewhat in proportion to his expertise rating among his peers. Nearly all the craftsmen were bolstered spiritually by pride in the trade they practiced and their own craftsmanship therein. The conversations among the men often centered on their accomplishments on this or that difficult job, somewhat like golfers rehashing their best performances. There was a recognizable similarity between the psychological climate of the shops and that of the artist's studio, although both parties would deny the kinship.

The most massive components of steam engines were in 1918 forged by the use of steam hammers. After the development of sophisticated acetylene gas welding and burning machines many of the heavier parts, that were forged at the time we are here concerned with, were torch cut from heavy stock, and, where required, extensions or additions were welded on. Today with the prevalence of diesel and electric engines some of the parts are no longer made because the engines are obsolete. An example would be the main drive rod of our largest steam engines at this time when rail travel was growing to its prime.

There was drama in the daily task of producing such a part: The dimensions of the material used and the machinery employed set the stage for a big show. A massive round rod of steel, if a piece about 24 inches in diameter and ten feet long could be called a rod, was the stock for such a job. An oil furnace with fire brick doors large enough to accept the cold steel was the forge. The first step was to heat an end of the stock and draw a short section of it down to a diameter small enough to accept the jaws of immense tongs.

These tongs were very special: just behind the jaws was a wheel, or ring made in two halves that joined, when the tongs closed, to form a complete circle. This ring was made of channel iron with the channel turned out to form a recessed track to accept a chain that ran through a wheel above on a heavy duty crane designed to handle the enormous weight of the steel and the tongs. An endless chain running through the two wheels gave a support that was rotatable. The tongs were intended for two men to operate and were provided with a long cross arm that gave each man leverage. They could work together to turn and hold firm the heavy metal on the steam hammer anvil as the hammer struck its powerful blows. They could move the iron back and forth as the overhead crane trolley responded to their reverse and forward body motions.

There was almost a poetic harmony between the steam hammer operator, always colored, and the blacksmith. The blacksmith signaled, with subtle motions of his head for heavy or light blows. There seemed to never be a misunderstanding of the blow that was wanted. The huge round steel would soon turn into a rectangular shape and sections would be left larger than other sections. In time these larger sections would be pierced with big punches, held in place by helpers. These pierced holes would be enlarged, stretched by tapered punches driven through while the steel was still hot or had been reheated. These were the holes that, after machining, would retain pressed-in cylindrical bearings that fit bearings off center, on the great driving wheels of the engine.

A project as massive as a main drive rod required reheating several times from start to finish but after the first heat the operation was relatively fast because of heat residual from the preceding step. Excess steel that had been provided, by design for a safety factor, was cut away by hot chisels built integral with long handles. A chisel would be held in position by the blacksmith, on the steel as it rested under the hammer, and controlled with the long attached handles. In harmony with the blacksmith's head signals, the chisels would be properly struck and the final trimming completed.

To observe from the side lines when one of these most extensive jobs were in progress was to witness a show that even the old hands would stop to watch. Often two large slabs of steel would be welded by steam hammer blows upon the pieces carefully placed in contact between the hammer faces. The pieces heated to full incandescence in the furnaces would be covered to saturation with melted sand or borax. These additions acted as a flux to promote the weld. When the prepared pieces became welding hot they were rapidly transferred, with the aid of two cranes, by separate crews who timed and coordinated their actions. One piece was placed in position on the lower face (anvil) of the steam hammer and immediately covered by the section to be welded on. The upper hammer head came down with a mighty blow that confirmed the weld. The spitting of sparks and molten flux that would spew out from the hammer faces in all directions would make a novice want to run for his life.

The men on the job wore gloves, helmets and heavy leather aprons, which picked up flux and sparks. These fried a bit and smelled atrociously. The show was always great.

Following this main event the controlling blacksmith continued working the welded pieces, under the hammer, into a finished single part.

Waycross, Georgia can be hot and usually is in midsummer. When the heat of numerous oil furnaces and coke forge fires raise the natural temperature a man working in a blacksmith shop, down there gets very used to sweating. I recall my feet slogging in perspiration, and my body sweating until I removed my shirt to wring it out. But a means of cooling off fast was provided by a very large fan called a man cooler. One had to brace himself against the force of the air from that fan. Its discharge opening was the height of a man. To cool yourself you stood in front of the discharge and, as the fan blew up a wind storm, you turned around frequently to receive the blast of air on your whole body. The sweat evaporated and your temperature dropped. Some said the rapid cooling was dangerous to your health but I never heard of anyone who had a bad reaction.

The blacksmith used a small but very hot fire. To build this in his forge he was provided with two steel bins beside his forge about the shape and dimensions of a medium sized watering trough for horses on a home farm. One container was filled daily, by his helper, with pea coal, the other was kept full of water, used also for cooling iron quickly and tempering steel. He did not heat with coal. For a clean fire he used coke made from pea coal in his own forge. The forges were each supplied with a controllable blast of air from a motor driven fan----push a lever back and the air blast grew stronger, pull it forward and the air strength could be reduced gradually to any desired level of softness.

To build a fire in the morning a two and one half inch square short post was set upright on the air intake so as to block it off and later provide a passageway for air through a bed of coal which was soon to be provided. Pea coal, wet down with a hose, handy at your forge, was shovelled in and ram packed tightly around the post. The post was then withdrawn to leave a hole nearly a foot deep through the packed coal. Grease soaked waste was thrown in the hole and lighted from a hand torch. As the fire started, small pieces of coke were added, a light air blast applied at first and then increased as the coke began to burn. More and larger pieces of coke were added as the fire grew.

Thus, from coke on hand the blacksmith was provided with the fire to begin heating iron required in his upcoming days work. The iron being heated, lying on top of the fire burning in the hole, was covered lightly with more coke and that coke was covered with wet coal. In time the oils in the wet coal, on top and down in the two and one half inch hole, burned off and left and abundance of light gray-white coke. As the day progressed the wall thickness of coke in the mound of wet coal on top of the fire increased, and the opening in front through which the iron in the process was passed in and out of the fire began to look like a door in a miniature Eskimo igloo. The whole arrangement functioned like a coke lined coke-air fueled furnace. In function it had one characteristic of a nuclear breeder reactor: the forge produced more coke than it burned. At times the smith would hold back on the wet coal on top so as not to get an over supply of coke.

For human interest examples, these could be as endless as there is variety in persons, Negro helpers came to work from time to time in euphoric moods boasting of their new wives. Sometimes there had been a marriage and innocent love was in bloom, but frequently the man meant he had a new girl friend that for a while at least was going to be like a wife to him.

Black men or white men could be heard quite openly discussing over their lunch pails some new house where the girls were very understanding, the drinks (corn whiskey in those days) and the hors d'oeuvres were special.

Others had their dreams of making money through ingenious schemes; I was caught up in one of these: An ex-prize fighter blacksmith talked to me daily for a while about the money to be made in ring fighting and the chance of my becoming a champion in my weight class. He would be my manager; all I had to do was learn to fight and train; he would get me matches, and in a short time we would be on the road to riches. I listened, was interested and began going with him every evening to the Railroad Y.M.C.A. gym for instruction and workouts. We reached a level of some pretty rough sparring matches. He was getting a bit old for the action and was lighter than me. The effect was that from time to time I would floor my instructor with a technical knockout.

He had more science and would deliver repeated blows to my chest that, one blow at a time seemed like nothing, but, in accumulation, gave me a chest so sore I could hardly breathe. He could repeat the accumulation trick with kidney punches that were almost disabling. The short of it was that I had some fun, learned a bit about fighting but learned better that my road to riches did not lie along a string of fighting matches.

Waycross was not a city with any night life or public amusements, other than one movie house for the town. Sea food was plentiful and a good short order restaurant was across the street from the popular pool hall. "Trouble in River City?" Not quite, but to look in on the place one would expect it. The after shop activities of the men who met "down town" was usually some fried oysters in the restaurant and an extended game of pool across the street. An occasional drink of corn whiskey might be passed around in the men's room.

There were also serious talks in the park on practically every subject including religion, politics, and a working man's code of ethics. In reflecting on these men I have often thought of a quotation, the author of which I have forgotten, "I might commit murder but I could not compute a false square root". These men were dedicated to their trade. There was only one way to do a job and that was, "do it right".
In my long association in the blacksmith shop and later in management of a manufacturing company I recall skilled mechanics as men who were noticeably vigilant concerning the integrity of their workmanship. Also, in these talks in the park, there were voiced the common aspirations of men who dream of rising to something higher in the world and, from the conventional point of view, some did.

The First Baptist Church in Waycross was, architecturally, reiterated Southern Baptist with the tower in the corner, instead of the steeple in the center, of the building. On the first level the tower provided a vestibule with double doors, on both sides of the corner, that opened onto a flight of several steps that circled the entire corner and descended directly onto the city sidewalks. The steps were more than ample to feed the doorways and were a customary come-together place for churchgoers on the way in or out of the building. They welcomed each other here with expressions of friendship and endearment before the service and chatted there for a period before going home after.

Across the back of the church, either entrance opened into an unfilled space from which the several isles were fed. The seats were light maple in color, bare wood to sit down on and multiple in capacity.

Basically they were constructed on a curved pattern so that the entire congregation faced the minister at his pulpit. The floor on which the seats were arranged slanted to the front center so that the assemblage gave the general appearance of an amphitheater. In summer, distributed along all the seats, were enough palmetto fans to accommodate their capacity. Motion, motion of these fans, dominated any summer audience. The men moved their fans rapidly from side to side and the women back and forth from and toward their chests. One could think of a room full of excited giant butterflies in action.

This was the building that symbolized the hopes of so many of the ardently faithful who became, in feeling, like an extended family during my father's pastorate.

It was also a focal point for most of the social life of the old and young alike: In summer there were watermelon cuttings in the church yard, ice cream socials in the building, and church picnics in the country. Some of the picnics were combined with hay rides and included members of the congregations of rural churches. These latter enjoyments included the phenomena of the natural attraction of the country girls for city boys and the reciprocal of the country boys manifesting their interest in the city girls. A good time was had by all.

My own interest in this respect was not centered on a country girl but on one from town whose father nevertheless drove a wagon for the hay rides. Her name was Hilda Dunn and she and her sister Helen were identical twins, so alike that Helen could meet me in their living room for a date I had with Hilda and get by with the deception for quite a while. Hilda is the first memory I have of "being sweet" on a girl and a risque affair it was: I can even recall the girls in our wagon having a giggling session over some conversation about their pajamas, which they modestly referred to as "PJ'S".

And there were "Cane Grindings". These were promoted by sugar cane growers and were extra curricular so far as the church was concerned. Baptist youth would attend with those from other churches and both were joined with the unchurched. These affairs were inspired by an ulterior motive: the cane farmers needed help grinding cane to produce Georgia Cane Syrup that was relished and consumed by nearly all Georgians and many in the adjoining states.

The setup for grinding was more a squeezing than a grinding operation: large wringers, like oversized clothes wringers on early model washing machines, were installed in a vertical position over an enormous tub.

Power was provided by a patient horse that walked in a circle around the tub. The horse was harnessed to a long lever that served to turn the rollers of the mill. Fiddling and dancing in the barn was provided to attract and hold the attention of the youngsters from Waycross. These merry makers paid their way by taking turns feeding long stalks of sugar cane into the vertical mill. Such celebrations combined with labor would continue until dawn for the pleasure and work of some that could stay the night without reporting in at home.

In the late evening an unorthodox liquor, actually a fermented cane juice, was introduced to enliven the dancing and assure continued help at the grinding. The parties were fun, the farmer got his due and only an occasional person got out of line with drink and over ardent emotions.

As I come to the heading, "revivals" in my outline I am moved to summarize before detailing by saying, the subject of evangelism, which it entails, cannot stand alone. It is but the tip of the iceberg of orthodox religion which, in its extreme form of inflexible fundamentalism, has had a very questionable affect on individual emotional life and society as a whole.

So far as the the evangelists who held revival meetings in our churches over my years at home, were concerned, I long entertained a modicum of respect. I have since become convinced that these people are running a big business. Redeeming downtrodden sinners is less their forte than attracting trusting good people who have already learned to be gullible and loyal. These people send in their money and get in return a bag full of superstition. At the least, their dogmatism is destructive of truth.

Some of the evangelical meetings were denominational and were held, with nightly services, for two week periods in the church. Some of the meetings were held in tents and were sponsored by several churches in the community. In either type the preachers I remember were fundamentalist scare artists, braggadocio about their records for saving souls, and competitive with other evangelists. They were men with little knowledge or respect for objective scientific truth.

They were purveyors of arbitrary dogma. I did not feel this way in Waycross: I mostly remember a feeling of surprise, even as a youth, at the character and ideas of these visiting evangelists. There was John Ham an ex-shoe salesman that was "born again in the faith", who, with rapid fire articulation, preached Hell fire and brimstone, and unabashedly called upon God to strike dead those in the community that opposed his teaching.

This was a disturbing performance to a teenager and, hearing similar pious arrogance repeated over the years in other places by other men, I became an enemy of this outrageous imposition upon the mind and spirit of mankind and wary of churches and religions, throughout the world, that emphasized the word "orthodox."

New Orleans has its Mardi Gras but Waycross has its Prosperity Week, or it did have when I lived there. The town went, as they say, "bananas", for one week: The street signs, the street lights, the business buildings and many homes were covered with carnival decorations.

Except for the stores and restaurants that catered to the celebrating crowds, many businesses were closed or neglected. The shop people, of course, were not so fortunate: The starting bell rang daily as usual and all hands were expected to be "on deck." But many came in with bloodshot eyes and suffered through the day in payment for the previous night's revelry. Nevertheless, when the next evening of pranks and merriment began many, who struggled to finish the day at work, were back on the street to make sure they missed nothing offered by their special week.

It seemed to me that not much of substance really happened but much was expected and all sustained a willing and expectant mood: The majority wore masks, many dressed in elaborate costumes and most seemed to be obsessed with weaving, in and out, among the revelers on the crowded streets. Men and women, strangers or acquaintances, embraced and kissed in their exuberance, danced in the street to the music of the volunteer combos and, from time to time, gave out with "Rebel Yells". I am sure that the tempo was increased by corn whiskey that was available from bootleggers who, with some circumspection, moved among the crowds and hawked their reinforcements.

The foregoing could picture a crowd out of control, in which damage to property or persons could occur, but I recall no unusual happenings. The week went by and, after a massive street cleaning job was completed, all seemed to quickly return to normal. If during the week you had kissed a member of the opposite sex, whom you recognized at the time was not on normal kissing terms with you,"never you mind" he or she would resume the pre-Prosperity Week status with no apparent recall.

In April of 1917 the war came to waycross as it did to the whole country. We, the younger ones, had heard the war in Europe discussed by our elders since 1914 but it was remote to any personal significance. Soon it was as close as the church meeting held to support and send off with honor some member or members that were leaving for the army and overseas to fight. There was pathos in these meetings and a distinct feeling that the young man, whose hand you were shaking in farewell, might never return. I can recall with poignancy a number of these ceremonial gatherings.

But we who were left at home did our part: we gathered around pianos and sang war songs about coming "over there" and not coming back 'till it was over over there. About a long, long trail of winding into the land of our dreams. There was also a girl we stuttered to call ka-kie- ka katie. And then there were more boisterous musical expressions like the one about a certain mademoiselle from Armentiers.

And how we sang!: There was a family that lived next door named Givens. The Givens girl could play with a vengeance. You entered their home into a large hall from which a stairway rose to the second floor. Under the stairway against the back wall of the hallway sat an upright grand piano that fronted on a space large enough for quite a few assembled singers who were there almost every night after dinner to sing again and again the many songs. New songs were coming out almost daily, about war and the longing of lovers to be together again. Some of our other friends had player pianos that ground out the same music and at times we gathered around these automatics.

I do not remember that, among the young people, the horror of war was thought about or discussed; I remember it as an ever present background fact of poorly understood but strongly felt excitement that fostered a sense of togetherness when we sang or discussed the news of victories overseas. Regarding normal routines life went on as usual among the stay-at-homes except when the the tragic news of casualties came home to a relative or close friend of the victim.

Had I known the verse at the time, "Oh what a tangled web we weave when once we practice to deceive", I would have quoted it time and again: I had represented my age in writing, on my application for employment, to be 17 with a February birthday. Eighteen years became the starting age for the draft during the summer of 1918! On the shop record I was decidedly eligible. In reality I was only several months into my fourteenth year.

This situation became a major worry to me. I sought advice from my elders and often received nothing in return but a lecture about lying in the first place. I am aware that at the time my concern was not the moral question primarily, but was about whether I would confess at the shop, and probably lose my job, or just hang on until the government came after me as a draft evader.

I do not recall that I had any sense of proportioning in my imagining what could happen to me if I was found out. I felt at times like it was a matter of me against the whole criminal process. Periodically and frequently I came back to this worry but never resolved the dilemma. I seemed to have worn it out, as time went by without my being challenged. I began, I suppose, believing that the government was not going to check the shop records for the ages of its young employees. I know that, after a while, the matter was forgotten and I worked with peace of mind, continued singing war songs on occasion, and recognized the sincerity of my patriotic feelings.

Our feelings against the enemy were heated up by propaganda films that came to the local theater; one, named The Greatest Thing in Life, showed German soldiers marching with Belgium babies impaled on their bayonets. This picture was the subject of many conversations expressing outrage and hatred. After the war the film was acknowledged to have been manufactured horror. My experience with such propaganda ploys during the war left an impression that even now makes it difficult for me to give full credence to almost anything said to denigrate, as being especially bad, nations with whom we differ.

And then in time the war ended. It was November 11th, 1918. As everywhere in the allied world, Waycross, Georgia went wild with rejoicing. Firearms, I hope with blank cartridges, were discharged in the streets, church bells rang continuously, improvised bands paraded, and, not so ingenious, noise makers were brought into action. Washtubs and cans were tied to the bumpers of automobiles, and horns of all description raised the general noise level of the shouts from the euphoric people pressing each other on the sidewalks.

There is no need to describe to anyone alive, and of a knowledgeable age at that time, the profound relief, the abiding sense of joy and excitement, and the continuing feeling of happiness, that possessed everyone on Armistice day and for an extended period after. And for those who were not there for the experience, no adequate explanation seems possible. For a time after the excitement subsided it was difficult to become used to the very fact that the war was over. The feeling seemed to develop independently in everyone that such a travesty on life as the plague of war must never again be allowed to happen. As time went by, many individuals and groups in concert swore an oath that they would never, under any circumstances, take up arms, whatever the penalty for refusing. Nations formed their league dedicated to peace and the general welfare of mankind, but alas, these good intentions were frustrated and eventually deleted in the maelstrom of world crisis.

Proceeding with this writing has impressed me with what a great difference is two and one half years between siblings. That was the small age difference between me and my brother Jim, but the worlds we lived in at the same time were vastly different. At this period except for an occasional event that recalls him to mind my recollection is of pictures in which his face never shows. I recall vividly when the time came for him to go to college, the talk around home for a while seemed to be about nothing else, the wonder of it. I was talked to by my parents, particularly my mother about how much better things would be if I would emulate my brother's ambition to make something of himself. At the time I thought making myself into a blacksmith was a pretty good show.

Later on, I understood that a family with a tradition, existing for generations, of ministers, lawyers and doctors among its members would not likely appreciate having a blacksmith in the family. I realized later the advantages of education and made up for the lost time. I too insisted on a college education for my own children. It turned out, as I believe we will see in what's ahead, that my years in the shops at waycross and elsewhere were a basic education that gave me a sense of direction, enabled me to relate theoretical engineering education to the real world, and gave me a feeling for the specificity of the attitudes and loyalties of laboring people as a class, which feeling helped me understand, when I needed to as an executive, their point of view on crucial organizational matters that might be in dispute.

There were some contacts with my brother in which the family would not have encouraged either of us to imitate the other: Occasionally when he was home from college for vacation we would get a bottle of corn whiskey and have a few social drinks together. Sometimes the social nature spilled over into some silly running around a rural field near our home making cat calls just to let off steam. And he did take me into his confidence about one or more of our good Baptist girls that he believed he was in love with. He was more inclined than I to take these matters seriously. Nevertheless, there was always Hilda Dunn that I kept on a pedestal as my special girl. How romantic can you get? We went to church socials together and had dates on her front porch mutually enjoying the swing.

I was just finishing the second year of my apprenticeship when Dad announced one evening at dinner, "Now hear this, we are all leaving Waycross by the fifteenth of the coming month. We are moving to a town called Beckley, West Virginia." Then he explained in detail that he had accepted a call to a good Baptist church in that city, that it was a "new field" for him to work in and he was happy to go and believed we would all be pleased with the new setup.

My father's announcement required a decision on my part: Would I go with the family or stay in Waycross and finish my apprenticeship? My father was most understanding of my desire to stay but was very persuasive as to why I should go. I think he always knew that eventually I would return to school for a "proper" education but he wanted it to be my decision when I did. He did not wish to use this move to pry me out of the shops and into the classroom. I have, in memory, always admired the patience with which he stated his case for such a return but, with a pleasant attitude, allowed me to make the decisions that determined my course at the time.

His persuasion certainly had its affect, but friends at the shop gave me other excellent reasons to go. I was flattered that the blacksmiths of my close acquaintance thought I was good at my trade and ready for a journeyman's card giving me full status as a blacksmith along with his higher wages. In the shops at Waycross I could not achieve that status until another two years of apprenticeship was completed; such were the union rules of the closed shop. The old timers explained that if I got a job in an open shop these rules would not apply, and, that after six months on the job, three union men in the shop could sign affidavits testifying to my ability to do the work up to union standards, and qualify me for a journeyman's card. I was ambitious and confident, and the argument was convincing; I decided to go with the family to Beckley and from there look for a job in an open shop.

There was one fringe benefit to my job in the shop that seemed at the time high privilege: I could, at frequent intervals, obtain a pass, a round-trip free ticket, to any destination on the Atlantic Coastline Railroad. That was something real. It contributed to a sense of importance derived from my work. I took full advantage: I traveled to Norfolk just to visit old friends for the weekend and saw my older sister at her home in Selma, North Carolina whenever I had free days and an excuse to make the trip. Losing this feature, which now seems of small value, when I was contemplating leaving Waycross, loomed as a serious loss of special status. This and similar extra features, used by me and my associates for evaluating a job, aided me later as a manager to understand better the psychology of employees regarding job perquisites.

Chapter X

Beckley, West Virginia

Before the parsonage was ready Dad evidently had duties in Beckley; he left mother in Waycross, Ga. and took me with him to our new environment. I was proud to be his companion, and was impressed and excited by my first experience living in a hotel.

I do not recall many special events during our advance sojourn but we talked a lot, man to man; I learned much about dad's thinking on diverse subjects. I realized that he wanted me to follow the traditions of our family, and become a professional, with a higher social standing than he believed blue color workers enjoyed. As a minister he preached to all classes, and was compassionate to their normal trials in life, but as a Virginia gentlemen his bias toward the patrician life was apparent. He even pointed out that, in the (rules?) even a dentist was rated lower than, say, a medical doctor because the dentist worked with his hands. I saw the point, but could not understand why not then a lower rating for a surgeon. We never cleared that up, but I did learn how much he wanted me to succeed in the world, and that according to conventional standards.

Dad's way was the obvious: go back to school, gain the education of one of the professions, work hard, and accomplish a high standing among your peers; with it accept the pecuniary rewards of such virtues. His views were nothing more or less than those of any loving father aware of the ways of this world, no matter his concern, as a minister, with the world to come.

Confronted with the reality of a son already launched on a different career, Dad took a surprising step that represented at least a movement in the direction he wanted me to go: He bought me an interest in a local blacksmith shop. In looking back I understand the very real compromise he made in that decision.

Unfortunately, a railroad or industrial blacksmith practiced a very different trade than a local smith who repaired wagons and shoed horses. The railroad smith could do the latter's work, but the latter would be lost among the steam hammers, bulldozers and drop forges, intrinsic to the work of the former. Dad, obviously, did not know this. His certainty that I would be pleased caused him to close the deal, for an interest in the shop, without conferring with me. He meant to give me a pleasant surprise. And surprised and puzzled I was, but not unhappy: After thinking the matter over I realized that dad thought my status would be improved by my being the owner of a business rather than an employed mechanic. I resolved to give his idea a try.

The only significant thing I had to learn about the mechanical work was how to fit and fasten a shoe on a horse. The forging work on the shoe, or on any of the wagon or automobile parts we repaired, was simple compared to the more complicated projects in a railroad shop. My partner was not a smith; he was the business head for the time being. I learned the shoeing quickly and was both flattered and put down a bit by Wilson's, my partner's name, remarks about my work at the anvil. He said. "You sure do good work but your anvil don't give out the right sounds".

By tradition, at that time, local blacksmiths were also showmen. They let their hammers bounce about on the anvil while they directed it into a staccato tune. This tradition has been honored in the music of the "Anvil Chorus." Local smiths had audiences from off the street; the audience stood, stared and listened. Through the ages the "mighty smith" has risen to the occasion, and let his anvil ring out. In the railroad shop the other smiths, our only audience, did not require or want a fancy display of technique; we spent our energy on the job.

But here I was on center stage. We had one older employed blacksmith who was a real ham and a good showman. He gave me pointers like a golf pro teaching a dub how to relax the wrist. I was shown how, at the end of a series of blows, to let the hammer bounce, and how to beat out a few deliberate refrains that, done right, really got the attention of the gawking observers. It was not long before I was also an attraction at my anvil and Wilson was able to say, "you've got it." That was a proud moment in my life.

But my adventure as a business man who could also play the anvil chorus was to be short lived. Our shop was located on an otherwise vacant lot. An impression of vacancy was given by the fact that the lot was considerably bigger than was needed for our building and all outdoor work. It sat back on the property with much unused space reaching down to the street. There was a sand-clay surfaced driveway that, in a curved pattern, led from the street to the relatively small area of the property that our shop put into service.

My father and I thought that our percentage of the business included part ownership of all the real property; this concept of the arrangement was probably a deciding factor in closing the original deal. I was not in the negotiations and have no idea whether or not papers were prepared that adequately defined all the terms. I only know a complete misunderstanding was uncovered as I sought buckets of water at a neighbors house.

A village blacksmith did not need frequent changes of the water he used for cooling works in process or for tempering steel tools. The evaporation from our trough was replaced by the bucket load from a neighboring yard. At the time, I did not think this arrangement surprising. It was simply a fact that there was no running water on our premises, and an accommodating neighbor had let us use his tap. Water was free to all in the community.

Much time went by before I carried any water. This task had been, and remained, a chore assigned to the hired smith. On a day he was off, I saw that our supply was low. I took a couple buckets to the next door tap. As I drew water in her back yard the lady of the house came out to meet the new man. As we talked, I told her I was the new half owner of the shop and all the property. She explained that I was mistaken, she owned the grounds, and rented these to Wilson, our partner. Wilson built the building under an agreement that this too would be her's, if he should close his shop.

A misunderstanding was obvious. I decided to drop the conversation until I had a chance to talk with Dad. The afternoon was a long one, waiting to unload what was on my mind. I saw our dream evaporating, and wondered what legal course Dad could or might take. The details of the later conversations, leading up to a satisfactory settlement, are not now important or well remembered. We believed, at the end, that all parties were honest, and that the mistake probably lay in the fact that both I and my father knew next to nothing about industrial property values, and that both sides were negligent for not spelling out, in detail, all the conditions of the sale.

It was agreed that the full purchase price would be refunded to Dad, and that I would be compensated, as an employee, for the months I had worked. If I ever knew, I no longer remember what funds changed hands in Dad's transactions. I only recall that the part owed me was small, was paid, and I was satisfied. I went my way, probably a lot wiser for the experience. I can reflect upon my association with Wilson and his hired blacksmith, and recall friends.

It was about this time that we moved into the parsonage, next door to the church, mother joined us, and we resumed family living. It was good to be at home again.

After things were settled at the Hoge-Wilson blacksmith shop, looking for a job became my daily occupation. Luck was with me. In only a couple days I went into the reception room for the two owners of The Beckley Machine and Electric Co., a Mr. Truman and mr. Evans. They were evidently equal partners: They occupied identical offices side by side.Their offices were entered through a common reception area where one young lady acted as receptionist and secretary for both men.

I asked to see the president, and, surprisingly, was immediately shown into Mr. Truman,s office. I had rehearsed my story and it must have been persuasive. I got a job better than the one I had hoped for. Mr.Truman called in Evans, the deal was closed, and I was made to feel at home. I left the place thinking life was pretty good. On the way home, I resolved to prove myself worthy of the confidence these two men had shown in me.

My interview for the job was on a Thursday; I reported for work at 7 A.M. the following Monday. The main building of the Beckley Machine and Electric co. was one long rectangular red brick structure beside a railroad track that hauled the company's freight. When I saw my own location I felt very special: my building was just that, a separate building for my operation alone. The small building was located behind the main structure and was fabricated of corrugated steel sheets. It opened onto a spacious construction yard that was also my territory.

The new blacksmith for this company was to be in charge of all steel fabrications, a variety of this classification of work was required by the mines, all welding, both forge and acetylene and, of course, all anvil forging. It was a unified operation and, I began to realize, an important one in the business of this versatile repair shop for the mines of the state, and particularly of the adjacent section of West Virginia called, for some reason not known to me then or now, the Gulf.

I was fascinated as I took in the large anvil, firmly spiked down on an immense truncated Beach log, a very ample electric forge, almost identical to the one I had left in Waycross, and large tanks of oxygen and others of acetylene gas. All this along with a complete set of hand tools, welding torches, and all the auxiliary equipment that one could wish for and need to practice the trade. I was ecstatic: all this, in a sense was to be mine in a special individual location, not in a line of other smiths, as in the Waycross shops. It seemed providential; I at last felt justified in leaving the railroad shop; I decided to do all necessary to prove myself and earn the journeyman's card in six months, the qualifying time required in an open shop.

Truman introduced me to a tall sinewy man, who appeared to be about forty years old, named Floyd Light; he was to be my helper. I had had helpers on all my previous work, but in this special location and unique status, I felt Floyd was more than just a helper, he was my one man organization. And he proved to be, his school education was limited. He was a devout Baptist, a member of my father's congregation, and loyal and helpful almost to a fault. In a short time I realized that a bond of respect, and even affection, had developed between us and we had become a team in which I took great pride.

Soon our shop became a busy place: this was to be straightened, that welded and many special designs forged to our engineers specifications. Our engineer was ingenues and thorough, and from his draftsmen came drawings that were easy to interpret, and well planned for forging. I felt a sense of pride in my work and went to the shop mornings with enthusiasm. There was a long period of successful jobs that built my confidence and made me a bit guilty of bragging, around home, about my good job.

But all was not perfect: On a special repair job, for an important customer, it was necessary to make an anvil weld of two pieces of tool steel for a steam shovel bit. I had welded many similar pieces in my apprentice days but I could not make these pieces stick. I would heat them to a welding heat and the parts would slide off of each other like something well greased. Over and over I tried with different fluxes and dangerously high temperatures, dangerous for the steel, but the bite, the tackiness to which I was used would not come.

I went back to the blacksmith shop I had owned a part of and talked to the blacksmith there. He was a powerful rustic man who seemed almost unapproachable but I remember him as a sensitive rescuing angel. He had had the same experience in his past; he was eager to help. "Test your coal," he said, "its probably loaded with sulfur. The high temperatures that soft steel or iron can take will burn out the sulfur but the lower welding temperature that you are using, by necessity, on tool steel melts and only partially oxidizes the sulfur. You cannot weld tool steel in a matrix of molten sulfur."

I could have kissed my mentor but of course didn't. I ran back to my shop. I felt he had saved my job. I had also had a practical chemistry lesson. I didn't test my coal but I ordered some fresh pea coal, and explained my problem to the dealer. As in other cases when help was needed everyone seemed helpful. The dealer must have preformed with care: My trouble had to be in the first coal; with the new batch I made a perfect weld the first try. I had not acquired the West Virginia penchant for corn whiskey but I knew my guardian angel blacksmith had; I bought him a bottle of what was recommended as the best mountain dew. And best it was; he insisted that we drink a toast to success and this I could not refuse or, after the drink, deny its potency.

We, Floyd and I, soon fell into a routine of daily work: There would be some simple frame construction that required cutting channel or angle iron into lengths and riveting; some mine would send in a broken cast iron gear that required acetylene gas welding to restore it to service. Pieces were forged that fit on coal cutting machines to protect a miners head or to brace a cutter in some unusual position. The jobs were interesting and I believe our work was good. I began to feel respected by the older mechanics of the different trades represented in the shop. Then a job came in that wasn't at all routine.

The gears referred to above were usually small, a foot or two in diameter, used on mine auxiliary machines. What was not routine was a gear about ten feet in diameter, with a proportionately large hub and a ten inch face, or tooth width. I do not recall the exact dimensions but the above is a modest estimate of a gear shipped in from a mine to be welded.

This gear was the reduction gear for a mine's main hoist. It was made of heavy cross-section cast iron. Its rim of large teeth was broken into several parts, two of the spokes, that looked like medium sized tree trunks, were broken from the hub, but were still attached to a section of the broken rim, and there were several sections of the rim broken out completely free from any other parts. The gear had been broken by a large steel object that fell into the mesh while the hoist was in operation. At the point where the object entered some of the teeth were broken off from the rim and some heavily gouged. Such accidents don't often occur, no replacement gear was immediately available. We were being asked to weld the broken gear if we could.

That was the question, "could we?" A conference was held between the bosses, a couple older machinists and me, who would be expected to do the work, to determine if the project was feasible. To make a long story somewhat shorter, I was pleased at my being in a conference in the front office. I was, nevertheless, adequately respectful of the challenge undertaking such a job would present, and was astonished that these older heads were looking at me and asking at the end of each observation, "what is your opinion--can you do it." I finally said with more confidence than I felt, "I think I can but I want a couple days to think about it and plan a step by step procedure." I was given better than that: we were talking on Thursday and even though we worked on Saturday, Truman said, "let's meet back here on Monday--we'll leave it to you, Hoge."

And leave it they did! I thought of little else for four days and probably for a good part of four nights. But Monday morning I did feel sure about the job; I had become thrilled with the challenge. I had not lost my respect for the difficulties but I was confident that, with a plan I had evolved, I could do the job.

We had our meeting which consisted of my report and their approval. I explained that I would reassemble the broken gear, lying on its side, on the sand clay surface of our construction yard. I wanted an opened ended order for firebrick, which I would need by the case, and the same for sand, which would be required in substantial amounts. I gave a full report of the use of these materials which will be clear here as we consider the job in progress. Truman and Evans were persuaded by either my confidence, or the explanation of details, and approved my plan.

Floyd and I gathered our materials, and precisely leveled a twelve foot square surface area in the yard. Preparatory for acetylene welding, we did much necessary grinding at the joints of the broken parts, and assembled the gear on its side. High precision in alignment was maintained in this operation. The assembly was made in a shallow coating of sand. Sand and fire bricks were used to hold lose pieces in place. This work was done in the tradition of laying flagstones in sand: sighting and tapping until all related parts are true and firm. As we got a large section of the gear assembled we encased that section in fire brick, leaving good clearance between the brick and the metal of the gear.

As we continued to assemble sections and encase them in fire brick, as explained, we were building a furnace with the gear inside. This was continued until the entire gear was enclosed. At four places, equally spaced around this circular furnace, entrances, made of firebrick, were provided so that high pressure gas torches could introduce long hot flames tangential to the circumference of the gear. With four such torches at work, under proper control, we knew we could heat the gear with an even heat throughout all the unbroken sections and smaller pieces assembled.

The above heating was essential, because to weld any cast iron structure preheating followed by slow cooling, is required to avoid cracking, by uneven stresses, in the process.

We were well organized and ready to begin the preheat by Friday afternoon. Wisdom would have dictated waiting until a new day before beginning, but enthusiasm and impatience turned the torches on just after a lunch of sandwiches Friday. Slow heating, at first, was necessary to avoid hot spots at the torches. I liked the sound, the roar of the gas combustion and was thrilled and relaxed to at last be on the way to the serious business of welding.

The circular furnace was not as efficient as we had expected, but, with allowing a little more time than planned, it worked well. By late afternoon the iron was adequately "soaked" with heat; it showed a uniform cherry red color. I began making the first weld about quitting time for the rest of the shop.

Each place on the gear that required welding was indicated outside the furnace by marks on the firebrick at a point prearranged for access. Bricks of the furnace at these points were placed so that they could be removed to weld, and replaced after welding. Where necessary, the ground beneath the joint had been dug out to permit the welding torch to operate to the extreme bottom of the joint. All went well. Only a few improvisations were required to correct some minor oversights in preparation. Time was the only commodity in short supply. So that I could endure the heat at the openings while welding, we would turn down the torches during the working period. When the weld at one point was finished, the opening was closed. The torches were turned up again, for a period of time necessary, to restore the lost heat.

The operation continued into the night (there were flood lights in the yard) with a regular rhythm of long intervals: take out the bricks, turn down the torches, weld, replace the brick, turn up the torches, wait for the heat to build up and then repeat the same steps at another point.

There were places where gear teeth had to be welded in, or, in some cases, built up entirely of molted welding rod put on in layers. About ten o'clock Floyd went for sandwiches and coffee at a fast food place in the neighborhood; we declared a rest period, ate, and I caught a half hour nap. Floyd could nap occasionally while I welded. That half hour was all the sleep I got Friday night. I would rest my eyes during the reheats, and may have nodded occasionally, but the show went on full out through the entire night. We were still busy when the workers came in Saturday morning with many questions about how the job was going. Floyd and I were too preoccupied to answer many; we had caught the rhythm, and that seemed to keep us going.

To cover all the details will spoil the story with boredom. We did finish the welding, from the top side, by late Saturday evening, and allowed the gear to cool enough for handling with a crane and asbestos gloved hands. We turned the gear over for the purpose of doing some cosmetic welding on the side that had been down and not fully accessible. This work was low in volume at any single place and could be done without a full preheat. We accomplished the final welding, along with other finishing tasks, including a cool down to a temperature safe to leave unattended, soon after midnight.

I arrived home about 1 A.M. Sunday morning. My mother and father got out of bed and came down to the dinning room to give me something to eat and express their anxiety over the long hours I had worked.

I never ate that supper. I fell asleep at the table, was guided to by bedroom, awake enough to walk but not to remember the trip. I had an uninterrupted sleep of many hours, my parents reported 16. I woke up starved and aching, but proud and happy in the knowledge that I had lying on the ground at the shop a fully welded gear that, after some chipping, grinding, filing and polishing, would go back to that mine hoist as good as new.

It was just a mechanical job, done well, I believe. But, at the time, it was so much more: I had slain the dragon, I had taken the city. I had learned again that successfully meeting challenges is much much more than putting together acts of the brain and muscles. It is the essence of the spirit.

There were things happening around my working area that were far removed from the business of the firm: There was a girl who made me aware that I was interesting to an attractive member of the opposite sex, and a very important one at that. Jinks Hoskins, a member of the high society of this small town, actually came to the neighborhood of our shop to observe a blacksmith at work. This was feminine curiosity. How could a young man, that she had met at my cousin Lyle's ice cream social, really be a living working blacksmith? She had never heard of anything like that from her patrician parents or in her social circle.

Beckley is built on hills. One street may look down a hundred feet to the next parallel street that would normally be one block over. Our shop was located on such a lower thoroughfare which was a dividing line between a residential district and industrial properties. There were vantage points on the upper level from which one could look down into the entrance part of my building or have a full view of my construction yard.

I soon became aware that I had an audience: the same car would be parked at the same place, at various times, on the street above. There was always, at the window of the car, the same head covered with blond curls, and possessed of attentive eyes peering down in my direction. My cousin, Lyle Hatcher, satisfied my curiosity: she explained that several of her girl friends had become romantic, or at least curious, about the teen age mighty smith, and that Jinks had made some sojourns to see and, I hope, admire from a closer distance. Jinks later admitted that she had been the girl in the car. My awareness of her interest, and her very real

charms, led soon to a lasting friendship. Among three fine
ladies I dated, somewhat in rotation, it was understood that
Jinks was special.

When I was informed by Evans that I was to go on a job
assignment, to a town with the very unlikely name of
Battleship, West Virginia, and restore a burned out
electric generating station at a coal mine, I realized that
Truman and his partner had confidence in my ability to do
the jobs required in my department.

I was informed that the building, housing the steam engine
driven generator, had been only partially destroyed. The
heat from the fire, however, had burned out the coils of the
generator, and completely melted the large babbitt bearings
supporting the main drive shaft of the engine. It was not my
job to replace the generator coils. That task was assigned
to a man from the electrical department of our company. My
responsibility was to rebuild, in situs, the two main drive
shaft bearings.

Battleship was located in a section of West Virginia known
as the Gulf. I had always associated a gulf with bodies of
water, but this gulf ran between precipitous mountains. I
went by train, and arrived at a station that seemed to be
hanging from the side of a lofty peak.

Within walking distance of the station I found the hotel, a
wooden frame structure with no pretense of elegance. I
walked through double swinging doors into and entrance hall.
The hall ended in a large dining area at its opposite end.
The area was composed primarily of a long table, home
constructed of boards mounted on saw horses.

I was met by a middle age woman who had obviously enjoyed
her own cooking. Her round red face, above a couple double
chins, was split at the bottom by a substantial smile that,
nevertheless, had a menacing aspect. I soon learned of her
importance. she was the only woman in town, and her boarding
house hotel was the only place that food or comfort could be
purchased.

She guided me up steps that rose from the hall. On the
second floor we entered a front room that was obviously
intended to be my haven in the town, which room overlooked
the railroad tracks. As an interesting sidelight, four men
were in the room playing poker, using the top of a pot
bellied stove as their table. They just looked up and said,
"hi!" and continued their game. I put my bag on the bed and
went back downstairs leaving them playing in my room.

This woman in charge was called Sally. Sally was rare and
entertaining. She can be better understood by an incident,

connected with my arrival at her place. It probably added a
little drama to her life way up in the hills:

After a couple days of eating three plain but substantial
meals from her boards, and listening to, and joining
occasionally, the banter between Sally and her rustic
clientele, I realized I was a participant in an ongoing live
coal mine-backwoods culture. The language was earthy and the
mutual responses were generous and loud.

On my third day I came to the dining hall ahead of the
scheduled time. Sally addressed me in a secretive voice
almost a whisper, "Hoge I know who you are and know your
problem. My advice is, get moving, get the hell out of here
quick. I won't tell anyone I saw you. You can trust me." I
had no idea what the woman meant, but, as I read some
headlines on the morning paper that Sally pushed into my
line of vision on the table, I began to understand. A murder
had come to light in Hinton, Wva., and the killer had
escaped up the valley on the day I had arrived. Sally was
sure I was the one. Who else could it be, a young city
slicker arriving with no known purpose? So far as she knew,
I had to be him, and that was it!

It took some time to explain to Sally what my job and
purpose was. She had some difficulty accepting my youth in
what she considered a very responsible undertaking. I
somewhat enjoyed her attitude here; I considered it a rather
flattering appraisal.

The main assembly of the steam engine to be repaired was a
flywheel eight feet in diameter, with a face ten inches
wide, press fitted to an also ten inch diameter drive shaft.
The electrical exciter for the main generator was direct
connected to the end of the drive shaft. The eccentric drive
for valve actuation was also part of this assembly. I do not
know the weight of this massive machinery but it would have
been stated in tons.

In normal operation, as the flywheel turned, approximately
one third of its diameter would be moving in a pit below the
floor surface. Our first problem was to jack the flywheel,
and the rest of the shaft assembly, out of the pit, and roll
the entirety away from the engine frame so that we could get
at the bearing cases to prepare them for casting Babbitt
bearings. There were trial and error arrangements for lining
up the several parts. This required repeated movements of
the shaft assemblage in and out of the casings, with great
effort and some swearing, until the shaft was true, level,
and well supported by improvised devices. The shaft had to
be held firmly in place, equally spaced within the two
casings. Accomplishing this without in-shop tools required
considerable improvising, a prayer and a bit of abiding

hope. But the deed was done with some pride on the part of myself and my Hungarian assistants.

incidentally, six of the ten helpers loaned to me by the mine management were Hungarian. It is interesting to me that my memory of these men is, primarily, that they were always sharpening large knives which they made from automobile spring leaves. They would swish these knives through the air and grin with satisfaction. I was glad to note that they were also men of friendly good humor, and were willing to take orders on the job, but they had a thing about those knives.

The steam generating boilers were located in a building smaller than the power plant proper, separate from but closely adjacent to the plant. The boiler furnaces were pressed into the service of heating the Babbitt metal to be poured into the molds we would prepare. Five eighths of inch steel rods were formed into pouring shanks to receive our crucibles, which crucibles were to be heated in the fired up boiler furnaces. This arrangement was quite efficient, enabling us to heat at one time the total number of crucibles required to avoid any interruption of a single pouring, thus making each bearing half an undivided whole. Each complete bearing was divided into two halves: the bottom half in which the drive shaft rested and a cap half that, bolted in place, retained the shaft in its running postion.

The technicalities of preparing the molds, pouring the metal and finishing may bore my readers, but the memory of the accomplishment causes me to include a brief description. The shaft in place was to be the core of the mold and the fixed casings the outer shells. The molten metal would require that the open space between these two be formed and sealed so that all the metal poured would take on the correct form and none could flow out through any leaks.

A pliable material that would sufficiently adhere to the steel casing and shaft was needed for this latter purpose. I decided to try octagon soap kneaded into a plastic. A small mold of the soap was made and tested. Melted Babbitt was poured in, the soap survived the heat and clung to the steel on which we had arranged the mold. It was usable.

One might question the soap standing the pouring heat. Babbitt bearing metal is a led-tin based material combined with Antimony. The grade used for general machinery purposes has a pouring temperature average of around seven hundred degrees Fahrenheit. This temperature is far below the twenty eight hundred to three thousand degrees of melted iron. Also the steel of the casing and shaft in the mold, we were constructing, would quickly chill the molten metal, and the soap would survive and do its job.

We ordered sent up from Beckley several cases of Octagon Soap and set our men to work kneading, a process in which hammers and improvised rolling pins were used. The plastic soap was carefully built around all escape points of the bottom casings first. Soap was also formed into cones, which were properly attached and sealed to openings into the molds, to form sprues to receive the metal during pouring.

When all was in order we fired the furnaces and introduced loaded crucibles for melting in each of the several furnaces. This was a time of nerve tension and excitement: We wondered if the molds would hold, was the shaft in perfect alignment, and would the metal freeze before the molds were full? There were numerous smaller worries that, at the time of our paranoia, seemed a menace. But the several hot crucibles per bearing were brought on in relays that maintained constant pouring. We rejoiced to see the metal rise in the sprues, and then begin to sink as the metal cooled and shrunk; we dared to accept success for the first half of each mold and a cast-in-position status for the shaft.

We approached the second half of the job with the confidence of veterans: I cut away the frozen sprues, chiseled and filed to prepare joints for the caps. Shims, for future adjustments, were cut and fit to the joints, and held in place with a small amount of our plastic soap. The caps were carefully put in place and aligned. Again soap was used to cover escape routes. The sprues in this case would be the oilcups cast in the casings. We lined the oil cups with soap to facilitate the removal of the cast sprues after pouring. We were ready to fire the furnaces again and proceed with our second pouring, which went through smoothly without undue excitement.

All of us who had worked together for days on the bearing project were impatient for the upper halves to cool for inspection. There was only one uncertainty left: had the filling of the molds been complete? We unloosened the bolts as soon as possible and lifted off the hot caps and saw to our delight two perfect castings.

Even at the above stage the bearings were not ready for use, they would be too tight for smooth and cool rotation. The usual procedure is to scrape the Babbitt with sharp knife-like tools. There are checking procedures in this method, not essential to explain here, that made it impractical to use the scraping method for finishing these large bearings. I decided to burn the bearings in by controlled tightening of the retaining bolts of the caps while the engine operated and oil was poured continuously into the assemblies. This could only be done by remaining in constant attention and feeding buckets of oil into the large cups on the bearing caps. In normal operation these cups, actually rectangular box shaped recesses, would hold oil soaked waste for lubrication.

I did this job myself, during an afternoon to midnight session, by running the engine at a modest speed and very slowly tightening the bolts on the cap. This required tightening until you could hear the oil fry, and were annoyed by clouds of smoke and the stench of burning oil. Restraint was essential to burn enough but not so fast as to melt the bearings. I used a two gallon bucket for the oil. The bucket was refilled often. I purposely over did the matter, assuring that no damage to my precious bearings occurred. And to get a perfect surface I probably kept the process going longer than was necessary. But a perfect surface we did get; when the caps were taken off, one could see one's picture in the mirrored surfaces.

We shimmed the caps to leave them just loose enough for running smoothly when the bolts were firmly tightened and normal lubrication was applied. We got the engine up to speed and made a few adjustments and declared the job finished. The mine boss came out with a jug of corn whiskey. All the participants had a belt, and there was a horse play victory celebration that lasted into the evening.

I cannot finish this without a personal reference that was important to me. The mine boss said he wanted to tell me something that he had held back until the job was done. He said that when I showed up for the job he had called my company, and asked Evans what the idea was sending a kid up to do a man's work. Did he know the complexity of the job? I was seventeen at the time. Evans replied, "leave the kid alone he'll finish the job and it will be done well." I believe I acted unconcerned with this exchange but actually I was pleased to learn my bosses attitude, and my self esteem soared as I listened to the flawless rhythmical performance of the engine. Maybe I had a second drink.

There is a sequel to this story. In those days, in West Virginia, public dances were held periodically at hotels in different small cities. Advertisements would be posted in nearby towns, and, what might be called, some of the best people would attend. Well known bands were hired, the music was good, the refreshments high grade, as was the liquor. A good time was had by all.

About two years after the above repair work was finished, I attended one of these dances at the Beckley Hotel. The mine boss from battleship was there. It was our first meeting since the job. With some trepidation, I asked how the job was running. His reply was, "Twenty four hours per day ever since you were there two years ago." It seemed, that not until I heard that remark was I really finished and free.

A church is usually the focal point of a community called the parish. The parish has its own history separate from the township in which it is located. A successful minister enjoys unusual respect from his congregation, members of his parish, and because of that his responsibility is great: Members of his church seek his advice in all manners of situations. Even though the Baptists have no confessional in the ordinances of the church many members confess their sins to the minister, and ask for guidance into a better life style.

Even though the elder John D. Rockefeller was a Baptist who endowed the famous Rockefeller Church on Riverside Drive in New York City, and there have been other rich and famous Baptists, the preponderance of the membership comes from the common people, the blue collar workers and local merchants. When I was a boy it was customary for the minister's family to be invited out for dinner on Sunday. Dinner was the midday meal served after the church service. I recall that there was a novel, I believe written by a minister's son, entitled "Chicken Every Sunday", that drew its title from the Southern practice of Giving the Minister's family fried chicken and Southern hospitality frequently for Sunday dinner.

These excursions into the homes of the parishioners gave me the opportunity to be with many different families on an intimate level. I remember so many *good* people into whose homes we often visited.

Even though the Minister's salary was not large there were other perquisites; the congregation would sometimes hold "poundings," and his family would receive, in an afternoon, an abundance of everything from cured hams to cases of canned foods. Also among the perks was the not small advantage of riding the trains at a substantial discount.

The church in Beckley had an exceptional choir with several leaders that were of professional quality. I remember Violet Cooke, whose piano transcended proficiency, and a building contractor, named Jack Freeman, whose tenor voice was operatic. Every Sunday there were visitors from other churches, and unchurched people, who came to hear the choir, Violet's piano, and Freeman's tenor solos. At Christmas time, the choir's "Messiah" was repeated for several days to accommodate a community demand that overflowed the capacity of the church. I carried a personal pride in these, and other accomplishments of the church, that received community recognition.

A minister's son is often importuned to be a role model, and is especially shamed for transgressions that would be winked at in others. On the other hand I think he has an advantage growing up in a family that is looked up to by the flock. It certainly does no harm to his self-esteem, which is supportive as he goes out to make his way in business or the professions.

Since religion was my father's profession I have discussed the churches of each community. The church at Beckley, however, is the last one of the five Dad was the pastor of during my life at home. He died at Beckley Sept. 12, 1924. There was a lingering illness which I shall not detail here. Doing some of the care taking, which I shared with my mother, I learned still more about the quiet faith and strength of character of the man.

I have explained previously in this book my pride in our family relationship to the church, the good people who were its members, and the high purpose of its ethics. Theological considerations are what brought the various churches into existence. However as I recall my youth they had little influence upon my daily thinking or behavior at that time. The latter was a product of things I wanted or wanted to do, my consideration of others and family rules which were strict enough to keep a youngster essentially in line. As to thinking, I don't recall that I had yet done much of that in the theological area. You were told what to believe there. It was later in life, when I sought truth for its own sake, that I developed convictions of my own.

There are many stories that could be told of adventures in the Gulf. For my company I did repair work in the mines of that area. There was a time when moonshiners mistook me for a revenue agent and marched me off their premises with a couple of gun barrels at my back.

Another time There was a mine at which I was welding for several days repairing a large steam shovel. This mine was a unique place where at lunch in the dining room, serving everybody at long tables at single sittings, there was always a two gallon water bucket sitting on the floor at each of the two entrances. There was a dipper in each bucket which was filled with what looked like water. One startling taste corrected your impression, and told you it was illegally distilled corn whiskey which had to be handled with care.

My days as a blacksmith, or general mechanic were coming to a close and I would like to hurry the process, by condensing and omitting some details. I want to get to a very important part of my early years, acquiring a deeper and broader education.

Time came, when for the purpose of improving my economics, and, I thought status, I left the Beckly Machine and

Electric Co., went to Charleston, Wva. and got a job as an Automobile Mechanic. A book could be written about the period in Charleston and, later, Hunington,but that would throw this one out of balance.

I worked for the Reo Motor Repair Co. rebuilding Automobile engines. It was an interesting job that took me into the real Mysteries of of good machinery. I commenced to understand precision and design and grasp the edges of their significance, I longed to know more. I got into induction coils and how they worked on sound electrical principals that to the uninitiated seemed impossible. I spent evenings trying to get real understanding of these laws of nature. I went to libraries for books to satisfy my passion for supporting knowledge on these mysteries beneath my daily work.

The Reo Company had also an establishment in Hunington ,Wa. I received in the mail an invitation from the Hunington Management, a Mr Cavendish, to join his organization in Hunington, which being a promotion, I accepted and moved to that city.

I consider these two cities in one package, one half to each, because they were the places where I agonized over education, a desire to know more and a desire to move up in general. Finally one fine day I was under an automobile installing a rebuilt motor when I was disturbed by some inner impulse. I stopped work and thought for but a few minutes when I realized I was overwhelmed my desire to go back to high school and on through college to an engineering degree.

I rolled out from under the car, went to Mr. Cavendish's office and said, "I am quitting, as of now. I'm going to school. Thank you for everything, but goodbye." It was hard for me to be so abrupt an final with Cavendish. I had been especially favored by him. We had a regular Thursday night date to eat frog's legs at a Chinese restaurant. There was other favorable treatment such as could only come from an older man who liked a younger one with fatherly interest. I could see that he understood and tried to lighten the tension: he said, "I'm going to miss the frog legs."

Back in our town there was, of course, the church, its choir, all the good people and their activities proclaiming the Faith and extending the earthly hospitality. It was my father's world, and he seemed happy in his work. Of real importance there was Jinks Hoskins, Lucy Ragland, Lyle Hatcher. I called them the three Graces and three Graces they were: wonderful young women that I had the privilege of dating. Back in those years it was understood that young men and women dated among their contemporaries unless they had developed a steady. Jinks was special to me but we were all good friends and "went out" together as seemed appropriate.

There were parties at the homes of friends and socials at the church or school. Some homes had a swimming pool and that was special. Others had tennis courts and we were invited and often played. We were very proud a few years later that a boy on our block became the governor of the state.

When I returned to Beckley my full attention was absorbed with the logistics of returning to school. I found that having had five years experience in the working world, being older and knowing exactly what I wanted was an advantage. There were three and one half years of schooling to make up to become eligible for college as a candidate for a degree. I was determined to get them out of the way in the one regular school year of 1922 and a summer session at a preparatory college. After much selling on my part, and sympathetic understanding on the part of the superintendent of the Beckley High school it appeared that that would be accomplished: First, considering that I had six months credit as a high school freshman and five years of work experience the superintendent thought it fair and proper to give me per se credit for the first full year. I would be required to cram up on English 1 and mathematics 1 and pass an examination that would be provided by the school.

I would be set up as a special student in the high school, taking the sophomore course complete, would have no free study hall periods, but would attend classes of the third year during those periods, and would from time to time be given appropriate examinations to confirm my progress. Other credits for the third year that I could not work into a schedule at the school would be handled by special coaches in the evening. I remember that my English coach was named Mrs. Givens. I had a another coach for advanced mathematics and a teacher of the educational courses at school as a coach for civics and such.

I would attend evening classes at these ladies' homes and from time to time have examinations to confirm my eligibility for passing grades. It worked. By the end of the 1922 semesters I was through the third year high school and off for a summer session at Princeton preparatory school in Princeton West Virginia (not the Ivy League Princeton). A full year of High School could be covered in the summer course for which I promptly signed. To summarize the point. I finished the summer course lacking only three required credits to to Enter Virginia Polytechnic institute as a candidate for the engineering degree I wanted. I promptly went to V.P.I. for a talk with the dean. I came away from Blacksburg an admitted special student, not yet a candidate for my degree. At the end of my freshman year I would be allowed to take a special College Chemistry and a Physics exam with another not quite so specific that, passing, would turn me into a regular student with all rights of candidacy reserved. I was on my way. When completed, the one year would have finished my preparatory work. I was euphoric, which euphoria I shared with good friends and a supportive family. A time came when I said out loud, "We did it, We did it, We did it."

Chapter XI

School Days and On

Here at the beginning of chapter XI, at the risk of being awkwardly so, I am going to be repetitive concerning my special educational program outlined in the final paragraphs of chapter X. I am going to do this to breathe a bit of life into that period.

In my school arrangement, with such a program of multiple years going on at one time, one might think of perpetual fatigue. That most certainly was not what happened. I had plenty of school work that kept me in the books until about twelve each night and busy all day, but busy on subjects that I found fascinating.

For example, I fell in love with the The beauty of plain and solid geometry. Studying such subjects was stimulating, not tiring. "When two parallel lines are cut by a transverse line the alternate interior angles are equal." and "The shortest distance between two points is a straight line." You start with such simple obvious statements and build on these with other truths, and, finally, you solve a complicated problem. Glory be! if everything could be so logical.

I had no personal history of school days here with the other students. I had come in as an outsider wanting very earnestly to acquire something that I realized was of paramount importance to the future of my life. Working to acquire this was my occupation at the time. I had no competitive problems or class standing, no athletic reputation or loyalties, was a single purpose individual.

As the Apostle Paul said, "This one thing I do." I was grateful for such an abundant orchard to gather fruit in. This singleness of purpose made an enormous difference in the quantity of work that I could handle and the degree of my absorption of the assigned work.

As I look back on the period I recognize myself in Plato's story about Socrates and the young man wanting knowledge. The young man had come to Socrates at the beach, and asked him how he could obtain knowledge. Socrates grabbed the young man and held his head under water for a stressful period of time, and then released him. He said, "When you want knowledge like you wanted air with your head under water you will get it." The story is less than plausible but I can identify with the intent.

I did develop an interest in basketball, girls basketball that is. I attended the games and cheered for the home team. The ladies on the team were very attractive in the uniforms of the period: they wore full dark blue bloomers and black stockings with a white shirt colorfully decorated at the neck.

I also attended the football games with some feeling of team spirit. I cheered with the rest. But there were auxiliary activities, not so compulsive, that I skipped and spent my time with my main purpose of earning the credits to enter college the following year.

Actually as I look ahead in the biography at this time, there is a period coming up in which I do not visualize my recording events in as much detail as has characterized much of the foregoing. The readers of these pages have all gone to school. Many of my special events as a student could get a, "So what?" reaction if turned into an elaborate story. Maybe a bit of a moratorium will have to be placed on extensive anecdotes. Only the quantity of work being carried was really unique. We shall see.

During the school term of 1922, spent in Beckley, there were school activities such as the senior play and church events that filled the social calendar.

The senior play gave me an unexpected local fame as an actor and a memory expert. On a Friday, before the play was to make its debut the next Tuesday night, the lead man came down with chicken pox. Because I was doing well in my many different classes, the director of the play said he assumed, I was just the one to memorize the lead over the weekend, have a Monday rehearsal, and probably save the day on Tuesday. I remember that the proposition was presented to me persuasively with sort of "you are our only hope" angle thrown in. The persuasion must have worked: I find myself hard at work over the weekend.

I crammed so hard Saturday and Sunday that I found myself coaching from the sidelines at the Monday rehearsal. The play opened Tuesday night with, what was declared to be, a smashing success; I then relaxed for the first time since Friday afternoon, and turned my attention back to my own program of study and being coached.

Some of the evening coaching was dictated by what could supply a credit and what was convenient to arrange, and not, necessarily, by what was most appropriate study for an engineering aspirant.

One credit was to be made in a class entitled "Education" which was designed for students who intended to be teachers. I was not that type of student, but, in my special program, a credit that would be accepted by the college was a credit. We learned about synapse, the bonding points between neurons, and associated data concerning the functioning of the brain. Though not specifically needed by engineers the subjects contributed to my general education. And the fact that they are still quite clearly remembered testifies to the thoroughness of the special coaching that was done.

Our school was active in competitive debating between the high schools and preparatory schools. There was a time during the year when a contest between our school and Bluefield high was to be held in Bluefield, a nearby small city. I became very interested in trying my ability in that skill also. I joined our debating society and put my name in to compete in the Beckley group to determine who would represent the school in Bluefield.

Both my mother and father were very interested in public speaking, and they were very supporting in this undertaking. My mother particularly gave me a few lectures on what to do and what not to do. She empathized and demonstrated the value of the peroration and how it gave strength and charisma to the simple facts of your speech.

I won the local competition, and, later, won the inter-school debate in Bluefield. The master of ceremonies of the debate in Bluefield, after the decision was announced said, in some closing remarks, that my performance showed the importance of experience. The debate was my first experience with public speaking. Yes, I felt flattered. I also realized I had had some good coaching back home.

From time to time, we had evenings of ballroom dancing at Beckley High, which dances were high grade social events. We hired nationally recognized bands, gave door prizes and special prizes to winners of competitive dances during the evening. Dress was formal, the boys were in their tuxedos and the girls in a great variety of beautiful dresses. I was among the students who put on the dances, but the only specific functions that I recall myself performing were handling some of the income, paying the band for their services, and being concerned with the accommodations of the musicians while they were in town.

And so, with the normally expected curricular and extra curricular events of school, the school term progressed. By the end of the term I had completed all assignments with high grades and was ready for the preparatory school summer course; the course that was to complete the making of me acceptable as an engineering student at Virginia Polytechnic Institute.

My mother volunteered her automobile and company to drive me to the Princeton preparatory school at Princeton, West Virginia, a town near Beckley; not the Ivy league Princeton of world fame.

Mother was a Baptist ministers wife, a total believer and a full practitioner and promoter of high standards of conduct. One did not use profanity in her presence. There was an exception in the language department on the way to Princeton: I was driving and suddenly was startled to see a truck coming toward me, in my lane, for a head on collision. As if by fate, on my left, at the instance, was a filling station. By reflex action I instantly, at high speed, swung my car into entrance driveway to the station, went through the station, between the pumps, and out the other driveway, back to the road again, but behind the truck that had threatened me.

As I made the wild sashay through the filling station there automatically burst from my mouth, "You S.O.B."-- only that is not an accurate quote. I used the words full out with a couple expletives to give emphasis appropriate to the occasion.

I drove on to Princeton without further event but with an enhanced sense of alertness. My mother offered no reprimand for my profane language, but I was to learn, from her later comments, that "the captain's lady and Susan O'Grady are sisters under the skin," and I liked her better for that fact. After I had checked into my boarding house room and we were having lunch before she headed home, she said simply, with what I could see was a controlled sly smile on her face, "You used pretty strong language back there."

By my grades one could gather that I did quite well in my studies at the school. My love for mathematics, particularly, continued unabated. In fact, about half way through the course, the trigonometry teacher was out sick for over two weeks. I was declared a substitute teacher, and put in charge of the course. I studied ahead of the scheduled pages, and kept the class in step with its normal timing.

The social life during the summer term included several fried chicken picnics with plenty of fun and food. There were also informal dances at my boarding house and a couple others. Friendships were made that were to last only a short time. The ties were not like those made over four years at one's Alma Mater, but enjoyable for the interlude.

I do not recall any special ceremonies connected with finishing the courses, but finish them we did with pride and satisfaction. Credits for college entrance were my objective and these had now been obtained. It felt good to be eligible for the first semester, of 1923 at V.P.I., which would begin within about ten days. I went from Princeton directly to Blacksburg. I talked to the dean of students at V.P.I. about three needed special credits, and made the arrangements explained at the end of chapter ten and was accepted.

My Memory of my four years at V.P.I. begins with going to the barracks to inspect the room that had been assigned me. I discovered a young man standing in the middle of the room holding a broom in one hand and a pocket knife in the other. He appeared to be busy carving his initials in the handle of the broom. I soon found that we were to be roommates by assignment. I saw no reason to object to the schools choice. In time I was to learn that the choice could not have been better. The young man's name was, and is, Henry Denny, and, as I write this, not so young, he lives in Charlottesville, Virginia. Over the years, we have seen each other many times on visits, and we talk on the phone when the spirit moves us.

At the time with which we are concerned V.P.I.was almost 100% military in format, and was one of the schools incorporated in the U.S. government Reserve Officers Training program, the R.O.T.C.: the students in this program were all male, were called cadets, lived in barracks, wore cadet uniforms, and followed a system of army discipline. There were a small number of nonmilitary students, both male and female, who lived off campus, of whom I was scarcely conscious during my entire four years.

We were aroused in the morning by bugle, had a limited time to arrive on the stoop fully dressed, and answer roll call. At the proper bugle call, we marched to the Mess Hall for a healthy breakfast. This was the framework and flavor of all our living arrangements. They went forward in support, and not in conflict with a high level of educational procedures. One R.O.T.C. class would remind you of the connection during the day. The vast majority of cadets were proud of their connection to the Corp. Nevertheless, griping was a pastime in which many, feeling restrained by the military, indulged. I could be found, at times, in that group.

Some students strove to excel in the military. They became the cadet officers. Others had special interests, such as music. They provided a fine marching band called the "Hity Tities." The Corp was fully equipped and well trained in all military exercises. The training took place on our well used parade grounds at school.

Every Thanksgiving day, the Corp went in body to Roanoke, Virginia, and paraded through its main streets and into the football stadium, on the outskirts of the city, to the sound of much applause. The focus of the performance was an annual

Thanksgiving day football game between V.P.I. and V.M.I., the Virginia school that matched West Point in its program of training officers for our Armed Forces.

I will confess that my orientation was academic. So far as the military was concerned, by my senior year, I qualified for the high order of senior privates, and felt a certain fraternalism with the other senior privates. Nevertheless, I enjoyed and took pride in being a member of the auspicious V.P.I. Corp of Cadets. I look back upon the experience with pride and affection.

But all was not discipline or organized academic work. There was time to relax and do what seemed to be fun at the time. The years in this respect do not lend themselves to being treated separately in sequence. There became a sameness about the diversions that one acquired and repeated over the years: One was living in the same room on the same campus, and following the same formal procedures. Informality and the use of free time soon took on a pattern and were continued with only minor differences at different times.

For example, on Sundays throughout my stay at the school, I was among those who checked out of the barracks for church attendance. Some Sundays I really went to church, others I joined friends for other recreational purposes. Often we took long hikes in the woods.

There was hazing in the freshman year. It was not original or unique. It was, with modifications, a standard military school brand. As a new experience, it was irritating: You could, according to the custom, be called "Rat," and be required to obey the commands of an upperclassman to render him some special service or carry out some awkward stunt or scenario. I only occasionally heard the name "Rat Hoge." Soon after becoming a cadet, I accepted, and at the same time ignored, hazing. I believe most freshmen did the same.

There was a modest amount of local social activity in all the years. The kind wife of Dr Newman, head of the English Department, added much to the enjoyment of cadets who were from time to time invited to parties in the Newman home. A highlight of these events was a slab of homemade ice cream that was split into enormous servings with chocolate syrup for a topping. At these parties we went with or met some of the girls who lived in Blacksburg. I was related to some of the local citizens and saw them often in their homes.

In general, it would be stretching the facts to make a big deal out of what happened between the Corp and the people of Blacksburg.

V.P.I., being an R.O.T.C. unit, was not allowed to have Greek letter fraternities. There were two dance clubs that, in addition to staging elaborate dances during various seasons, functioned as substitute fraternal organizations. There was the Cotillion club and the German Club, both of which put on fine dances and functioned in a competitive ambience. The cadets danced in their dress uniforms and the girls in their finest ball room clothes. We were told by friends of the corps and local ladies who chaperoned the dances, that they were elegant to observe, and elegant they were. I was a member of the German Club.

Happiness, however, was not without interruption. My father died at the end of my first year. I was entirely self supporting for my last three years. I earned the money working as an automobile mechanic during the summer holidays and doing some repair work on professor's cars at the school.

For me the academic work grew more and more interesting, and, with the passage of time, we students looked and acted more like engineers. My grades were consistently good. I graduated with Phi Kappa Phi honors, received the key, and a special certificate. Phi Kappa was, at the time, the Engineer's Phi Beta. I received my college degree of BS in Mechanical Engineering.

Actually I was glad when the four years were over and I could begin the serious business of building a career. I look back upon those school years primarily with happy recall of many wonderful friends. Prominent among these is Henry Denny, that young man I met as my room mate that first day at the school.

During my senior year I experienced the system of being recruited by large national corporations. It seemed somewhat of an honor to receive such special attention. After considering several offers, I accepted General Electric Co and was scheduled to go to Lynn Mass, for training.

Probably because I was going to the land settled by the Pilgrims about 1610 I felt like a Pilgrim. I was leaving the old South for the first time, and going to yanki country, and that New England. I felt wonder at what I would find and a full sense of adventure which it was for me at the time: I was starting a new career, one I had spent another five years preparing for and now it was here. It remains one of the most important moments of my life.

I went by train from Beckley, Wva. to Norfolk, Va. where I was met by my next door pal, when we lived in Norfolk.

The years had gone by for him also. He now owned and operated a successful furniture store on Granby St. We went to his store, went to lunch from there ,and waited out the time of several hours before my ship sailed for Boston. Yes ship, I went by ship from Norfolk to Boston, a daily schedule in 1927. Charlie, my friend, took me to the docks and put me aboard, for what turned out to be, a wonderful interlude.

My arrival by ship accented my feeling of a pilgrim going to a new land. We arrived in Boston harbor in the morning fog and to the sound of many fog horns, including the one on our ship. It was all very new and very exciting to me. We took over an hour to complete our landing and come ashore where I was met by two other cadets from V.P.I., Sterling Weld and Red Kunkel who were also going with General Electric in Lynn, Ma..

Lynn is a suburb of Boston, and was the location of the General Electric factories. By our prior arrangement, Sterling and Red had gone on before me, found us an apartment, and made some deals with two other beginners from other schools. For economic reasons, we were to have five in our rather large facilities. One of the other two did not last long and I remember almost nothing about him, but one was from Alabama, with a speaking accent you could cut with a knife. He always mentioned that he had principles. One of them must have been "I don't wash dishes" but more on that later when we are in the apartment supposedly taking turns with all chores. I remember all about Alabama to this day.

Another thing I remember now and have clearly over the years is an occurrence on the sidewalk in front of our apartment. At home I came from a religious background of fundamentalism. I had just graduated from a college where the background was very much scientific; the latter appealed to me more than the former. Actually I had spent much time and energy trying to reconcile the two, which is impossible without changing meanings throughout. So I am not surprised to find myself walking toward the apartment and thinking, what really does happen to one's self, one's soul, when he leaves the scene of life.

I was doing just that when I abruptly stopped walking, almost as though I had been arrested by a force, and I talked plainly to myself, "Don't you realize that a supreme intelligence who could make a universe, make people, and put them in the universe, is an intelligence who has no reason to leave unfinished what is to be done with the people when their experience on earth is finished. Trust that it's in the plan and that it is okay."

I was convinced then, and still am, that that is a simple and sane answer. I moved on in confidence. Over the years I have been back in mind, time and again, to that same place on the sidewalk, before our apt in 1927, and am always satisfied with the same answer. I have seen no reason to change it.

But there was a darker side to that apartment. With all its baroque exterior, and fine construction within, it had rats in the walls. Yes, families of rats lived in the walls of the entire building. They were considerate. They never came out when you were home and awake.

However, when we went to Boston for the theater or dinner we would come home late. As we opened our door to enter, we would often break into a social gathering of rats on our kitchen and dining room floors.

There was a hysterical scattering: Rats would head for their holes behind furnishings or in the plumbing. On one occasion, a drawer in a chest of drawers was open. I saw a rat dive into the drawer. I slammed the drawer shut and trapped the rat inside. I do not recall why we went to bed without getting the rat out of the drawer. I do remember that the next morning we found about a two inch hole in the front of the drawer.

Trying to get rid of the rats actually became a sort of game. The building superintendent cooperated: he put weasels in the walls that were supposed to attack and drive the rats out. The affect was not noticeable.

Red Kunkel and I each got a fire place poker. We kept them in the kitchen. If either, or both, of us detected a rat, or rats, in the kitchen, we ran in, slammed the door and attacked the rats with our pokers. Attacking a cornered rat with a poker is an indelicate business. I shall not contribute to this age of violence by giving a blow by blow description. We sometimes made a minor contribution to clearing the rat problem, but the risk and effort was way out of proportion to the accomplishment. We soon surrendered the kitchen to the rats. All of us kept out of each others way. No great harm was done, and we and the rodents lived happily ever after.

You would naturally ask, "Why didn't you just rent a rat free place." I answer, "As beginners at General Electric, our salaries were $90.00. per month."

With a salary of $90 in 1927, you could afford two bran muffins and a cup of coffee for breakfast at some quick lunch counter. You could eat an inexpensive, GE subsidized lunch in their cafeteria, and for dinner you could cook your own in your apartment. We cooked for five every night. We took turns. We had some good meals. We had some atrocious meals. Occasionally we went to Boston and ate a sea food dinner that was superb. These dinners were expensive with a top price of three dollars. To save money often two would split one meal.

Believe it or not, on ninety dollars each month, we kept our health, were never hungry, took in theater plays in Boston, had dates, went on holidays in the mountains, and lived a generally happy life. Among the five of us in the apartment, there was a lot of sharing in the cost and the pleasures.

My first job with General Electric, (or G.E. for future reference} was in steam turbine research. My training included testing blade designs, made by older engineers, working on designs myself under guidance and supervision. It was school again, but doing the real thing. The training was intense but the newcomer was expected to learn and move fast. I was less than a year in Lynn, and much happened.

Very soon I was taken through a series of Psychological tests. I went off the curve and the board on which the curve was drawn, indicating high ability, but they did not recommend that I stay in turbine research.

My papers were marked "executive type" It made no sense to me: I had been a mechanic for years was trained in engineering had thought of myself as an engineer, and preferably a research engineer.

A couple psychologist explained to me that a good executive and a good research man have the same type of minds, and with the same opportunities, the same intellectual interests. They differ in their emotional interests. The successful research engineer tends to the introvert the executive the extrovert.

They persuaded me to switch to G.E.'s application engineering program, coupled with sales, and hopefully, in time, business management. I did so and never regretted it. But I never lost my interest in science and engineering for its own sake.

I started this change by transferring to the Electric Motor Division. My work was at the end of the production line. Several of we trainees tested every motor that came by to assure that it performed up to G.E. standards of quality. We took the work seriously, and later on in life when I was buying motors It gave me confidence in G.E. products. When these factory departments finished with us we were well trained in application engineering with a strong emphasis on sales, and were ready for district office work.

I was soon chosen for district work by the Texas Division of the company. Arrangements were made by Bob Shields, manager of the division. Our discussion of the matter was over a dinner table in a Boston hotel, at Bob's expense, or rather his G.E. expense account's. We had a gorgeous dinner and I commenced to sense that I was going to like district application engineering sales. I had a feeling I was about to join the elite. In a relative way there was some truth to the feeling, but not without a lot of hard work. I was, however, to remain in Lynn for more training for several months before the move.

During this waiting period time came for a vacation. With a friend named Wayne Wilson, who had the distinct advantage of owning a Ford Runabout automobile, I headed for the White Mountains. We both declared we were tired of dating, dancing and the dating game.

We were going to forget the girls and go mountain climbing. We, some how, raised the money for a couple weeks at Cold River Camp, an Appalachian Club mountain climbing resort at Chatham, New Hampshire, right on the Main border. The first night, after dinner, we went to the recreation hall. There was music, there was dancing and there was a man named Bill Whitney who came into the hall with two girls. That was a fateful entrance: we became life long friends. He eventually married one of the girls and I the other, but much was to happen before that denouement.

Even though our plans to go mountain climbing for a vacation deliberately excluded girls, it seemed the most natural thing in the world to ask these girls for dances. I found myself immediately attracted to the little one. As I found out later she was five foot two. I saw instantly that she was perfectly proportioned. Her name was Marjorie Meader, but her friends called her "Marge." I immediately felt friendly, So Marge it was.

I do not remember how many others were present in the recreation room that evening. The other girl that Came in with Bill Whitney was Betty Welch. Betty and Marge had an apartment together in Pawtucket, R.I. They both worked for the Y.W.C.A.; Marge was in charge of Physical Education. Betty some other department. Bill Whitney was a friend.

That first evening, in addition to dancing, Marge and I got well acquainted: we worked out that "good morning" in Chinese would be, "!Ole Ole Unk Yung!" Of course that's not a true translation, but it satisfied us then. The next morning found me out under a window of the girls building shouting !Ole Ole Unk Yung!, followed by Marge joining me for breakfast. We repeated this performance mornings during the vacation.

Very soon after day one an assault on Mount Washington was scheduled. There was great excitement of the " I can't wait" type. The lodge was to supply several trucks to take the climbers to the foot of the mountain. We were to team up there. I came with my partner and her name was Marge.

I had learned a lot about mountain climbing from Bill and Betty. The important thing is that the summit of mountain is up there and you want to get there. When you do, after hours of hiking trails, struggling up vertical cliffs, Yes, through beautiful scenery, arrive, you are at the top, you can't go any farther, you relax and look. "My God how beautiful!"

On mount Washington, the tallest peak in the presidential range, for example, you can see the coast of Maine, and about all of New Hampshire. You see on, it seems, forever through three hundred and sixty degrees. When Marge and I reached that summit we were tired but we did not sit down we turned and looked, turned and looked until we felt we had seen it all. We then sat down and decided to stay a while.

We Had come up Hunington's ravine. a 12 mile climb, up grade all the way, over winding paths, that continued to lift us from the earth below. I do not remember the exact time for the climb, but we started after breakfast and we ate a late lunch on top.

On the trail we came to one place where we had to cross the face of a vertical cliff for a long distance. The distance seemed very very long when one considered that there was about fifteen hundred feet to fall straight down if one's foot didn't stay firmly on the toe holders which never exceeded one inch protrusion from the face of the cliff.

I went across first. I do not recall too much concern on my passage, but then I looked back. Marge was starting over. I really felt concern. That little woman looked so little and helpless against that high cliff that I prayed and prayed again, I detected nothing about her but a steady nerve and surefootedness. I watched in silence as she progressed. When she reached where I could, I took firm hold of her arm and saw her through the last few steps. She had not been afraid she was calm and at ease. I was in need of relaxation. I held her in my arms to quiet my nerves not hers. I was to find, over the years, that that was the kind of girl she was from beginning to end.

But, as said earlier, we were now on top resting planning our return trip to the valley below, over an eight mile descent down a steep grade. Before starting down we wanted to take a 2 mile side trip to see the palace in the clouds. This took time. We had to come back one mile to Tuckerman's ravine. Tuckerman's was the eight mile return route down.

We had used too much time on top. We started down in the late middle of the afternoon. We were sure to be caught in darkness before getting off the mountain. Somewhere in the deep woods we began to lose the light, for a while a full moon helped but the tree tops became so heavy that there was complete darkness.

I could hear water falling, My spirits lifted. It might be a stream or a river on the mountain and water would keep going down hill. It would eventually reach the valley floor. If we kept the water in ear shot we would also reach the valley floor. That's what we did and in time we saw highway lights. We came out of the woods and found that the stream we followed with our ears was named The Cascades. It flowed within feet of the place where our return trucks were parked. Before we got there we met a party of several climbers coming toward us on the trail. They were starting out to search for us. Many of our friends from the camp had waited. We were reunited in the back of a truck and driven home. It was truly a happy ending.

Soon the kidding started and recurred from time to time. Friends would smile and say, "Convenient for a young couple to get lost on a mountain on a full moon night." We did no explaining. And no explanation was wanted.

There were smaller mountains in the vicinity of our Cold River Camp. As the days went by we climbed all of these. There was a cold river fed by melted snow in the higher mountains. In the river there was a pool named Emerald Pool. It was like a giant emerald against the mountain, a sparkling green at the end of a water fall.

As we went out climbing in the morning Betty and Bill, Marge and I, and usually some other couple would take our bathing suits and hide them in the woods around Emerald Pool. We would join others for the climbs. In the late afternoon, on the way back to camp, we would route ourselves by Emerald Pool and spend and hour or more diving and swimming. The diving was from high up on the mountain side. The pool was very deep and very cold.

Wayne Wilson, my friend whom I came to the camp with, would, with or without a companion, often join us. He was usually a loner but was welcome in our group. His idea of fun was to take a golf club and some balls up a mountain and make long drives from the peak. It was fun, I drove a few myself.

At the pool Wayne would dive from very high up and would yell to support his nerve. Often our diving sessions sounded like a tribal affair before the battle.

The energy output for mountain climbing is great. It is invigorating exercise. As the days went by our appetites reflected the output. The clubhouse gave us steaks for breakfast and packed larger and larger lunches for the trail. Our dinners became royal feasts, "eat all you can hold."

Evenings after dinner were spent around the recreation hall
or the club house. On several occasions we attended local
square dances by invitation, walked to and from the dance,
and felt a strange comfort and excitement over the night
time experience of mountain roads on foot.

At last it came, the evening at the club house before our
vacations ended on the morrow, and we went our separate
ways. I recall one thing clearly and fondly about that
evening. I am sitting in a club house chair, Marge is
perched above me looking me in the eyes, she is singing "You
may search this wide world over but you will never find a
girl like me." As she sang her eyes were sparkling with a
separate laughter of their own. That laughter in her eyes, I
was to learn, was a life long characteristic. In the 1980's
I painted a portrait of Marge, true to her appearance at the
time. The portrait is distinctive by those same laughing
eyes that were there in 1928. Our personal singing interlude
ended and we joined the others for a farewell party.

The next morning I went to the girls building, and shouted
"ole ole unk yung." Marge came out; we went to breakfast
together. We both tried to avoid thinking of the last day,
but it wouldn't go away. We talked of my going to Texas in a
few months, and how we would have some dates before that
time. Still, I'll confess to stupidity and a $90.00 a month
salary; I said nothing about marriage. Actually, at the
time, I just did not consider such in my picture.

After breakfast Wayne Wilson brought his Ford around, and
Bill Whitney his car. Marge was going back to Pawtucket with
Bill and Betty. I to Lynn with Wayne. Many friends were out
to wave good bye. There was much sweet sorrow to the
parting, but we knew we had made some friends that would
last a life time. Among many kisses and hugs we separated
and took to the road with Wayne's runabout responding to
Wayne's urging.

On the way to Lynn,, time for lunch came around. We had
passed many eating places; we were out among farms again and
passed one that had a sign out, "All you can eat $1.50."
That seemed for us, we turned and went back to the property
entrance, and up to the farm house. A very nice lady let us
in and seated us in her dinning room. She went to the
kitchen and came back with two of the largest beef steak
tomatoes I had ever seen that looked as if they had ripened
on the vine. They had. She sat one in front of Wayne and one
in front of me and returned to the kitchen. She had not
counted on the appetites of two men that had been climbing
mountains for two weeks. She left sharp knives and forks for
us to eat our tomatoes, and that we did so fast that it was
like the disappearing act of a magician's show.

The lady returned with some chicken, and looked in amazement at our empty plates. She asked if we would like more tomatoes. We, somewhat apologetically, said that we would. She brought two more very large ones. They too had soon disappeared.

She brought in large plates of chicken and vegetables; these were soon gone. She returned with more, which we ravishingly ate. The act became embarrassing. We finally did quit the main courses to eat some wonderful pie for desert, two pieces each. To ease our consciences we each left tips about equal to the price of the meal. I can still relieve my hunger when need be by thinking of that wonderful meal on the farm.

The next day, back in Lynn, it seemed odd not to be with Marge for breakfast and the day ahead, but it was back to work and familiar routines. But all was not lost: A friend of mine, named Bill Dooling, had a girl up the north coast near Gloucester. Marge began attending a small boarding school in Gloucester for some special diving and swimming training connected with her work at the Y.W.C.A.. Bill and I would cut the expense by renting a car together, and arranging our dates to coincide. Thus we saw the ladies of our choice quite frequently.

Marge's parents owned a cottage farther up the North coast. I visited Marge there for a couple weekends, became acquainted with her family, and enjoyed the romance of being with her in her home and alone together on the beach.

Once when some holidays were joined with a weekend, Bill and Betty from the Cold River experience arranged a party at Lake Winnipesaukee in central New Hampshire. Some friends from the Cold River experience were invited, including Marge and me, with transportation provided. It was a glorious four days. The girls cooked wonderful meals. We males helped all we could with the dishes and the housework. We swam in and boated on the lake, and had plenty of private time together. It was a wonderful renewal of our vacation days at Cold River Camp.

And so, I did see Marge from time to time after Cold River before going to Texas. But I also had an active time schedule for Lynn alone.

When I first came to Lynn, I no longer had a church affiliation, was no longer in agreement with many Southern Baptist dogmas. Again my friend Wayne Wilson was an aid. He had been attending the Unitarian Church. I joined him for a Sunday service. When the service was over I realized I had been listening to beliefs which were already my own, acquired from much hard thinking and reading among the thinkers of the time. Important among these was Harry

Emerson Fosdick. I became a Unitarian and stayed with that identity for many years.

Radio at this time was a new science, and I was very interested. I finally built a radio for my own use, mounted on a three quarter by twelve inch board.

One thing that would seem very strange to present times was how I tuned in the stations. I used a coupling coil which I hung on a cord above all the assembled parts on the board. The cord ran over a pulley hanging from the ceiling. To tune in a station, I carefully raised and lowered the hanging coil. The oscillating inductive vibrations of this coil in apposition with one like it on the board would change until they matched, exactly, the vibrating wave length being broadcast by some station, and, behold, the music came in. I provided marks for previously tuned stations on the board, and a black mark on the cord. By matching marks I could chose stations with ease.

I was occasionally asked to give radio talks, and enjoyed doing that. I took parts along and built a radio as I talked. In 1928 radio was a new marvel, and I enjoyed an aurora of being a marvel by association.

There were amateur plays at the Edison Club and at the women's club. Both Wayne and I were active performers. We played parts in several shows.

I enjoyed the activities of the area with friends. A young lady at the church was a major in music; we frequently attended the Boston Pops together in Boston. The same show that still goes on and can be seen and heard on TV. I believe from what I see now that the room in which they play has not changed since 1928.

There was much much more, but the flavor was the same: Socials, at our apartment, given by the famous five, trips to Boston to the theater and dinners. Drives, up the New England coast sight seeing or to meet Marge, and down the coast to Plymouth Rock where the pilgrims landed in 1610. There was plenty of learning activity at the G.E. plant that ran through all these days.

But the time arrived when I was scheduled to go to Texas, and I went. My leaving was hurried, and Marge and I had to be satisfied with a telephone good by,

Even in the 1920's General Electric was a large National and international company which, if corrected for 70 years of inflation, would have measured in the billions of dollars. Likewise their district offices would have to be scaled to the times.

Sales was through these offices, each of which was an autonomous organization. I do not remember the total number of districts, but each had its own engineering, warehousing, and marketing. Texas, the largest state in the Union, with Oklahoma, a small state, and a small piece of Louisiana composed territorialy the Texas or Southwestern district of the company. The number of states in the other districts varied with the size of the states, and the area's demand for G.E. products. I was the Motor and Control Specialist for our district.

G.E. had so many diverse products that the general salesman, working on a large job often needed special engineering and marketing help for one or more of the products involved. Giving that help was an important part of the specialist's job.

G.E. had dealers designated by the company product or products he handled. The specialist in those products supervised the company's relationship with those dealers. Within the framework of the above discussion I was the motor and control man, the specialist, in our district.

My office was at the Dallas headquarters, but my regular activities kept me on the road visiting the branch offices and the dealers in those areas. We had branch offices in Houston, San Antonio, Oklahoma City and Shreveport Indiana. During this period, 65 years ago, the electric power companies sold electric equipment made by such companies as G.E., Westinghouse, and others. I considered the power companies my best dealers. I frequently brought products and gave talks to the utility salesmen of cities like Oklahoma City, Houston and San Antonio hoping to increase their sales.

A certain deference was shown to the Specialists from the home office. Parties would be arranged at some one's home or at hotel dinners. The locals would arrange a date for me, and I came to know some very nice girls in the branch office areas. I can recall a red head in San Antonio, a brunette in Dallas and a stage struck dancer in Oklahoma City.

There were others I don't recall so clearly, because, particularly in Dallas, my boss, Bob Shields, would from time to time try to be a match maker, and would arrange a party for me to meet, "just the girl for you to marry." There would be good Texans at these outdoor patio parties. We would spend much time on balmy evenings singing, "The stars at night shine big and bright deep in the heart of Texas." They were good people and I recall these as happy evenings with people who it was a joy to know. And so, I was never bored. I was intensely interested in my work and had good companionship.

There was always a special compartment in my mind and feelings occupied by Marge Meader back in New England. I could not have forgotten her easily. I received a letter, fat and inviting, in a pale blue envelope, everyday without exception. My personal mail was delivered to my apartment. I hurried home from work each day to get that letter.

In this period of time, which I think was a superior way, both boy and girl, even with someone special in their life, were free to date whom they wished. Marge did not hesitate to send me photographs of canoe trips up the Ipswich River with friends, one of whom would be her date. Believe it or not I was not Jealous and she was not jealous of me enjoying Texas hospitality.

When I was transferred to Texas my salary was raised from $90.00 a month to $175,00. I felt a bit affluent. I even thought of myself as being a candidate for marriage, if I wished to try that state. I had not given that matter serious thought before.

But I was thinking seriously this evening sixty five years ago as I sat on the front porch of the home in which I lived. I did the unusual for me, I went in the house to the phone, and called Marge in Pawtucket R.I. That long distance call cost me $3.10. Three dollars and ten cents, the last of the great spenders.

I made it brief, I said, "Marge will you marry me I love you." She said, "I love you too. I thought you would never ask. Of course I'll marry you." That was just about all there was to it and the deed was done. We got as far as Marge saying she had three hundred dollars in the bank, and I had about three hundred in Texas which I would send to her. She would put our funds together and by a Chevrolet, ready for me to come over, marry her and drive our own car back home. We set early August, 1929 for the wedding. Good night sweetheart.

I have heard much about the heartless big corporations; that has not been my experience, and it wasn't then. As soon as Shields learned I was going to New England to get married he figured out some work for me to do in Schenectady and Boston around the wedding dates. He advised me that the company would pay all my expenses of the trip to Boston and Whitinsville, Marge's home town, where we were to be married in the Congregational Church.

I am not going to give a blow by blow description of the wedding or be sentimental about all of It. It was a good wedding, but getting married was, for me, a new experience. It seemed a bit like an ordeal to satisfy an audience. You danced to a tune with steps set by others; when all you wanted was to take your girl and head for home.

I was happy to be married to Marge. I got through the wedding and gave I hope a good performance. I was glad when we ran out of the church to escape the shoes and tin cans, showered with rice, and jumped in our well marked car, "Just married etc." We took off for the North Coast of New England and New Hampshire for a Honey Moon in our beloved mountains at Cold River Camp. We had discussed the wedding being there at Emerald Pool, but for adequate reasons had decided on the conventional wedding at the church.

Marge and I had in the car everything we wished to take with us to Texas. The plan was to do some mountain climbing, swim some in Emerald Pool, visit with friends in the area, and just enjoy being with each other. When the honey moon was over we would head for Texas.

In 1929 the cost of traveling was what it was and was accepted as such. Looking back the figures seem impossible. Gasoline was 10 cents a gallon plus a few cents Government tax. Breakfast on the road would be about 15 to 25 cents, lunch 50 cents and dinner about one dollar. Motels were one dollar per night for the couple. And yet one thought of the expense.

The time came and we set out for Texas on what proved to be an uneventful trip until we got to Arkansas.

In 1929 cross country highways were not what they are today, but all the states had a road across them that, though narrow, had an asphalt covering. All except Arkansas. It was beginning to build a road. Clear across the state they had put in a foundation of broken granite; the granite pieces were about 1 inch cubes that tore at your tires. When we reached the Texas end of Arkansas our two rear wheel driving tires were ruined. We had to buy two new tires, and that was a hardship. But we made the Texas border and quickened our pace as we headed for Dallas on the same latitude.

We arrived in Dallas late in the afternoon. Even though we had been travelling all day, I could not resist driving Marge around the city on a sightseeing tour of the wonderful place she was coming to. I did not yet have an apartment for the two of us. We went to a first class motel, built of stone blocks, with rooms like the Ambassador in New York city. I suppose we may have paid two dollars a night in such luxury.

Chapter XII

Texas, and to Clark Controller

A very important thing had happened: Marge was now with me in Texas. On the day following our arrival I went to my office to face my accumulated mail; Marge searched for an apartment or small home that suited our needs and our limited budget at the same time. I didn't know it then, but I was to learn Marge was a natural when it came to finding ideal living arrangements at affordable costs.

When, after work, I came back to our motel accommodations Marge said, "I think I've found a place you will like." I said "O.K. let's go to look at it." It was delightful. It was a single building, furnished, one bedroom apartment with an ample kitchen and bath. Its living room, through a large plate glass scenic window, overlooked a junction of two fairways of the Dallas Country Club golf course. The building was set among some young trees off the course.

The owners lived nearby. Marge had made arrangements that we could stop at their home, and complete our sales agreement which included a monthly charge that we could afford. I do not remember the exact figure, but it had to be within the late twenties or early thirties for that to be possible. We paid them a visit, closed the deal, and went out for dinner. After dinner we moved our few belongings from the motel to the apartment. That night we were settled in our first home.

This began a delightful period of togetherness. We had no children, as yet. On all my trips to the branch offices, which were frequent, Marge became my traveling pal. We acquired a young Collie dog; we named her Napoleon. She was a real pal to both of us. The Texas and Oklahoma hotels had kennel accommodations, therefore, Napoleon lived in style; she was well cared for, and joined us when that was appropriate.

Marge and I enjoyed good food on the road, such as the giant shrimp around Corpus Christi, and excellent steaks anywhere in the cattle country of Texas. To have the wives of the business and engineering personnel become acquainted and friends was considered good for morale. Wives traveling with Specialist on company business were considered, in those remote days, a legitimate company expense; not today.

Branch managers and other local personnel frequently used the visiting specialist and his wife as an excuse to hold a good party. Friendships were developed.

Our first branch office visit was to the Oklahoma City territory. The Branch manager's wife held a party for six couples to introduce Marge to the principals in the area. She put some of us up for the night. I do not remember why but I recall sleeping that night on the floor all very cozy with my new bride.

The following day we proceeded with my visits to the outlying towns under the jurisdiction of the Oklahoma City Office. My first stop was Chickasha, a two hours drive west of Oklahoma City.

The local salesman and the power company representative were trying to promote a cooperative cotton gin. The cooperative feature would mean that the Cotton farmers owned the company that ginned their cotton. The first necessity, that of selling stock securities to the farmers, was on hold on religious grounds: The whole rural community were members of a church that considered it sinful to own stocks and bonds in corporations.

The day we arrived there was scheduled, at the town hall, a speech by a minister of that church who made a moving speech. He explained owning stock cooperatively was not sinful, because the users of the gin, and not a foreign organization, would, as a group, own the gin. That satisfied the church, and the ministers sermon satisfied the people.

Outside the town hall the committee promoting the gin had a station set up to sell stock. Enough farmers subscribed to assure success. From our narrow point of view all was a success: the power company sold the large motors and control. The power company was our agent so we left Chickasha with a nice order given to us by being right in our religious associations.

Our next stop was a town that shall remain nameless because of what I will report. All the people I met were in a state of excitement. There had been a lynching the day before. A Negro had been arrested accused of raping a white woman. I went to the jail with the city manager of the town and was allowed to see the evidence of the confrontation, at the jail, between the Negro and the mob that wanted to remove him for a lynching. Some of the mob worked at removing bars. The Negro's only defense was some hot water from a tap in his cell. I was shown that he ran around a circular path. On each turn he would draw hot water, into a small pitcher, make a turn where men were trying to open his cell, and throw the water in their faces.

It was a bold, futile attempt to, in desperation, do anything to turn back the fate that he saw for himself in the cruel determination of the mob tearing at the bars. They won; what we saw was several bars broken out of the concrete, and bent apart. The Negro had been forcibly removed, taken to the countryside, hanged and mutilated. To see the evidence of the struggle and hear the story was like witnessing the event. I felt sad for mankind. I passed up business activities for the day and headed for Elk City. Oklahoma.

Elk City was a customary center of activity for me contacting power company offices in the surrounding area. My plan was to contact our dealer in Elk City in the afternoon, stay over night, and go to Amarillo Texas the following day. I made my call on the dealer, but soon learned that a hurricane and cyclone had hit nearby in a community south of Elk City. I decided to visit that community the next morning; there were numerous cotton gins in the area, and, following a cyclone, any one, or all, could be a prospect to replace electrical equipment destroyed in the storm. I felt a little like an ambulance chaser.

I found the next morning that the storm damage extended for over one hundred and fifty miles into the vicinity of Lawton in South East Oklahoma. The Power Company was on the job throughout the area reestablishing service and taking orders to replace damaged equipment which orders went to General Electric. I tied in to expedite these orders.

In one of the hit communities I pulled into a filling station with surprise that it was totally undamaged. On all sides of the station all was destruction: An apartment building had been torn apart. Only segments were hanging from broken walls. The street on which we approached had been bulldozed to assist traffic. On the other three sides of the filling stations homes had been leveled to the ground. There was a storm cellar at one home with a trap door at ground level. We were told a sad story by the filling station attendant, that two young men had taken refuge in the cellar, and closed the trap door behind them. The cyclone had created a vacuum that pulled opened the trap door, and, literally, sucked the men out of the cellar. The beating they took in the wind was fatal.

On the same street with the filling station, what had been a cotton gin, was a scattered mass of debris. Two inch steel shafting that had transmitted power to the machinery of the gin was twisted like cords of wire. One respected the power of the wind.

The point in all of this recital is that the filling station sat among these ruins with not a speck of damage. I asked the operator how this could be. He said, "I pay the preacher."

On our out of town trips Marge would, from time to time, ask questions about what I did on the calls I made at power company offices, dealer establishments, cotton gins and machine shops. In trying to answer these questions I discovered I wasn't doing much, the
business of the day had its own momentum. I was simply an element that showed up, often at the right time, and was there and willing to do what I could.

I commenced to learn the human side of doing business. Your customers appreciate the attention. The information reached me through the G.E. managers that our business with power companies was being improved by my presence in the field. In those days many cotton gins were driven by gasoline engines. Electric motors and gasoline engines were direct competitors. The power company offices in our area appreciated my preaching the Gospel of electrification, and had reported that back to my bosses. I discovered that my passion for the miraculous in electricity was contagious and I earned credit for being a good engineer and salesman by just talking and doing what came naturally.

Elk City was on the well known northern route across country, route 40 or 66. Amarillo was to the west, in the panhandle of Texas, on the same route. That was my next destination. The morning after our visit to the hurricane area found us on route 40 (or 66) headed west. We left Elk City after an early breakfast and were riding at a good speed through a beautiful morning of sunshine and light cool breezes. Soon I realized that some young trees along the road were bending in stronger breezes that seemed to be increasing rapidly in intensity. I noticed in the distance what looked like a dark curtain coming toward us. After the promise of the early morning, it seemed impossible that I was talking about preparing for a storm. The tornados of yesterday south of Elk City were now on its north.

We did not experience a cyclone, but the winds soon reached above hurricane velocity of 73 miles per hour. Darkness seemed to descend upon us out of that curtain I had noticed in the distance. The young trees bent over in the wind so that their tops were horizontal. And then it came, the sleet or rather the ice chunks. They came in mass, many much larger than golf balls, some as large as base balls. They pelted the car with a force that should have broken the windshield, and dented the body. Marge and I left our seats and crowded under the dash board. With the car stopped we waited and held our breath, as it were; we expected a crash of glass, we hoped for an end to the display of violence.

And it did end as suddenly as it had come upon us: the ice storm shut off with faucet speed, the wind died down and the sun came out. The pressure of alarm faded with the change, but our troubles were not over.

In 1929 the roads of Oklahoma were often maintained and surfaced by blading the natural clay. In dry weather the surface was smooth with a softness that made for driving fast and smoothly. In wet weather one could be stuck in the mud or slide into a ditch; progress was slow. The tons of ice that had fallen in our brief storm quickly melted in the sun, and wet weather with its curses was upon us.

The company supplied me with a dodge automobile which was famous in those times as a workhorse. For "just in case" I always carried in my trunk a tow chain. It turned out that the "just in cases" with me and my dodge found me towing others out of a ditch or a mudhole rather than being towed out. I explained this to Marge, and we continued our trip to Amarillo, through the mud, in the spirit of the good Samaritan. We actually did, right at the Texas border, throw out our rescue chain to a Texan who had backed too near the edge, and slid into a shallow ditch. He bought us a beer in Amarillo,

This trip to Amarillo with Marge along was my first visit to that city. It was also apparent that those who proceeded me had neglected an important area that focused on that city. I was determined to bring its power company merchandising and the electric dealers into the G.E. fold. I recall that visit as among friends that wanted a closer relations. My approach was like granting "most favored nation status" in international trade. It paid off in reciprocal business favors as well as sales volume.

We returned directly to Dallas from Amarillo, by way of Wichita falls where the wheat fields looked like brown seas with waves moving rapidly across them in the wind. I made my customary calls in that city. and a few other towns enroute. In the flat country around Dallas, the towers of the city could be seen for nearly twenty miles as you approached by automobile. When this happened on our way back from Oklahoma Marge cozied to my side. That city skyline seemed to hold our promise of happiness. I stopped the car long enough for a pledging kiss. Our safe return was, to us, a triumph.

Not all trips to the branch offices were as complete with odd happenings as the one to Oklahoma just described, but most had a special flavor that characterized Southwestern United States in 1929. Texas, Oklahoma, and environs was unique; Texas was cited by some as a country unto itself.

The proximity of Mexico was a Texas feature. One could cross the border at many places and buy a drink during our

prohibition years. That was a small detail. Mexico has a
culture as foreign to an American as Spain or even India.
People go there and experience a real change in the
environment. Move the time over to early in 1930 when it
was time for me to pay a visit to our branch office in San
Antonio. Marge and I were talking on a Sunday. Wednesday and
Thursday of the coming week would give me time to complete
my business in San Antonio. I made that a schedule completed
by deciding to take Friday off, and join it with the next
coming Saturday and Sunday for a trip to Mexico. Monterey
would be our destination below the border. I would cover
Waco, Texas Tuesday enroute to San Antonio. That gave me
Monday in Dallas for office work. So we would soon be off
for an adventure close to home.

Texas was the first place where I experienced filling
stations that cleaned the windshield of my car and checked
the air in my tires. Texas seemed ahead of other states in
what are now routine practices. San Antonio also had motels
with bellboys, drug stores and restaurants on the premises
and service that is not exceeded today. It is difficult to
recapture the surprise and pleasure when these were first
experiences.

Tuesday in Waco, and Wednesday and Thursday in San Antonio,
I had very rewarding business days which I will not detail.
While I worked, Marge shopped or went to a park where she
captured an armadillo. Some workers in the park helped her
put the animal in a bag. With the help of bellboys at the
motel we kept the animal alive and well. But that is not
the subject of this story.

Friday we left our dog in the care of a bell boy at the
motel. Very early, we drove from San Antonio to the border
at Laredo where we were to enter Mexico at Nuevo Laredo. As
we went through customs someone was picking a banjo and
singing a plaintive Mexican song. We felt like it was staged
to give us a warm welcome to their country. It became more
interesting that the performer had no reason but his own
love of music to be playing and singing in a business office
in the afternoon. Believe it or not I can still be warmed by
recalling that haunting melody.

In 1930 a passport was required to cross the border.
Obtaining one was expedited by our embassy in Laredo. We had
to get passport Photos--the works.

In those days the pesos was strong you could buy only two
for a dollar, all delivered to you as silver coins. My
pockets were weighted down by exchanging forty dollars.

We were, at last, in Mexico and free to go. The road to
Monterey from Nuevo Laredo is claimed by the Mexicans to, in
part, be the longest straight tangential road in the world.

What is meant by tangential is that the road not only has no curves it has no hills however slight. The road is for fifty miles absolutely straight and exactly the same distance above sea level, perfectly flat without the slightest rise or fall in altitude for those fifty miles. One could drive safely at great speed, and we did.

As far as the eye could see on both sides of our road were flat planes of pure dessert. Cactus dominated the dessert growth that spread across the land. At the end of this fifty some miles of tangential country we came to the mountains. While our fast drive on their special road had been interesting, the mountain roads were a welcome change.

We also had a change in the car. Marge complained of discomfort. She was in the early period of pregnancy, and nausea seemed to be her response to the winding roads. I cut the speed and stopped a couple times for her relief. I began to worry: Should we see a doctor? Was I being a responsible husband taking a pregnant wife on a jaunt in Mexico? Marge knew more about having babies than I did. She assured me that her reaction was entirely normal and to be expected, and that she had no intention of being a shut in at home during the term of her pregnancy, and that we did not need a doctor for what she called "this nuisance." We drove on through scenic mountain country for the remaining hundred miles.

My first impression of the city was that all their streets were one way streets; I was constantly going against traffic while people blew their horns, made frantic direction signs, and shouted in Spanish. In the midst of the confusion one good Samaritan pulled his horse and wagon over to my slow moving car and stopped. I stopped also, as did much of the surrounding traffic. And, blessings upon him, he asked, in perfectly good English, "Where do you want to go?" I gave him the name of the hotel at which we had reservations. He said, still in beautiful English "Go to the next corner, and turn left, go one block, and turn right, then straight ahead for three blocks. You will see your hotel on your left." He advised us that we would be with the traffic this time. After the prior confusion and the feeling of being lost among a babel of language, English sounded truly beautiful on the lips of this rustic man.

In coming to Mexico Marge and I had thought that the unusual would be fun. A gin fizz at an open bar, and certainly a bull fight were unusual. We promptly had the fizz at our hotel and acquired, from an Irish Mexican, tickets for the Saturday bull fight.

The Irish Mexican was in the lobby of our hotel waiting for a tourist to buy his tickets. He not only sold us the tickets, he volunteered to be our guide for what, we thought, was a small fee. We had not expected an English speaking guide with a combination Iris and Spanish accent, nor one with his enthusiasm; he right away explained the joys of bull fighting. The previous Tuesday fight was an example. I have never forgotten his punch line. At the pitch of excitement he exclaimed, "It was wonderful! the bull damn near killed the toreador!"

We had made an early start from Laredo. There was still time for afternoon sightseeing in Monterey. A young man was available, for a fee to drive your car and show you the sights. We hired him, and he did his job well. But my memory has to do mostly with chickens and sadism, Monterey seemed to be overrun with chickens. They were in the road in all parts of the city, and our driver's delight would have been to run over all of them. He chased them with the car until I demanded that he quit the practice. Still when chickens showed up he inclined the car in their direction.

We returned to the hotel without any chicken fatalities. In the late afternoon the promenade began. It was a sort of a dignified wholesale courtship blessed by the church, and, apparently, universally practiced evenings at the public square. Single lines of girls would walk in one direction while single lines of young men walked in the other direction. The lines went round and round the square, one in a clockwise moving circle and the opposite sex counter clockwise. They would look each other over, and exchange smiling signs of recognition. I did see one or two boys bold enough to join the girls line for a turn around the park. I do not know how or why the exception, which it was. It was rarely done.

Later in the evening there was a motorized version of the promenade that seemed reduced in numbers and contrived. The girls were standing beside the circular road through the park, and the boys would drive by and exchange rather subdued greetings.

I thought as I watched either of these sexually created customs that I liked the American ways better. A front porch swing in the summer time, an intimate stroll through the park or other ways that my readers can think of seemed to have many advantages over the promenade.

Our hotel was a Spanish style structure with the building completely encircling a central court yard of fountains, Sculpture and flowers. We enjoyed the atmosphere as well as a good Mexican dinner at a table in the court yard. We tried for the first time the famous cactus whiskey, tequila, and saw no chance of becoming addicted,

The following day, Saturday, was a full day with a bull fight in the morning, and some visits, arranged by our

Irish-Mexican guide, to some representative homes in the city. I am not simpatico with bull fighting, we've all seen it in the movies, and we saw no more in Monterey. The general ambience of the crowd was not unlike a crowd at a baseball or foot ball game. The sport was different. I shall leave the subject there.

The visits to the homes were in an atmosphere of warm hospitality, Among the rich, the homes were not unlike the fine building and grounds of our hotel. Among the poor they were unique to us. The layout was small one story buildings around a courtyard without any sculpture or decor. Floors inside the homes were red clay hard as stone and swept clean. In the kitchens always, and sometimes in the living room, a few pigs would be sleeping. They were free to come in and go out as they pleased. The system seemed to work. We never had a feeling of being in a filthy situation.

The next morning, Sunday, we got up early for breakfast and a drive back to San Antonio. Nothing had changed about the trip except one thing with Marge, and that was good. Her stomach no longer rebelled against car motion, it objected to sitting still. So we kept moving on the road, it was anti-nausea. Once when we stopped at a filling station she had to retreat and relieve. We were by now old timers with pregnancy foibles, and took such matters in our stride. Of course, that was easy for me; I felt no pain. We made San Antonio by early after noon.

Our bellboy caretaker had some bad news for us: A guest at the motel had driven off with Napoleon. In fact he whistled at the dog, and she hopped on board with joy as the guest was leaving the motel in the morning of the same day as our return in the early afternoon. Fortunately, the bellboy knew the guest's name. The desk clerk at the motel told me more. The guest was out of New York; he represented an organization that sold moving pictures to theaters. I called his home office in New York, and mentioned that I was in the theater business and would like to get in touch with their representative. Could they tell me where he was expected to be on Monday. I received a quick answer, "Brady, Texas."

Brady was 100 miles from San Antonio. I discussed the matter with Marge. We decided to drive right on this Sunday afternoon to reclaim our dog. This though we had just completed a 250 mile jaunt from Monterey. However the driving was not tiring, and, in those days of little travel and good roads in Texas and on the main arteries of Mexico, it was fast. We did not agonize over the decision. We arrived in Brady in time for dinner.

Brady was a Texas town of the old west. The sheriff wore his pistols in hip holsters tied to the legs. Boots and spurs, put determination in his walking gait. He wasted no words

in conversation. I began to tell him how our dog had been
under care at a motel, etc., and he interrupted with the
question, "Did some son-of-bitch steal your dog." I said
that about covered my complaint. The party I sought was
registered at the hotel. The sheriff planned our strategy:
we would get up early the next morning, and confront the
party before he left the hotel for work. The time was about
5;30, the sheriff knocked loudly on the door, and a middle
age man opened the door after being told it was the sheriff.

The man protested that he had no dog. I spoke loudly, and
Napoleon barked loudly in the bath room. The man had lost
his case, but the sheriff said there had to be a trial, and
that arrangements had been made with the Justice of the
Peace.

A time was given for after breakfast at the court house. All
were present and accounted for at that time. There were two
men in the offending party. The men were already judged
guilty. There was some serious speech making by the Justice
of Peace about the crime of stealing dogs. The accused
entered a plea of nolo contendere. I was asked to put a
value on the dog, and was advised to keep it under twenty
five dollars to avoid turning the theft into a felony. I
said, "Fifteen dollars." Each man accused was judged guilty
and fined fourteen dollars.

The two men apologized after the trial, all was forgiven
amid hand shakes and explanations. I was sorry for the trial
and judgments but Brady justice had to be served, and, quite
likely, the gentlemen did not, after that, drive off with
someone's well groomed dog as though he was a stray.

A day late from our planned trip to San Antonio and Mexico
we headed for Dallas and home. I had paid the San Antonio
bellboy for his services, and, as an extra blessing, we
decided to leave our armadillo in his care. He could release
him to the wild or make of him an unusual pet. And I would
see the bellboy again in the future.

It is difficult to realize now but in the 1930's the
electrical industry was far advanced but it still felt like
a new industry. There was much about our merchandising
practices that was experimental. There was room for young
men, like me, to make important suggestions for change, and
they were listened to. I made so many suggestions in the
mill supply field that I feared I might wear my welcome out
in Schenectady. My first trip out of Dallas after the San
Antonio visit was to Shreveport Louisiana to work with a
couple Mill Supply houses to represent us in multiple lines
and not just product by product.

I had corresponded and talked with the various line managers
within the company, and received limited delegated authority

to appoint these mill supply houses as agents for their products. I had original proposals concerning quantity discounts on multiple product lines and service supported by the strength of increased volume. The subject was hot in the industrial department of the company, and I was, by the nature of the case, being maneuvered into a leadership position.

While in the midst of a discussion of the greater General Electric representation program I was handed a telegram relayed to me from the office. It said, "Come to Schenectady at the soonest.---C.F.Pitman. Mgr. Motor division." That was an order; I began immediately to close out my Shreveport business, and head for Dallas.

I was moved emotionally. I sensed that I was being recognized for some work, before I knew the exact purpose of the call. On our trip home in the car I talked continuously to Marge how people had said to me that I would be lost in the crowd in such a large company. Here was proof that large companies did care about people and did have opportunities for men willing to work and extend themselves.

I had been in the district less than two years and was apparently being considered in some special way. I was certainly counting chickens before they hatched but I had heard some peeping. Shields had passed on to me favorable comment he had heard on visits to Schenectady. I had a gut feeling that I was to be put in charge of the department responsible for Motor division resale activities, and I was to expand that to bring in the multiple lines.

And that was it: I went to Schenectady, talked to Pitman at length, and accepted the promotion. My department was to be responsible for resale contracts with Manufacturers, Manufacture agents, power companies, Motor Dealers, and the multiproduct dealers, expected to be primarily Mill Supply Houses. I was to edit a magazine named The Motor Dealer.

But very soon, after we had moved to Schenectady, the blush came off the Rose, and, frankly, I was disappointed. The great depression was in full swing, and it was used as an excuse not to raise my salary to suit my increased responsibility. "Wages are frozen throughout the company." I was told, "You should recognize how fast you are moving up as a young man, and be happy for the honor. In a few months we will review your income." And review it they did. With all the general salary cuts applied during those coming depression days I soon lost forty percent of that with which I started.

The five additional years that I spent with G.E., 1930 through 1935, were in the rock bottom of the depression, and there was much human depression in the form of lay offs and salary cuts. Our social life was, bring your own sandwich, and play bridge for the evening.

I had learned from a physicist named Ernie Therrel how to create sculpture. It became a life saver to me plus a minor source of income. A large percent of my spare time was devoted, at first, to portraiture. I did portraits for a price. Do a small kid, precious to his relatives, and many members of the family would order a small plaster bust in a bronze finish, I would collect twenty five dollars for each copy. Do a bass relief; twenty five dollars for the first one, and fifteen dollars for all copies. These were also in high grade plaster of Paris with a bronze patina.

I did not realize it at the time but I had discovered a latent talent in myself that was to play a large part in shaping the rest of my life. I could lose myself in sculpture and later painting. As the years went by, a working studio became a permanent part of my personal infrastructure, and, as we shall later see, art became a second successful career when I retired from engineering and corporation business. But now we were at the beginning and not the end of the business career.

I hesitate to open up the details of these critical times. Not unlike a soldier who doesn't wish to discuss the gory details of battle. Living and working through the depression conditions of the 1930's was a fight for survival. You saw good friends, as capable as you, lose their jobs, and, if they were so fortunate, go home to their parental rescue operation. You also saw a predominance of people who stayed on the, job kept up their spirits, and seemed to live above the fray. One thing that could be learned through this period was that, with most of us, fear of what might happen was the real source of pain. Away from the fear, life went on in a normal fashion. Strong friendships were made, and special events were celebrated. I can look back, without the fear, and truthfully say, "those were good times. Just living was a masterful learning experience."

Among the things I was learning was that Large corporations, out of a certain necessity, at their home offices, become bureaucratic. However, original ideas are welcomed, but must be promoted through the established order, and the established order can be quite precise. For an humorous example, not as I cared, I was told that I was a junior executive, and did not qualify for a key to the management toilets. They were for senior Executives.

In Texas a predominant part of my activities was travel to the branch offices of the Texas district. In Schenectady an important part was travel to the district offices of the entire country. So, the existing resale agreements were served in the customary way, while I promoted the multilineal contracts with mill supply houses. In the latter I had the full cooperation of the district and the line managers. In time the program succeeded to the benefit of the agent and the company.

As I wrote the above I was impatient to move on. I had returned to the home office in March 1930, and I wished to leap the months to September 29th, 1930, and the most important personal business of our lives. I was the silent party with Marge in a conspiracy to have a baby, and she was delivered that day. Coliver Nancy Hoge was to be her name; the Nancy was Marge's middle name, and the Coliver? Thereby hangs a tail: her name was to be Cold River in happy memory of Cold River Camp days in the White Mountains. We decided to disguise the name for a certain privacy that I am now glad to ignore. We dropped the d in cold and the R in river, and combined what was left of the words. We gave her the name, Coliver. She will respond to the nickname Collie

That day is fresh in my memory. I was so excited that a blind man could see my confusion with his cane. They wouldn't let me in the delivery room. To prove that I was matter of fact about the whole business I went by my office during my waiting period to show my nonchalance. I met Jack Hume V.P. of Industrial Sales. He was not fooled. He said, "Why don't you get back to the hospital before you collapse." And that is what I did. I did not have long to wait. Soon they rolled Marge out of the delivery room with a baby at her feet. I have never before or since experienced such Euphoria. The baby already had a personality; it showed in her face, and it was beautiful to me. She is and has been throughout her life the person I saw in that moment of enlightenment.

The job went on, and the depression went on, and the stress on our marriage went on. There were cuts in salaries across the board followed by more cuts across the board. Finally, instead of the substantial increase expected from my promotion to a department head, my monthly take home pay became one hundred and eighty dollars per month. I no longer drove my car to work.

I walked in zero weather. To protect my face I made a plastic mask on a stick. I would hold the mask before my face and let the wind blow. There were things I wanted to do but couldn't afford and other things that Marge wanted to do but lacked the funds. There came times when we were working at cross purposes, irritated with circumstances, and even with each other.

We decided to take control. We devised the family meeting. Tuesday evenings were reserved for open season on our problems. Each of us was to bring into the open our economic condition as he or she saw it. We were pledged to do all we could to understand and help each other, and face our economic realities, whatever they were. Nothing of an economic nature could be mentioned at any other time, and that meant absolutely nothing. Immediately things improved: instead of every meal being spoiled by mourning about conditions, we relaxed, talked on interesting subjects, including how much we loved each other, and how lucky we were. We developed our own idea of positive thinking, and positively practiced it. There soon came a time when, except for our Tuesday meetings the depression was simply out of our minds. We lived above it.

I practiced my art hobbies and Marge made rugs with a beginning interest in pottery. When we could we took short holidays in the white mountains and Marge saved up for an occasional permanent or something else to add to her female charm. We lived and loved and quit suffering under what could not at once be corrected. The depression no longer haunted us. We lived daily. We were consciously happy.

We are here talking about February 1933 and it was on the 18th day of that month that Marge's labor pains became close enough for her to go to the hospital. After about two hours she was delivered of the most beautiful baby boy ever born.

We were both so happy that we wanted to mark the day in a special way. Our policy on naming our children was to give each a family middle name, and a unique first name with a strong personal meaning. Trying to devise a unique name we recalled the days a couple years earlier, when we were fretting over the economic strains of the depression and how that had led to some personal stress between us. The present compared to that was like a reunion in love. We thought "Renon" with an accent over the e could be a manufactured French word to always remind us of this reunion, and maintain its association with the happy event that had just occurred.

The social life during the five years we were in Schenectady was enjoyable. There was a large number of our contemporaries with General Electric also at the beginning of their careers. We were all at about the same low level in income. During those depression years our at home reciprocal parties or dinners were done on budget.

Starting with Leonardo de Vinci engineers have shown interest and ability in the arts. Among the host of engineers working on company products their were many who had a mature interest in Sculpture, painting and other arts or crafts. There would always be available an interesting meeting or class to suit your interest.

In the cultural atmosphere of Schenectady I found a real outlet for interests I did not realize I had. I developed a mind set toward the graphic arts that abided to blossom in a post retirement profession. So in art hobbies many of us were continually busy and escaped the real pain of the depression.

There lived in the suburbs of Schenectady Clement Wood and Gloria Godard. They were married to each other and both were writers not lacking in fame. Among many books, Clement wrote "The Outline Of Man's Knowledge" used as a textbook in adult education classes. Gloria wrote "Better to Burn", a very popular novel of the times that was a critique on the current sexual freedom that was breaking out all over.

I did for this couple my first commission in sculpture. It was a nude in bronze, lying face down beside a pool below a waterfall on their property in the Bosenkiln district near Schenectady. "If I do say so myself" it was good and others said the same.

So again, much of my time that could have been spent worrying over the impending disasters of the depression were spent in art work for its own sake. I recall this period as being as intellectually stimulating as were my college days.

Nevertheless. I finally realized I wanted to leave G.E. Not because of the financial stress of the depression but in spite of it. Bill Miller, the senior vice president of the Industrial Department said that the only thing wrong with me was that I wanted to be president before I had served my time as office boy. And, he may have been right.

I had confidence in myself and I saw things that needed to be done for the good of the company and its customers. I strove for more authority and responsibility to accomplish these things. My impatience matured into a conviction that I had something in the services I could render, that should be sold at a higher price, and have more room, in job assignment, to operate. I wanted to express what I felt about myself. I resolved to sell my services like a commodity, and to do so only at a fair price. And not to let the fear of being destitute in a depression, or any other fear or favor cause me to make, or continue in a bad bargain. This became a cornerstone of my personal career.

Marge not only encouraged this attitude she promoted it. When I would say, "We can't, in the current economic situation, risk our secure job seeking improvement." she would say, "I am sure there is a right place for a man of your ability; I have no fear of going for it." This coming from a person fully exposed and one who loved you was a profound source of courage. In many things I was caused to wonder if I had courage or only had a courageous wife. We had coming, just ahead, repeated tests of both.

Action on this thinking was not immediate but the delay was a gestation period for a plan of action. The action came but not with any dramatic plan. It was an act of desperation. I began to realize that I wasn't going to make any great effort to move ahead as long as I had, though minimum it was, the security of the General Electric to fall back on. On my way to work one morning I found myself almost speaking aloud, "I am going to resign this morning, make it final so I can't Change my mind or have anyone change it for me. I am going to take the plunge with determination and faith that I will be guided, and find the right way."

When I went to the boss's office to carry out my intention. Hank Henry, the assistant manager was in charge. Pitman, the department manager, was on vacation. Hank tried to get me to wait until Pitman returned in about five days. I said, "No I might change my mind." After being so bold, and leaving the office, I realized I had not arranged for any closing out period that would give me time to contact prospective places for either temporary or permanent work. I went back to the management and asked for two weeks which was willingly Granted.

I made up brochures on myself and mailed them to many of my customers who knew me and my work. I made telephone calls around the country. I got no immediate favorable responses. There was one contractual situation, for which in my job, I had been responsible, that was very attractive to me for, at least, a temporary job. We had arranged for The Gee Electric Co. (this was not a G.E. company.), a mill supply house in Wheeling, Wva. to be our agent for that district. In the contract Mr. Gee, the owner of the Mill Supply, was required to place on his payroll a G.E. trained man to be responsible for all G.E. work. The contract had not been implemented in that respect, I saw it as a natural for a man of my experience.

I felt confident, I called Mr. Gee, made an early morning appointment, and drove all night to fill it. Mr. Gee was very considerate. We spent most of the day relaxing, as best we could, and talking at his club. It finally became clear that he wanted me for the job and that I very much wanted to be the G.E.trained man responsible for all G.E. industrial sales in parts of Wva. and the Pittsburgh area of Pennsylvania. But we could not agree on the salary.

This was a test of my resolution that in the future I meant to insist on selling my services at what I considered a fair price. Here we were at the end of the day and almost the end of my two weeks grace period before I was off the G.E. payroll. I had about forty dollars to my name, and quite a few unpaid bills. Mr. Gee said,that among men that had been with him for years making less, he could not risk paying the salary I wanted. I still was determined not to go back on my resolution, and agree to less. We ended the talk with mutual respect. Going home I drove again most of the night, with an hours sleep in the car beside the road.

When I arrived home in the early morning, before it was light, I open my front door; a telegram had been dropped through the mail slot in the door. I picked it up from the floor, and opened it with excitement, it said, "Mr. Hoge, we accept your proposition." signed Harry Gee. To say the least, I was a bit euphoric. Our first steps toward a new freedom had just acquired the gait of the conqueror.

In my talk with Mr.Gee, I had proposed a one year understanding with which Mr. Gee agreed. We did not make a written agreement of the understanding, but both parties understood that they could terminate the arrangement, at the end of one year, without prejudice. I wanted that freedom so that I could, at that time, reappraise my position after experience in the company, and, if that were indicated, move on without a feeling of guilt that I had let the man down. I had already doubled my salary by the move, but I felt the need to learn more before making a long commitment.

Within a few days we had closed our accounts in Schenectady, said our goodbyes, and moved to Wheeling. Marge had again shown her expertise, and found a good house, within our budget, and located in the suburban hills just out of wheeling. That latter was important. Wheeling was surrounded by industrial plants including some steel mills. In the morning, driving to work, the sun could be out in all its brilliance, but, as you descended the hill, and approached down town, you would see ahead of you a dark area, like a ceiling, over the land below, and you would enter this covered area and see the sunlight all but disappear. They call it smog. You wanted your home above that elevation. We had a charming place.

As I look back upon these times I am learning some truths about myself: I was, during an extended period at this time, a young man playing a dangerous game. The depression be damned, I was determined, and impatient to get ahead, far ahead of what had been.

Faults unrelated to my job were appraised for their meaning in our life style. A neighbor in our location had a female dog that was in the heat when we arrived. Male dogs were creating a real disturbance around the neighbor's home. There were dog fights night and day. A couple police came out and shot several dogs, and piled them by the curb to be picked up. The police decided that was their duty to the peace and security of the neighborhood. I grieved for the people who lost their pets in the shooting and felt the whole affair a blemish upon our home setup that had been so charming.

I very soon decided that I was going to stay with Gee
Electric the promised year but no longer. The work was the
interesting engineering and sales work of G. E. origin. I
had no trouble with that. I had trouble focusing on any long
term position, in this local company, that satisfied my
aspirations. When and if Mr. Gee retired, he had family, and
he had old timers in the company. Being the General Manager
of a family owned mill supply house, at close quarters, no
longer looked attractive.

Marge was my secretary at home; within the first month of
the new job, I dictated to her a letter to myself, for our
files, "lest I forget." The letter said that it was already
decided that we would leave at the end of the fiscal year,
and that I must by then have a job with avenues ahead that
led to, more desirable denouements. This meant a national
organization, more specific than General Electric, and
smaller. Perhaps one could be a bigger frog in a smaller
pond.

There was a man named J.P.Jones; he was manager of the G.E.
Cleveland, Ohio district office. We were friends, our
offices in Schenectady had been just down the hall from each
other. I decided to seek some guidance from J.P. I drove to
Cleveland on a Sunday. We met at the Carter hotel, had a
drink for old times sake, and then spent the afternoon
talking. J. P. knew the companies of his area, and he Knew
me. His advice was invaluable, but, so far, in all cases
inconclusive. Finally he took on a wise look and said, "You
know what I would do if I were in your place?" "I would go
for the Clark Controller Co., any job, and commit myself to
the long pull. One could grow with the company." This rang
the bell. I had experienced Clark competition in the steel
mills; their equipment was good to superior; their methods
progressive I had previously thought of them as a
possibility.

Clark Controller had formed in recent years from an
insurrection in another controller company. The new company
was led by Mr. P.C. Clark, not an engineer, but a business
man with an adventurous spirit. He took with him into the
new company good engineers and personnel that were likewise
adventurous. As we considered this prospect we concluded
that, without recognizing it, this was an ambience I was
looking for, and one for which I was suited. The talks ended
there.

Mr.Clark had lost his wife. He lived at the down town
Athletic Club. I called him then and there, and asked for an
appointment the next Sunday in the early afternoon. I
explained that I was working during the week and needed a
Sunday date. He said, "O.K. two O'clock here at my Club." In
my conviction that this was a natural, I, at first, felt

that I was already hired. I thanked J. P. as though for an accomplished fact. We parted in that mood.

That mood was short lived, I returned to Cleveland feeling that if I was not accepted, it would be a disaster. In my spare time, for the coming week, I tortured myself with doubt and planned a sales approach on Mr. Clark. I arrived at the Athletic Club in Cleveland before two o'clock with a well organized plan of attack. Mr. Clark hoped if I had eaten lunch, he had, that, as a desert, I would join him in a rice pudding for which his club was famous, and it was a rice pudding to remember, as I have, for a life time. I drool as I write.

Over the rice pudding we got acquainted. We then went to the main living room of the club, and seated ourselves in the typical overstuffed club chairs. Clark passed the cigars, and held out his lighter; as I lit my cigar, he said, "I assume that you would like a job with our company." I said." Yes.", and I thought to myself, now make your pitch, and then I heard Clark say, "you're hired." I said, "You can't do that I have not explained my virtues." He said. "But I have done just that." and it was a fait accompli. I had just joined the company with which I would stay to retirement and in which I would find more than the answers to my ambitions. There would be a time, after Mr. Clark was deceased, when I would have all the responsibilities, for the company, that were now his.

Chapter XIII

Wheeling, And Back To Main Line.

Mr. Clark and I finished our meeting with some discussion of my past experience and present aspirations. I explained that I could not go to work for Clark until my agreement with Gee Electric was satisfied. This did not mean that I would have to complete the full year agreed upon. It did mean that I would have to assure that the General Electric agreement was satisfied, in that the G. E. part of Gee Electric was a working reality. That would take time. Mr. Clark agreed to the delay. He directed me to see Pete Williams, V.P. of sales and Andy Mellon his Assistant to work out the details of my coming to work.

I will relate my contacts with these men when I am telling of my transfer to the Clark Controller Co. First there were jobs and experiences with Gee Electric that certainly contributed to my education.

A large part of my work in the Wheeling setup was customer relations with Wheeling Steel, Weirton Steel, Wheeling Corrugated and other prime companies very significant to the industrial business of the time. I would make regular calls to answer questions about our products and to engineer applications essential to making sales.

There were plenty of local plants that were also important users of industrial electric equipment. The application engineering associated with these contributed to keeping me busy trying to win or keep good G. E. customers. A couple jobs can illustrate the point.

But first let's have a short course in Electrical Engineering. The electricity that is distributed to homes and plants throughout North America is alternating current with a frequency of sixty cycles per second. Elsewhere it is fifty cycles. In one cycle the voltage polarity of the current changes from, say, 125 volts positive to 125 volts negative and back to 125 volts positive. Current with a frequency of sixty cycles makes that cycle of change sixty times in one second. That's pretty fast slight of hand.

There was a time when twenty five cycles saw limited use for special engineering purposes that had to do with the rotating speed of certain equipment. Some of this twenty five cycle current had general use also.

There also came a time, just about when I was with the Gee Electric, that the remaining twenty five cycle power was being converted to Sixty. To continue operating equipment, such as motors, affected by frequency, the equipment had to be rewired or replaced. In a sizable plant, careful study and much work was required to do a thorough job.

One of these jobs was changing over the electrical equipment of a meat packing company. I brought mechanics in from the shop, and for over two weeks, on a contract, we replaced motors with loans while we rewired the company's equipment. I was about the premises of the meat packing company daily supervising the operation. And, that is where my incomplete education was repaired.

I will save the reader the details of working on the equipment, but give some details of how the place worked on me. I had always enjoyed a good steak and had eaten my share. But I had not visualized the mayhem and slaughter that preceded those steaks.

Cattle cars were brought into the building, and parked at a strategic place for cows and steers to run out of the car and down an inclined platform to a floor below. As the animal passed through a restricted entrance to the lower floor there was a man above his head with his legs spread apart so he could swing his sledge hammer. As the animal passed under the man, down came the sledge with the skill of practice, and the animal collapsed. A chain was placed around its body, and a crane lifted the corpse and swung it into a room where a group of men, with very sharp knives, were waiting and ready. Each man knew his job and went to work.

It seemed almost instantly that that living breathing animal had become sides, and smaller cuts, of beef. The sides of beef were hung on a moving chain that held the meat about a foot above the floor. The moving chain carried the sides into a refrigerated area. All was efficiency in the slaughter house, and the workers were a team that seemed to enjoy, and take pride in their work.

We had changed over the motors of the blood pumps, and they were working at top speed. Blood was pouring through grating covered drains in the floor. Other corpses were coming in from the sledge hammer area, and other workers were keeping the production line in motion.

Watching the beef operation, and the pig sticking conveyor belt, which I will not detail, left me with a mixture of emotions about life and mortality, and a sadness for the animals that went so trustfully to slaughter on a production line. No conclusions could be drawn. There is a Chinese proverb that says, "if you want to enjoy your meal, don't look over the kitchen wall." As soon as I could I quit looking and became practically a vegetarian for a time.

We had a job, similar to the one at the meat packing house, at the State Penitentiary located in Moundsville, Wva., a few miles south of Wheeling. I commuted with the institution daily, for about two weeks, supervising the change over, from twenty five cycle to sixty cycle, of all their electrical lighting and rotating equipment. These were two weeks of learning a lot about Penitentiaries and how their inhabitants view life.

There was a waiting room at the penitentiary for people visiting inmates. I waited there for my guides every morning, and sensed the tension among visitors who might have been bringing bad news or good, concerning their efforts to win an early release, or a probation hearing, for an inmate, .

One of the first things I learned about these people, deprived of liberty, was that all of them wanted to talk about someone on the outside who was on the verge of accomplishing, for them, one of these goals. It seemed they all had an abiding and pressing need to feel that someone was trying, and about to succeed at winning a parcel of freedom. I had two convicts as helpers on the job. They talked daily about the approach of freedom through the efforts of family, friend, or hired attorney. I became very aware of how precious freedom is, and prized my own more highly.

One of my helpers was ideal for the job. Before incarceration he had been an electrical contractor, and was familiar in advance with the work. As to his crime, he had been convicted of killing a man over the man's relationship with his wife. He acknowledged his guilt, condemned the crime, and stated he could never do such again. He hoped and believed that his complete rehabilitation would soon lead to freedom or probation from his life sentence. He and others would talk about this seemingly universal hope with obvious emotional longing and faith.

My other helper was in on a long sentence for armed robbery: he believed that a store keeper had defrauded him of nineteen dollars. I never learned the particulars of the fraud, but the young man had forced the store keeper, at gun point, to open his cash register, and count out nineteen dollars which the young man took to even the account. regardless of any strained justice, he was, of course, guilty.

I spent my days with these two men. We climbed through passageways behind the cell blocks that abutted each other in the center of large exercise areas. The wiring followed these courses. My electric contractor cracked macabre jokes, about how one could be murdered in tunnels like these, and just disappear, never to be found.

I spent time in the the tailor shop and the women's building converting special machines. The women enjoyed teasing this man from the outer world. Mostly, it was good clean fun. There was work to do in the heating plant, and in the auxiliary power plant. In general wherever electricity had a job to do.

There were folklore stories told about the place: I heard several times a yarn about how an inmate tailor in a planned escape swung his large, razor sharp, tailor's clever, and beheaded a guard blocking his way.

But, not all was of crime or fringed with violence; there was culture with a capital C. Marge and I were taken in by the theater. We attended several plays at the Penitentiary that were the outstanding works of conscientious actors. We forgot the environs. We became acquainted with some of the actors and were impressed with their sincerity. Likewise their painters and sculptors. After I had finished my job at the institution, we returned at times for a play or a visit to the art workshop.

The down town part of Wheeling, Wva. is low, river valley, country. The Ohio River flows through the center of the city. There is an island in the river in this area. The island is integrated with the city by two bridges. There are business offices and residences on the island, and, important to my story, there is, or there was, a tabernacle that belonged to an evangelical religious congregation.

This was in the summer of 1936. The meteorological report was for above normal rain fall and the probability of flooding on the Ohio. Water had already invaded the edges of Wheeling Island. Down town business offices were already putting important papers and property above any probable flood level.

And the rains did come and there was a flood to remember, nearly three feet of water and mud in my office. When the water receded there was a very wet mud about a foot deep that the office personnel, including the writer, had to shovel and scrape from the first floor of our building. It seemed that everyone was in the mud shovelling business, and all busy. professional help was unavailable.

We kept our office open on the second floor of our building to take emergency calls, and the calls came. A sample was an urgent need for a couple heavy duty motor starters. They were not only heavy duty they were just heavy, I found.

To deliver the starters to the electrical contractor on the job, I despaired of our regular delivery service, and took them in my automobile over the highway that runs along the banks of the Ohio river on part of its journey from Wheeling to Wellsburg. There was no access from this road, to the power station, where the starters were needed, except over an elevated railroad bridge, (the kind with rails over wooden ties), that itself was a couple feet under water.

Feeling, with your foot under water, for ties to step upon, while carrying a 60 pound steel box loaded with Electrical equipment that must not get wet, is invigorating but not recreational. It was a long bridge; the electrical contractor met me half way. The first time across we felt "Mission accomplished." But we had to do it a second time. I cannot speak for the contractor, but for myself. I almost cried contemplating that second trip.

On the way home along the river I found that the flood level had risen. In the low places, along the road, cars were stalled or abandoned. In my wet and hungry condition, I was determined to get home. I had with me, in the car, a pair of cutting pliers.

I turned off my engine as the car entered a lake of water spread across the road. I got out in the water, opened the hood, and cut the fan belt on my engine. I removed the belt so that the fan would not run and spray water on the spark plugs and the whole ignition system, killing the engine.

It worked: I accelerated slowly, the car moved forward, without hesitation, and soon came out on the road above water. Mine was the only car that made it at that interval. And I made it through all the other sink holes on the way home. With no fan to cool it, the engine heated and steamed, but it took me home to security, food, and rest.

The next day flood levels were higher. The conditions throughout the area were the constant subject on the radio: bridges washed out, important buildings inaccessible, and road traffic impossible. The threat to the tabernacle on Wheeling Island had constant coverage from the church radio. In eloquent language, it was pictured as the stalwart, steadfast servant of the good, standing firmly against evil. The speaker would periodically, with dramatic finality, declare, "The old tabernacle stands firm!"

Following one such declaration, a voice in the background was heard shouting, "There she goes!" And a description was given of the building floating down the river of rushing water. I hope that the faithful, who must have been shocked at this denouement, remembered, for their forgiveness and solace, the Biblical quotation "The Lord makes the rain to fall upon the just and the unjust."

Our social life in Wheeling was not extensive, and, in the time available, what there was had a limited opportunity to develop. I have pleasant memories of dinners with the Gee family. There was a group of younger people who sponsored art exhibits and promotional dances. Someone had been kind enough to put us on their mailing list. We accepted all invitations, and all events were entertaining and educational.

Marge and I shared our hobbies with others who enjoyed similar inclinations.

On one occasion of informal cocktails with Mr. Gee, he expressed satisfaction with the general progress of the department responsible for G. E. products, and particularly the volume of business that had developed from our programs. The time had arrived, and I, reluctantly, told Mr. Gee of my plans and present arrangements with the Clark Controller Co. I explained the concept I held of my opportunities with Clark doing business on a national and international level, compared with a more limited prospects for an employee of the Gee Electric.

Mr. Gee was most gracious: he sincerely offered me inducements to stay with Gee, but he took on a fatherly attitude, and said, "Clark Controller is a very promising company. With your young age, training and ability I think you will go places there. You have my blessing." He assured me that his agreement with G.E. was now secure, and I was free to leave when I completed my arrangements with Clark.

Without delay, I called Pete Williams, V.P. Sales at Clark, and made an appointment for the coming Sunday afternoon. Andy Mellon, Sales Manager, would be present for talks on my starting setup. The meeting was to be at Mr. Williams home in Shaker Heights, a suburb of Cleveland.

When I arrived, it was all very reassuring about my possibilities. Pete's home was impressive in a luxury neighborhood. The two men came across as serious industrialists, but warm personalities. I soon felt confident that I was entering the right organization and a good personal relationship. Both men emanated a challenging esprit de corps that made me want to join. They questioned me at length to determine my experience, and general knowledge of the Control Industry.

It was agreed that I would make a temporary move to Cleveland. I would spend six weeks working in the Home Office to acquaint myself with Clark products and methods of doing business. I would report for work within the coming week. It was further agreed that, after my training period, I would be appointed manager of the Philadelphia office, and would, of course, move my family to that city. Since I was driving back to Wheeling, I took a most decorous drink as they were passed around to celebrate our understanding.

When I arrived home Marge was waiting up for the news, and was delighted with my report. We both had hopes it might be New York, but, we said, "you can't have everything.," and what we had, in my being Manager of an important district office, was beyond our total expectations.

In two days I was back in Cleveland with my suit case, and had engaged a room at a boarding house three blocks from our plant on 152nd street. It took only a few days on the job for me to realize that I must have been guided to this relationship. Clark Controller was indeed a special place: The management cared about its employees, and a sincere fraternal spirit was a chief characteristic among the employees. The fact that the company was young was evident in the progressive and venturous attitude of key personnel. The ambience was refreshing.

I was given a desk among the Application Engineers, and jobs were selected for my desk that were educational to a new man headed for a district office. Mellon even had me write a speech that he was to give on the dynamic lowering circuit of a crane hoist. As a district manager, I would have a lot of that sort of thing to do myself.

About three weeks into my training period Mr. Williams called me into his office with an obvious burden on his mind. He explained that Holly Holcumbe, who had been the previous manager of the Philadelphia Office, wanted to come back to the company.

He was highly rated in the company and among the customers in the Philadelphia area. Pete showed his embarrassment as he said, "Frankly the company wants him back, and we want to be fair with you. The question is what can we do about it?" He began talking about my going to New York, and how the present New York Manager was headed for a regional manager's job soon. I realized he was saying that I could go to New York now with a special status, and be in the right place at the right time, when some changes took place. And then some good things could happen to me.

As I sat there, with grave countenance, listening, I am sure Pete never knew how pleased I was. New York was my dream. It was Marge's dream. As Pete talked, I visualized a home for my sculpture and painting in my studio in Greenwich Village. How could all these things be falling into place at one time?! How could all my diverse interests be landing so neatly in one place? I was overjoyed.

I said, "Mr. Williams I have confidence in you. You make the decision and I will abide by it." He said,"I think the present best interest of the company will be served by taking Holly back as Manager. I think your future best interest will develop in the New York picture." And I really did agree with him. I told him so with sincerity and a warm hand shake.

We were soon off for the Big Apple. New York may not have been waiting for us, but Marge and I had been waiting for New York. Our temporary home was a comfortable hotel room provided by the company. During the day I traveled about the district with Ed Jung, the district manager, being introduced to our customers, and learning the general lay of the land. I also became acquainted with our office personnel and the the procedures of the office. In a few days I felt like an old timer.

During these same days Marge went apartment hunting and studio hunting, and demonstrated her usual skill.

Her solution for the studio was perfect: she rented a loft on Green street neatly situated between Greenwich Village Park, on the New York University side, and the Bowery on the Southern side. A loft, for any who do not know, in New York, is an entire floor of a building that is condemned for most purposes, but is approved for several usages, among them art studios and related work. I would have much more room than needed for my sculpture tools and casting equipment. Beautiful and more beautiful! The rent was fifteen dollars per month. Before we were set up in an apartment for home we were established in Greenwich Village with our equipment moved in.

But we were not to be without a home long, Marge found an excellent apartment at 158th Street and Riverside Drive. Marge had scheduled the date of arrival, with the mover, before leaving Wheeling, and when he arrived the apartment was ready to receive our few furnishings. With all completed as planned we were, at last, New Yorkers.

For awhile, there was not too much, that was exciting, to relate. Business and engineering were, in a sense, routine: travel, by car, through New Jersey and upstate New York, making an engineering proposal here, closing a contract there, keeping open contacts with calls on key people. and buying a lunch when the time and circumstances were right.

There were challenges in the variety of engineering or equipment jobs and maintaining customer relations. However, the greatest challenge was having to keep up my enthusiasm in face of the fact that Clark was a newcomer, compared to Cutler Hammer, G.E., or Westinghouse. I would go for days, sometimes a week, without a serious inquiry. Facing days with no results was hard to get up for in the morning. I was opening new territory for Clark.

Williams and Mellon understood the situation and did not hold low sales volume against me. I was being judged by the number of prime companies I was bringing into the fold.

After several years, it was pleasant to note that a high sales volume, as well as gaining prime companies as new customers, was credited to my efforts in the field. Also, as williams had predicted, Ed Jung was promoted to a special regional manager, including having an oversight of some important customer relations in the Philadelphia district, and some special accounts, he had handled for years, in upstate New York. I was promoted to New York District Manager. Ed Jung had always "run a good show;" therefore, as District Manager, I made only minor changes in job assignments and operating procedures.

From the lack of comment it may seem that the Art String to our bow was missing. Not so, for one who is interested, New York is an open feast for Art and science. There are multiple galleries, museums and shows for all the disciplines that support and are supported by Art and Science.

It seemed in our time there that the table was always set. We partook of the feast by attending Broadway shows, the Opera, and special events. We were in and out of the galleries and museums so frequently that many acquaintanceships, particularly in the Village, grew into friendships. Likewise, among the artists my contacts were frequent and interesting and friendships developed. I could count some of the famous of the times in that latter category.

When Malvina Hoffman had her much publicized show "The Races of Man" I assisted her personally with its installation in a gallery on 57th Street. Robert Aiken, who created the facade of the Supreme Court Building in Washington, carried out the whole project in large miniature in his Greenwich Village studio. By this time I had graduated from my loft building studio on Green street to one on 12th Street. This being a couple blocks from Aikens studio enabled me to look in frequently on the Supreme Court project. It also facilitated Aiken being a constructive critic of my work.

George Gray Barnard peopled the estates of millionaires with Marble sculptures. He became known as "the man with the million dollar chisel." The heroic size bust of Lincoln, and the larger than life "Two Natures of Man," both in the Metropolitan Museum, are his work. Using his own art collection, he also recreated "The Cloisters," a 16th

century monastery, in far-uptown Manhattan. It is now an exstention of the Metropolitan Museum of Art.

It was Barnard's nature to do things on a heroic scale. To express, in sculpture, his hope that there would be no more wars he rented an abandoned church, with a very high ceiling, and used it as a studio. In the studio he created an enormous sculpture for marble, composed of 19 nine foot figures and associated compositions . I knew this man well, and gained inspiration and direct assistance from our personal contacts and visits to his works in progress.

I was at this time, of course, not personally connected with the whole art scene: I was not competing for commissions or even prizes and honors at art shows. I did not, with minor exceptions, place works in art galleries for sale or spend my days creating works of art for my own or other people's amazement. Sculpture, painting and photography were, with differing emphases, each part of a composite hobby that was a source of relaxation and actual support of my engineering and business activities.

As an example, at the end of our one year lease on the apartment on 158th Street we rented a house in Nyack, N. Y., within good commuting distance of the city. The house gave us room for a studio at home along with a photographic dark room, and a workshop for ceramics and mold building.

We kept our studio apartment on 12th Street. It made an ideal place to meet our business customers, as well as our artist friends. Marge and I would set up, in our New York studio, a cocktail party for several business associates and their wives. This, with its close Greenwich Village art association, alone was unusual entertainment for many of our friends in the business setup. We would follow the cocktail party with dinner at one of the Village's, or city's, night clubs, or attend some art event. These evenings had the double characteristic of being enjoyable and, for my business, profitable.

What I am trying to say, and not succeeding too well, is that my aspirations were not a house divided against itself. I was not working at my job just to make a living while I yearned to be an artist, the classical frustrated artist. Engineering was, in time sequence, my first love. Its creativity found itself at home later in the graphic arts. I was as pleased with my patents as I was to be later with my prizes or honorable mentions at art shows. Likewise, playing a significant part in the building of a district office and a company that turned creative ideas into real functioning equipment, at the service of industry, and through industry, of people, became a crowning pleasure.

A challenging characteristic of industrial electrical control is that it is designed to determine the behavior of another company's, or person's, product. Designing custom built control, the control engineer often participates in the design of the product, or system, that is to be controlled. He must always work closely with his customer's engineers and clearly understand their needs. The variety, to me, always was stimulating to a high degree.

The Tube Reducing Machine Co. was my most interesting account. Its Chief Engineer was named George Coe. George was a genius. He designed the Reducing machines proclaimed in the company's name. His machines reduced the wall thickness of tubes all right, but they could do much much more. One of the machines I worked with him on turned out the propellers for large bombers, such as the B29.

Highly controlled roller arms, that had surface configurations, acted as swages on thick walled tubes. They applied great rolling pressure to shape and draw those tubes into a precise form, with accurately controlled wall thickness that progressively changed to match the changing stress along its entire length. The finished piece was a long and specifically shaped bomber propeller. It was uncanny to watch the incredible ability of the machine forming metal as though it were modeling clay. Even closing the end, welding was not resorted to: In that section, the swaging action continued to reduce the tube hole size until there was no more hole, it just disappeared, and the end was formed as designed. Although not exactly like it, the action made me think of a snake starting at his tail, and continuing to swallow himself until he just disappeared.

This is a case where it seems easier to describe the machine action than the electric controllers making it so. By automatically altering, during operation, the torque and speed of motors, and the strength of thrustors, working with cams and other mechanical devices designed into the machine, we were able to keep his swaging action working, with close tolerance, according to plan.

George was favorable to a couple martinis and a good dinner. He changed trains in New York going from his plant in Jersey to his home in New Rochelle. My office was in the Lincoln building, across the street from the Grand Central Station. When a job was hot, and overtime work was needed, in the late afternoon George would occasionally stick his head in my door and say, "What about a drink." I knew the situation before hand and was as interested as he in having an extra discussion of the job along with some food and entertainment. We picked Billy Roses Beef Trust restaurant theater for several sessions wrapping up the ends on the bomber job. They used paper table cloths which were convenient for design sketches. We would tear off our sketches and take them home for refinement. On our last session there we substituted mint juleps for martinis. We went home quite happy with our evening's work.

During this period Marge was expecting, and we were looking for a house to buy. A friend and real-estate broker named Walter Lake was the agent for the house we were renting, and was also trying to accommodate, our taste and ability to pay for a purchase. He and his wife, Elmer, were really close friends who remained in that status for life. Our business conferences were a bit unusual: neither of us were drinkers, but I would bring out a bottle of good brandy which we would sip and negotiate houses. I had the idea that the brandy might make Walter generous and he liked the relaxation in the late afternoon.

First the pregnancy came to maturity. Marge and I both liked the Doctor in Schenectady who had delivered Coliver and Renon. In conference with him, it had been decided that the timing and medication could be taken care of, and he could be our doctor for delivery at the Schenectady Hospital, some miles north of Nyack. When the signals said the time had come we were ready to go. Everything worked out smoothly according to plan. I took our portable radio along. Established in the hospital, with some good music playing, Marge said, "How about a dance." Although short in time, the dance was a happy celebration of the blessed event anticipated. And it was a blessed event, another beautiful baby girl, second to none in the universe.

To build up her strength, in those days, a woman was required to stay in the hospital for ten days after giving birth. I returned to Nyack and my job, and also to moving the family possessions into another house only three blocks away. This action was consistent with Walter Lake's keeping us in a rental with no lease until he could find a house for us to buy.

The move timing coincided with the birth timing purely by inconvenient accident. I called in the movers, moved, set up the furniture, and hung the curtains in a very pleasant second home for us in Nyack. We had a good housekeeper who was competent with Coliver and Renon in Marge's absence, and would help Marge with Margo. If it was a girl, we had decided, her name would be Margo Hatcher.

Regarding the house we were leaving, I had agreed that, in the event of a move, I would leave the premises "broom clean." The house was large, and I did the sweeping.

And so the time passed quickly, and I was in Schenectady on a Sunday morning to pick up our precious cargo for a trip home. Margo was so alert and so energetic that I was surprised she did not speak or run to greet her father. In ten days she had become a distinct personality passing her smiles and innocent love around to all who would receive it. Marge was well and strong and apparently ready to take the family back into her care.

I said that the housekeeper was competent, but she was odd for a housekeeper: she invented devises. Lottie, which was her name, suffered constant anxiety that someone might steal her inventions. At the time these consisted of an inkwell and a soap dish. I do not remember much about the ink well but the soap dish had a special drain for water. The idea didn't look very special to me.

Since I was an engineer, Lottie wanted me to have drawings made, specifications written, and contracts drawn so that she could send her models to manufacturers without having them steal her ideas. She also had to take a nap at a precise time each afternoon. With a new baby in the house, that was not always conveinent. She also required numerous special foods for a health diet. All of these things seemed out of proportion to the magnitude of the subjects. But time went by and Lottie faded out of the picture I do not recall why or when.

The right house to buy came along. We all recognized it when we saw it. The house was a depression foreclosure held by the local bank. The price was right, without Walter and I doing any brandy negotiation. Walter arranged a favorable mortgage with a private citizen. We signed all the papers, called in the movers again, and were soon set up in our very own first home. I commenced to feel the pride of ownership without spending, on a monthly basis, much more than rent had been costing. Values were such that you could do that back in the depression years of the thirties.

The house was located well out of town on Upper Broadway. We had the distinction of having Helen Hays and Charles MacArthur for neighbors; also Ben Heck. Helen liked to be called Mrs. MacArthur in her home area. She was a good neighbor: even cabitzed on my remodelling. She would take her constitutional walk up Broadway, and would stop to see if I were placing the flagstones right in the walk, or doing a good job laying brick in the front stoop,

I am a little ahead of my story, but after years turned baby Margo into a little girl she and Jamie MacArthur played together. I remember a birthday party for Margo when some one knocked rather loudly on our door to overcome the indoor party noise. It was Helen reporting that Jamie had a cold. He could not attend the party. She brought Jamie's present to Margo, and "would we be so kind" as to let her take home, to Jamie, any party favors going around. Of course, Marge made up a package, including birthday cake.

Helen said she so admired our remodeling, and could she look around. We furnished some cake to eat while we guided her about the property. The house had ten rooms, some large and some small. By the time of this visit, in the 1940's, on the first floor, we had joined a parlor and a living room to make one 31 foot living room. We had put in French doors to the dining room, and remodelled that room and the kitchen.

An interesting side comment is, we were required to pay the Cabinet Maker, who built our kitchen cupboards, seventy five cents per hour. I liked his work so much that I paid him one dollar an hour. He cried in appreciation of our kindness. Today you can get that sort of work done for thirty to fifty dollars an hour, and no one will cry if you add a bonus. Someone might think you stingy if you don't.

On the second floor we had built a new bathroom and darkroom, and a studio looking out of a picture window on to the Hudson River. We had cut into the roof, and put in a deck, adjoined by a staircase to the studio. The deck was equipped with ornamental safety railings and more good views of the Hudson.

Going back to the first floor, there was a second small living room that joined a back porch. You descended steps from the porch to a very large flagstone patio that did not come with the house. We built it. When I say "we," I mean the hands of Marge and Bob, not hired hands.

There was a young man, named Arthur Keenen, whom I hired from time to time for help on any job. For common labor, like removing old plaster, and cleaning up, in general, there was a second man. At seventy five cents per hour for the first man, and thirty five cents for the second, who could afford, often, such help?

Both the large living room and the small had attractive open fire places. The facade of the fire place in the large living room was painted a very disagreeable dirty gray color. We scraped and used remover to discover that the carved grapes and other fruit were in marble, and quite obviously hand done by an artist. We cleaned, repaired and polished the facade and mantel, and enjoyed for years the unknown artist's work.

To finance these alterations and additions we used the New Deal F.H.A. loans with low interest rates. And for that we remembered Franklin Roosevelt in our prayers.

Winston Churchill had said about the war, "Give us the tools, and we'll finish the job." America was trying to do that in 1940. Our business with the steel Companies in the Chicago area became so large that we needed a branch office in Gary Indiana to handle the volume that came from that area alone. Also control Engineers were scarce. Williams asked me to go to Gary and open a new office and staff it.

I commuted to visit home occasionally. When the office became a going institution, I was sort of left holding the bag as its manager for the spring and summer of 1940. The whole Gary chapter happened when the remodeling of our home, as described above, was in progress. On one visit home I put our remodeling on complete hold. One incident was, we had opened the wall of the studio to receive a large picture window. I covered this exposure to the elements with a large heavy duty tarpaulin nailed down around the edges with moldings

Marge brought the family out to Gary. We set up very good housekeeping in a summer cottage at Miller beach on Lake Michigan. The whole family enjoyed the beach, and I had a good commute to the office. During this period, the company protested that finding a permanent manager suited to the special requirements of the steel industry was difficult. I protested that I wanted to go back to New York as soon as possible----or sooner!

The Gary office's jurisdiction covered a portion of the territory that wraps itself around the southern end of Lake Michigan. It included South Chicago and the Illinois territory between that and Gary on the western side, and Indiana as far as South Bend on the East, also the South West corner of Michigan.

That entire area is highly industrialized with steel predominating along the Chicago Gary axis, which part was by far my principal concern. Steel mill job propositions were usually complex and were not developed by a single person; departments got into the act. In these situations my work was largely calls on Engineering and purchasing to keep the focus of specifications on Clark and to expedite the program.

An important part of my work was public relations, among our customers and prospective customers, that expressed itself in golf games and entertainment. Because of the frequency of occasions, I had numerous bar tenders on the loop posted to serve me tea when, with a guest, I ordered bourbon. I would usually start with a scotch to be sociable, and switch to bourbon, preordained as tea, to be sensible and stay in charge of the evening.

At the mills I cultivated the superintendents of maintenance to be favored on replacement equipment, chief engineers for the new projects, and purchasing agents for both eventualities.

I can see now Charlie Curtain, Senior Purchasing Agent for a
large steel company, welcoming, with a friendly Mien, the
young man from Gary into his luxurious Chicago office. He
knew I had just stopped by to see if that coming crane
control was to have a Clark Controller nameplate on its
enclosing cabinet door. He was like someone teasing a cat,
but with a fifteen to twenty thousand dollar chunk of
cheese. When jobs reached the closing stage, and there was
some bargaining to be done, as to price and extra features,
he really enjoyed the matching of wits. He also liked the
inducements: I always brought good cigars, and I drank a lot
of tea with Charlie.

I stayed with the Gary situation until it began to feel like
something permanent, and that was not my intention. I was
sure also that the management in Cleveland felt things were
pretty well settled: no hurry to find another manager. I do
not recall the exact time I spent as operating Manager of
the Gary office, but it was, many months, all that summer
moving into fall. The family, and especially our kids, were
having a glorious time living and playing on Miller beach.
Lake Michigan there is like the ocean shores. I was, daily,
straining at the ties that bound me to Gary when I wanted to
be, and belonged to be, in New York. I finally realized I
would have to make a decision and risk the displeasure of my
bosses. Again quoting Winston Churchill, "there were many
agonizing reappraisals."

I made a decision: I was finished with the temporary program
for me in Gary. I was going back to New York on my
management job there with Clark Controller or with another
company. While realizing, with a bit of pain, the chance I
took, I still felt confident: I called the president of an
electric company, who had talked with me previously, and was
offered the position of General Manager, we left it
tentative. My heart was still with Clark.

Mr, Williams came out for a visit to the Gary office. The
time had arrived; after spending an afternoon visiting
important customers we went back to my office to relax,
clean up, and go to the Chicago loop district for a good
dinner. Pete was the visiting Headquarters man, and he
admitted that he loved to spend money, and enjoy the night
spots with his district managers.

But this was not to be our night. I opened my painful
subject: did he have any one in sight for Gary? He did not.
As I expected, he thought maybe I was liking the place with
all the interesting jobs I was into, and he was very happy
with how the Gary office was increasing our share of the
business in the steel industry. I realized that, from a
business point of view, he considered Gary, combined with
Chicago, his number one area.

I explained that, over the weekend, I was going to my home in Nyack and think, but I already believed that, with reasonable notice, I would leave the company rather than stay in Gary. This was a matter that included where we thought our kids would have the best opportunities growing up, and where Marge and I could lead the fullest life.

That intended trip and thinking turned out to be unnecessary. Mr. Williams returned to Cleveland, and talked the matter over with Mr.Clark. I received a telegram from Pete saying a lot of considerate things, but the first sentence settled the problem: it said, "Bob Hoge, we want you and want you in New York." It seemed a salary increase was already in the works for me. That adjustment was also made. I had good reason to believe that the decision was Pete's, but he wanted to make sure Mr. Clark agreed before telling me.

I said a fond farewell to my friends in the area, packed our automobile, and with my wonderful family headed for Nyack and home.

I shall skip details about the rapid growth of business taking place all over the country as it was stimulated by the war in Europe. New York was no exception. We were getting million dollar orders for entirely new business, like firing and lighting circuits for battle ships.

After Pearl Harbor, and we were in the war, all orders seemed to be multiples of what had been. Its a sad commentary to note that the great depression wasn't ended until the war came along.

After we entered the war, eventually overhead travelling cranes were not just in short supply, none were available. An entrepreneur name Jack Burke was moved by the business opportunity, and his patriotism, to form from scratch a crane manufacturing company. He enlisted a venture capitalist named Leonard who supplied the money. They formed the Leonard Burke Company.

In time I learned that Burke was a creator through fantasy, a promoter on a large scale; that is said as a complement. He would visualize, in great detail, the product he was going to design, the factory he was going to build, and would seem to believe himself that they already existed. He would explain them as though they did. He would sell a job based on his intention to produce, and on his drawings and specifications in the beginning stage. He would then work continuously to deliver, and, as far as I know, he always did.

Those associated with him would be conscience bound also; everyone involved would go to work creating what Jack had dreamed up and sold.

Before any crane had been built and tested, or even a factory existed, he was out to obtained a multi-million dollar order from The Higgins Ship Building Corp of New Orleans that needed, as a beginning, 105 seventy five ton cranes. Higgins, of the ship building company, was also a dreamer. His plan was to build Liberty ships on a dry ground production lines, like manufacturing automobiles. They would need many cranes to support those heavy ships as they moved down the production lines to launching.

The way Burke operated is illustrated in my experience. A Mr. Burke came to my office and explained in detail the design of his travelling cranes. I knew about the shortage of cranes in the war effort. Burke said that I was reputed to know quite a bit about cranes. He explained that the purpose of his visit was to get me on his team, to not only build the electrical control equipment, but also to help him with his new organization of electrical engineers. He said he was recruiting good engineers, but most of them would be new to the design and production of cranes. This was the necessary approach, if he was going to help relieve the shortage.

He said his steel girder men had decided to build in an ignorance factor, deliberately designing in some excess capacity to make up for the limitations of experience and testing time, needed for more precision. On a few special cranes, where they would have no time for testing, they intended to use simple box shaped girders instead of ones tapered to form beams of constant strength, and curved for good looks. The procedure would take some extra steel, but it would produced absolutely safe girders. He said he had, for the steel work, men of experience designing for steel; some especially for cranes.

I was familiar with the hoists, trolleys, electrical motors and controllers and could be of specific help there. Jack explained that for that help it would be his intention to give Clark Controller all of the electrical business generated by his company. This would be our understanding. He just casually mentioned that The Higgins Ship Building Company of New Orleans needed now the 105 cranes mentioned above; an order the size of which no one in the crane business had ever heard.

Jack was on his way to New Orleans that evening. He gave good reasons for the short notice, but "could I go with him to talk hoists and control?" Only alternating current motors were available, so for the hoists we would be required to use alternating current control with mechanical load brakes instead of dynamic lowering direct current controls with D. C. motors. I said, " We can supply the alternating current control, but mechanical load brakes are in short supply." Characteristically Jack said, "we'll build our own and they will be the best, tell them that."

From almost any point of view, this was a crazy proposition. My home was in Nyack 16 miles up the Hudson River. I must get some clothes and a tooth brush, and leave within a couple hours. I was being asked to take this stranger at his word and, at my expense, go on a week or ten day visit to New Orleans. Leaving in the evening we would spend a day and two nights on a train. Plane seats were commandeered--none were available. Nothing was for sure in the business prospects, it would be our job to bring those things into the real world. But I developed a certain confidence that he could organize, supply the creative energy and "dream and dream until the dream creates the thing it contemplates" (with apologies to the author of the original of my quote.)

I thought as he talked, this has the marks of my kind of thing only more so. I thought with one man who's crazy a second not quite so far gone could pull things into line; maybe they really could fly over the rainbow. I would be leaving my territory, and invading another, without home office approval. I would be far exceeding my usual expense account. All of this would be done on a project hard to explain to the home office. My neck would be way out. If I didn't deliver, I cringed to think of what might happen in organization discipline. I said to myself, and then aloud, "I'll do it!"

I called Marge with the news that I was going, by train, to New Orleans in a few hours, and explained the situation to her in some detail. She thought well of the plan, and volunteered to pack my bag and bring it to the office. I was glad for that and for the fact that I would see her before leaving. Our train was to leave just before the dinner hour, so neither of us could have the pleasure of the other's company at dinner, to ease the impromptu separation.

We arrived in New Orleans the morning of the day after tomorrow (two men from La Mancha?), maybe. Jack had made reservations for two at the Roosevelt Hotel; we were soon checked in and ready for business, but it wasn't going to happen that way. In New Orleans, before business of some magnitude is transacted, sociability is extended and expected.

Improvisation was also evident in the Higgins Corporation. A father and son named Moses were in charge of all Purchasing activities. They had been drafted by Higgins from their substantial local business in small craft and appliances. We found that they had been given just about full responsibility for acquiring the large amount of tools and machinery needed to build large ships on production lines. They started their work with us by an invitation to Antwaun's for lunch; for the time before lunch we were guided about the shipbuilding works by an attractive young lady.

We met John Moses, the father, and Joe Moses, the son for lunch and liked both men. I do not remember if John and Joe are the right first names. We were surprised by the custom of bourbon before a large sea food lunch. The weather was hot; it took me only a couple days of such lunches before I went out and bought a thin summer suit.

Following for a few days were yacht trips on lake pontchartrain, swimming sessions from their yacht, and visits to their home for tennis and dinner. Jack and I supplied a case of good champagne for the yacht and the dinners in town. But here also the customer tried to share the hosting with the drinks and wine.

After several days, when we were purified by the ritual, the Moseses began to talk business. We talked early, and talked late and soon approached some happy conclusions. What they would be was indicated in a unique experience in sales: Joe Moses called me, from a comfortable chair in his waiting room, into his office, and said his assistant was absent, would I take his seat in another office, and act as purchasing agent, and review the proposals of some accumulated salesmen for differing things. He wanted me to reccommend who should get the business on various jobs. He surely expected me to interview myself and recomend Leonard Burke cranes with Clark controllers. I realized that we had a lot more than a foot in the door.

That afternoon, in a final session of all interested parties, we closed the business with an understanding that Burke would build the 105 cranes.

The next morning Jack went to the plant and came back with the finished contract and a Higgins Shipbuilding check for one million dollars earnest money. We decided to leave on a late afternoon train for Cleveland, Ohio.

In New Orleans I had prepared a contract for Burke to sign with me. The contract included Burke's assurance that Clark Controller would be his sole source of supply for crane control. In exchange for our setting up a special production line for the large control panels, which would save him time and money, he would make progressive payments in advance of production and shipment. I knew that the latter provision would please our budget director.

There were good reasons why we headed for Cleveland instead of New York. Jack wanted to meet our home office executives and I wanted to show off the main contract, the million dollar check and my special agreement with Leonard Burke. The news had circulated: I was not only forgiven for running off base, out of my territory, but I was for the moment sort of a sales hero.

We arrived in Clevelad after breakfast on the train, and went directly to the plant. P. C. Clark invited us to his office, and reviewed the main agreement and the one I had drawn for Jack to sign. He was very pleased with the "orderliness" of everything, and surprised at the volume of business they represented. Jack was met and welcomed by our principal executives. A number of preliminaries to a special manufacturing program were tentatively discussed and arranged. Mr. Clark hosted a lunch at his club including key men from sales, engineering and manufacturing.

That same night Jack and I had dinner at the restaurant in the railroad station, and I put him on the eight o'clock train for New York. And so ended an episode.

I was going to stay in Cleveland for a couple days to review the Leonard Burke and other jobs with Pete Williams and Andy Mellon, who, of course, were my bosses and the ones due a full report. During the day Mellon had said, "I told everyone to leave you alone in New Orleans and you would get the job, and you did. Nice going." He said that in a manner that displayed confidence. It was a nice moment for a relatively new kid on the block.

Chapter XIV

More New York and Back to Cleveland

When I returned to New York, jobs were waiting; the pertinent papers were piled on my desk. I picked the most urgent, a special crane modification for loading war material to and from a staging area in Bayonne, New Jersey. My introduction to the place was dramatic in the extreme.

After being cleared for the restricted area, I walked out on a long loading dock that extended from the land out to the edges of the Hudson River Channel. The cranes of my concern were located on this dock, but, for the moment, I was captivated by the scene before me: a water front replete with huge barges loaded with battle tanks, trucks and heavy crates being moved by tugs into position to transfer their loads to waiting ships destined to war zones.

Near the outer end of the dock I became aware that a loaded barge on my left, unattached from a tug nearby, was moving slowly but ever so steadily toward the dock not far from my general location. I stood fascinated as the barge, eventually, with a deliberate steady motion relentlessly pressed into the side of the dock pushing over double pilings and tearing out very heavy planks. Its slow smooth motion was unabated. The barge moved through the dock, tearing apart bracing and flooring as it advanced, coming out the other side, and leaving behind it a well cut passageway through what had tried to stop its motion.

Except for the passageway the dock seemed undamaged, and I, in my location, was unhurt, and the cranes, the objects of my visit, were safe in still a better location. As for the loose barge, we could see tugs moving in to put it under control.

As a student of kinetics in Mechanical engineering, I probably should not have been surprised at this performance, but I was, to fascination, with the invincibility of the power of momentum, even in the slow motion, of a great mass. The barge seemed to have an intelligent purpose, that was not to be denied, that it irresistibly carried out at a calm smooth pace.

I watched the excitement for awhile: some dock workers running and shouting, and a man, obviously the boss, commencing to give orders. I walked back to my crane location, and turned my attention to the job that had brought me there.

The heavy military equipment that came through this loading area because of the war necessitated changes in the dock cranes. I was dealing with armature shunts on the hoist motors, and field resistance on the trolleys, primarily to increase the capacity of the cranes, with some significant changes in certain functional sequences. The capacity alterations required the addition of banks of mill resistors and a couple of make and break contactors on the main control panels. The functional sequences called for a change of cams in the crane operator's cam switch that directed the electrical controllers what to do and when. My job was to determine what was needed and give my factory an order and specifications, and this I was busy on for several days.

For the engineers who might read this, I performed a bit of heroics to give the loading company partial relief while we waited on factory shipments: I altered the cams in the large master switches with sealing plastic, the kind used to seal legal documents; by the simple act of warming the plastic, and remodelling the cam shapes, sanding and polishing. I produced cams that had the looks of duplicates to factory-made. I wondered if the material would last a few days.

Actually when the new cams were received from Cleveland we had one operator who said he liked the feel of my altered switch. So, on his crane the new cams were not installed. Over one year after the job was closed he was still using the home made cams. I inspected the the switch; the altered cams were still functional, and in reasonable condition.

Among my business relationships in New York, there was one situation to which I had to become sensitive that was a side effect of current politics: Soviet Russia was a customer and a prospective larger buyer. Their purchasing in New York was handled by a purchasing agent known as the Amtorg Trading Corp., staffed by some Soviet personnel, including party members that spied on the purchasing agents to protect them from contamination by the capitalist with whom they dealt.

I developed a business friendship with one of the agents, who was also a Russian, assigned to my class of business: we frequently had lunch together, transacted our business and talked on whatever subject came to mind. On one occasion I called his office, he was not in; I asked that he be told that his "friend" Hoge had called and would appreciate a call back.

He called me back, all right, but in a fire storm. The essence of his heated remarks was that I should get it through my head that he had no "friends" in this country, particularly among people he might buy products from. I will not try to recall his words, but the theme is still clear. He wanted someone to realize his purity. I could only think that he was talking for the benefit of a wiretap on his line. And that must have been the case. At that time, I was aware of the allegation that soviets were sometimes brought home, and shot for disloyalty. After the lecture, and some time went by, our meetings were as friendly and productive as ever, but I never went off limits again.

Wire drawing was a process important to our business. We developed our engineering and sales proposals jointly with a company named Wean Engineering Co. who manufactured the drawing machines. I had made it a point to become expert in the electric control circuits necessary for good performance on multi-die machines. At Wean Engineering's request, I was available to them in other Clark district offices adjacent to the New York district. For example, I would work in the Boston District or the Pennsylvania District bringing sales to maturity and supervising installations.

As an example of war time business, there arose a need for special wires for which die machines and electrical controls had not been developed. Wean Engineering co. made alterations in their machines, and sent an altered machine to one of our wire drawing customers. I obtained approval to work in their shop, operating the machine, drawing wire with the workers, and developing the essential electric controls on the job. We had the show on the road within the month. Soon after development, we altered the equipment and procedures in all the wire manufacturing plants, with whom we were associated, in New Jersey and New York State.

I would like now to ignore the actual sequence of events, and review some that were educational as well as good business and, maybe, fun:

I enjoyed entertaining, at the Worlds fair, foreign visitors seeking American equipment. It was as though they established the fair just to give us a special place to aid our sales. There were many Englishmen with whom we were working. In periods of relaxation, when some would boast about how everything in England was superior, I would take them for a stroll beside the giant statue of George Washington, and suggest that maybe not everything. It was all done in good humor. I used to enjoy the English wit in their responses.

Clark supplied various controllers to the Pennsylvania Railroad shops. There were extensive repair shops underground beneath their central passenger and freight station in Manhattan. There was a multiplicity of railroad tracks accommodating trains being served. When I first visited these shops I was astonished to see facilities for repair that covered a very large area which was freed from the congestion of a sky scraper city by being spread out beneath it.

My territory was the entire state of New York, and I paid regular visits to cities like Albany, Utica, Syracuse, Rome and others. I drove those upstate roads in snow, rain and sunshine. I have crossed the state from Albany to Rome in the late afternoon and into the night when the temperature was 0 degrees, and the road was like a tunnel, with its roof off, through the drifted snow. The traction was packed ice with sifted snow lubrication.

At this time, social gatherings in Greenwich Village were often political events in disguise. Also the park area around the intersection of fourteenth street and fifth avenue was safe haven for outdoor meetings. Every evening, soap box orators would be haranguing the crowds about the stressful subjects of the day. Often, several speakers would be talking at the same time. You could move around and get several points of view almost simultaneously the same evening. Nearly all were politically left wing ranging from light pink to red.

At a party in the Village, we met a couple who seemed to be, at least, stable. The husband gave me his business card that testified to his being a consulting engineer in the very active field of Time Study of manufacturing methods and production lines. In conversation, we found that we covered about the same territory and companies, and he thought it would be enjoyable if we rode together occasionally on our business calls upstate----In my automobile.

Days later I received a phone call form my new friend, who's name I have forgotten, explaining some tentative days that he might be going to Utica and Syracuse, and would I, by chance, have a similar schedule. Actually, I did, and with slight adjustment we got our days together, and he was to be my guest on the road. We arranged to meet at my office. At nine o'clock on the day of departure he showed carrying two rather large wrapped packages of literature, and thereby hangs a tale.

Our trip together was pleasant but uneventful; so there is little need of details here. I discovered several weeks later, on a repeat visit alone to some of the plants we had visited, that his packages of literature contained communist propaganda. I was glad that, in these large plants, we had not visited the same people, and that I was not associated as his transportation.

On my return to New York, I talked to the man, and, with the passion of an idealist, he honestly told me his story: he and his sister, who was the woman with him at the village party, not a wife, were journalist on the Daily Worker, the communist principal newspaper and propaganda sheet, and both were full time communist. I supplied no future transportation.

And so the time went by, with jobs that were learning experiences, vehicles of self expression, or both.

It was a company practice to have, at appropriate intervals, sales meetings that included the whole national sales force. These meetings were held at the Athletic Club in Cleveland, and were filled with both business and pleasure. They enhanced the esprit de corps.

Also a very strong factor in my fraternal feeling within the company came from the visits of Andy Mellon and Pete Williams to New York: they would come individually. We would talk and transact business during the day and go out on the town in the evening. Often Marge would join us for dinner in the city. I felt at home and was glad to be there.

But, as it must, sadness came into our picture, P.C.Clark, who was well advanced in years, died. He was loved throughout the company, and had been a great leader. These facts were paramount in making Clark Controller the special place that it was. Confronted with a great loss, the company became rife with reorganization and new programs to repair the damage.

I did not yet know about the reorganization planning taking place in Cleveland when I received an unusual phone call from Andy Mellon. It was unusual because he asked if he could visit with me at my home in Nyack, said he wanted to relax for a few days in New York City, would be bringing his ten year old son and would like to visit with Marge, me and family in Nyack, a day or two. We made it two. Our son was ten at the time. Mellon hoped I could take the time off from work, and we could, in the relaxation of my home territory, find much to talk about. He would like to begin this program several days from his call. Who was I to say nay to the boss. And I was to find that he was "the" boss.

Andy had not been at my home more than a few hours when I found out that he was to be our new president. Profits were not good at the time and we talked over whether he should cut dividends to stock holders---a far cry from my sales work. Nevertheless, I gave him my best advice.

We went for extensive walks along the palisades of the Hudson River, and talked of the intricate aspects of high finance and corporate structure. We analyzed personnel problems in the framework of specific situations and jobs to be filled. And here it came out why Mellon wanted to pay this visit: I and my family were being observed, in situs, for me to come to Cleveland in an executive capacity.

For years Williams and Mellon jointly represented sales management in the company, with Williams emphasizing personnel matters, and Mellon the mechanics of selling the product, and the concerns of competition. In the new setup it was projected that I would be the Sales Manager. Mr. Williams would be Vice President of Sales.

Mellon's son played with our son, and made himself at home, but my recall is simply of a mature 10 year old boy who reflected the strong personality of his father. We enjoyed having him as a guest. Father and son departed for home at the end of an obviously successful visit.

It was not long before I had a call from Williams, he filled in the details such as the date for starting my new job and what my salary would be, over 300% of my present one, and would I accept the offer. I accepted.

Marge and I had had a lot of talks about how we loved our home in Nyack, and the whole New York area, and how we hated to leave. But we had decided before Pete's call that, given reasonable terms, we would accept the promotion with thankfulness.

After saying yes, there was a finality that called for a celebration, we went to New York for an evening of dining and dancing in the Rainbow Room atop the R.C.A. building in Rockefeller Center.

I was expected in Cleveland at an early date, and there was a house full of personal property and a family to move, and a transfer of responsibility at the office. The latter was not too difficult. Ed Jung just added to his load for the immediate future. He and I had some conferences to bring him up to date on active propositions. At home Marge, as usual, would make the moving job much easier.

We spent hours talking over the significance of the change. We knew we would miss New York, our visits as a romantic couple to the Broadway shows, the Metropolitan operas, the Museums and galleries, Benny Goodman at Carnegie Hall and the symphony there. We began to experience parting as "sweet sorrow" as we talked about our own special New Years parties at the Roosevelt Hotel with Guy Lumbardo and his band playing "the sweetest music this side of Heaven."

We reflected on special bistros in the village with small bands playing behind the bar, and impulsive musicians, at the tables, breaking in with their instruments, and turning the place into a jam session. We talked of Julius', on Seventh ave. in the village, with only a single pianist playing the Broadway melodies, but serving the finest steaks in town. I thought of Samuel Hoffenstein's, "I would rather listen to a flute, in Gotham than a band in Butte."

The kitchen was in the dining room. You picked your steak from sides of beef hanging in the refrigerator. They cut it to suit your capacity and taste.

We talked of Times Square and Central Park like they were play areas in our own back yard, and the pleasure of just going into town. At times the whole place would seem to be our special raison d'etre, and here we were getting ready to leave it.

It was time to go: New York was real to both of us, but there was romance in the reality and a state of mind that colored what we experienced. We had seen and heard the magic of art, the majesty of things done on a grand scale, and quite fully appreciated the distinct personality of a great city like New York. The things that mattered now on a personal level were going with us: Our love for each other and our children, which was basic to all else, and our personal interests and ideals,

Anyway, prior to Mellon's visit, I had found myself thinking well beyond my present job: The depression, that was ending with the war's demands on industry, had left me with definite ideas, or rather ideals, for future corporate policy. Also the unusual combination of my having been a blacksmith, a mechanic, and, later on, an assistant to top management in General Electric caused me to think and study overall company policy, and to develop ideals for organization and policy. Marge and I had decided it should be my goal to find a way into general management. What had developed seemed a timely step, an answer to a silent prayer.

Soon, after the mechanics of moving were completed, we were in Cleveland, living in an attractive residential hotel in Painesville, and negotiating for a house to buy.

We bought the house. It was an attractive English Tudor style in the suburbs, with a thirty foot living room, a play room of the same size, an ample dining room and two bed rooms. The maid's quarters, included a smaller living room, a bed room and bath. The garage was three stalls with very fancy roll-up doors. There was approximately an acre of land. I have given these details in order to mention what could be bought for $21,000.00 in 1944, and that that price home was unusual enough, in those days, for the local newspaper to run a short article with a head line, "Clark executive buys $21,000.00 home," And, what is more, one of our directors said, "We could have labor trouble with that kind of publicity."

As I now recall it, the demeanor at the plant, in spite of the war, was the same deliberate care taking approach to building reliable functional control, but, because of the war, the whole place had expanded, and office, as well as factory space, was at a premium. In order to give the new Sales Manager a private office some remodelling along the executive corridor was in progress. I was placed in temporary quarters which were adequate but a bit below an ambience that would say, here abides an important man. Yes, as one climbs up the ladder he sometimes notices the superficial as well as the official.

We went to work without delay. I had for long been a believer in profit sharing as a fair and effective form of compensation. As a war measure the government placed controls on wages and salaries as such, but, believing it helped the war effort, allowed incentive compensation plans to increase income.

This meant to me a new and fair bonus plan for the entire sales force. The plan would take into account that, in our national business, the purchasing department of a customer might be in one of our districts, the engineering department in another, and the plant where our control would be installed in still another. Three of our districts would have responsibility for relations with that spread out customer.

If it were no more than good public relations with one of its divisions, the district responsible should share in the profits on sales to that customer. Calculating a fair distribution of profits through a bonus plan was complicated, but the formulae were developed, and a new plan went out to our district offices.

It caused a pro and con debate across the country which was generally favorable. The dissidents, where more central purchasing divisions were located, soon came into line when they began to receive checks for business shipped into their territory for which the order was received in another. With more grace, they shared the profits with another district on orders placed in their's that were engineered or shipped elsewhere.

The plan worked, our district offices cultivated (gave service to) divisions of national companies even though that division could not place an order in that district. The customers or prospects liked what they saw, and requested of, or specified to, their purchasing divisions Clark products, and the executive and purchasing divisions were vocal in their appreciation of the complete organization contact. I did feel considerable satisfaction, as score one, on my undertaking to increase Clark's percentage of the market.

But smooth sailing was not to be for long. Mellon had for years been outstanding as a brilliant engineer, and sales management assistant to Williams, and equally as a popular personality throughout the company. A reversal was taking place, he was not popular as president. He did not run true to form. In speeches before company meetings his attitude would often seem arbitrary and dominating. He might end his urging with a statement like "do it that way or else." It was never quite clear, what the "or else" was to be, but it was pretty well implied in the the build up to his conclusion. This approach was completely foreign to the Clark Controller policy of general good will, and foreign to Mellon's, prior to his becoming president. Mellon had great dreams for the Company, but instead of leading he was trying to force the future.

It would serve no purpose to detail the the road to the crisis that developed at that time. The revolt was general, and, with some urging from the Board of Directors, Mellon resigned. He landed on his feet as second in command at a large national company. This was a setup he understood well from his years being the right arm of Williams. I had occasion to see him often and he was again a top performer with his impatience held in check by a strong boss.

Reorganization was the order of the day at Clark Controller: Mr Williams became president. I became de facto General manager as well as sales Manager, and was elected to the board of directors. It became apparent that all the principal departments of the company were headed by men reaching their retirement age. I was an exception and became a focal point for what became an aggressive post war drive for company expansion. The older department heads would rather wait and see before committing the company to a drastic program.

The real difference of opinion was whether there was to be a depression or economic domestic growth when the war ended. I believed it was a good gamble to bet on growth and to prepare the company for that by building inventories, hiring and training personnel and in general preparing the company for advantage in a growing market. Most of the younger men in the management felt the same way.

The older department heads, with just as much sincerity, believed the best interests of the company lay in a policy of down-sizing and preparing for the the strains of depression. Probably temperament, as well as hard facts to judge by, influenced all of us. Whatever, a lively debate ensued.

Much time went by, the war was drawing to a close, and our regular board meetings and special meetings were almost preoccupied with discussions of policies to meet the post war world.

Our board was composed of six executives in the company and five outside men. Three of the five were presidents of other companies with headquarters in Cleveland, one was our attorney and another an investment banker. Among the six inside executives I became a minority of one, like a voice crying in the wilderness, to make ready for a golden opportunity. There were various degrees of agreement and disagreement among the outside men.

Finally the issues became clear cut, I put together a composite policy which I tried, unsuccessfully, to sell at a regular board meeting. The meeting was adjourned until the following day without any action.

The next day, just before the continued meeting, one of the directors came to my office, and, with an air of considerate confidentiality, advised me to back away from my insistence upon the plan I was trying to have adopted. He said, "You are going to have ten men against you, and that in a serious way." At the meeting I still sincerely championed the plan as the way to go.

One of our outside directors, president of a large Cleveland company, suggested that what we were discussing was a sweeping and fundamental change in the posture of the company.

He proposed that a committee be appointed by the board, and authorized to make a study through questioning key men in the company for their opinions as they saw things from the vantage points of their jobs. The committee endeavor to arrive at a consensus, and make such recommendations back to the board as seemed appropriate. This suggestion was adopted. The chair appointed the three corporate presidents to such a committee, and asked them to submit a proposal in one month at the next board meeting.

The outsiders were frequently seen on the inside during the month. It was a nervous wait, but at the next meeting a comprehensive proposal was made as the unanimous opinion of the three.

They stated that my plan seemed to be consistent with a wide spread attitude in the company, and, in the committee's opinion, and from the facts also, seemed to be what was needed for the coming market, and that it be adopted.

They further stated that they had had a side talk with Mr, Williams. He would welcome a change in responsibility. It was proposed that Mr. Williams become chairman of the board, a position we had not previously filled on the board, and that I be made president and chief executive officer with a full vote of confidence by the board.

All proposals of the subcommittee were unanimously adopted.

While the company negotiations and reorganizations were taking place we sold our home in Mayfield, and put the family in comfortable temporary rented quarters in Willoughby. We felt more secure without a Mortgage over our heads while the strenuous talks went on. And, becoming more familiar with the Cleveland area, we had, already, developed a strong desire to move to Gates Mills, a very beautiful and generally desirable residential section of Cleveland. After the reorganization was completed we found the house we wanted there, and began a home building and family raising program that was to mature and blossom, in that location, for twenty years.

What I recall as a starting point for my administration as CEO of the company was a talk I made to all employees over our public address system. It was later referred to, with good humor, as my inauguration speech. I emphasized that a national, or rather multi-national, organization of our kind was also a social institution with obligations to customers, employees, stockholders, and the branch of industry in which it operated.

For the customer, the the company would always remember that the "priceless ingredient of every product is the honor and integrity of its maker." Also his expertise.

For employees, it would consciously strive to make its premises a place where they could grow in their chosen work, and realize their maximum potential.

For the stockholders, we believed that sound policies for the company and its people would result in a fair return on their investment. But the sound policies for the company must always recognize the essential nature of profits.

For the industry in which it operated, even though a competitor, it would always be a good neighbor that enhanced the neighborhood.

This four cornered structure of policy was enlarged upon with deep conviction, because I had long had dreams for working people, and just people, as well as for what makes for good business and good engineering.

Immediately we, the V. P. of Manufacturing, the Personnel manager, and I, met with the shop committee in several sessions reviewing the existing contract with labor.

I initiated the meetings to explain in detail our concept of good relations. It included management voluntarily upgrading some practices to assure that Clark Controller would always be known and referred to as a "good place to work." Many points of agreement would continue to require the good offices of negotiation to arrive at mutual agreement.

To illustrate the point we proposed, what we called, "my Days." It had long been the universal practice to dock hourly workers for time taken off for personal business. On regular national holidays the hourly worker was paid for the time off. This had long been, by negotiation, in the contract. But, if a special national holiday was declared, the hourly worker took the holiday, all right, but without pay.

It was my proposal that we put it in the contract that all workers had 5 my days each year which could be taken off in whole or in hours. If he had a dental appointment he could punch out and note "my day time" on his card. He could do the same if he wanted to play golf, or he could save his days for an extra week, or extra days, of vacation in addition to the negotiated vacation time.

In a similar manner we reviewed other procedures to determine that they were expressions of our general policy.

In due time I had meetings with all departments. The Engineering department was next. I and the Chief Engineer invited discussion. When I talked with labor I had remembered my days as a blacksmith and felt simpatico. As I talked and listened to responses from our large group of engineers, I felt very much at home with my contemporaries of more recent years. I had worked with many of these men on my own engineering projects.

We arrived at an agenda for the department that was a core to build on. I'll mention only one small item that had a large personal meaning to the group. Company practice for years had required engineers to punch a time clock when coming to and leaving work. This was not an uncommon procedure in the industry.

The question was raised from the floor, "As professional people should we not do creative work without so much clock watching both morning and evening?" I responded immediately. "You should and you will from now on. You are professional, and professional behavior can be expected coming and going in your relations with the company. As of now, to illustrate the point, there are to be no engineering time clocks in the company."

A young man, with a degree in industrial engineering came to the company looking for a job, and wanted to see the president. Our personnel department told me of his insistence on an opportunity to tell his story, in his way, to the CEO.

I liked his style and agreed to an appointment. As he talked I recognized his intelligence and saw his place in what we were trying to do. I hired him as Assistant to the president and put him to work on a staff basis analyzing our company operations and reducing them to curves, charts, tables and numbers. The young man's name was Al Thalman.

For example he brought into clear focus the monthly volume of sales, manufacturing and shipments needed just to break even on a profit and loss scale. Al made some wonderful large curve charts that showed plainly the variables of overhead, labor, and material and where we were on the charts and the attractive changes in the rate of profits after we passed the break-even point of our business.

They were professional charts accurately supported and displayed. I used them to set our goals in talks with all departments throughout the company, and to design our production bonus as a true profit sharing one. A formula was developed that indexed profits to the volume of shipments. It was surprising what the company could pay working out beyond the break-even point.

All at the factory, except top management, participated in the monthly bonus which was paid as a percent of salary. sometimes 50%. Always some percent when we passed the break-even.

We placed posters throughout the shop showing the production goal, well above our break-even point, for each month, and from time to time the company gave a banquet, at one of the best hotels, as a reward for achieving these goals. I sometimes felt that the people loved these parties as much as they did the extra money.

The shop committee, in spite of all that one might have heard about unions opposing some production drives, supported these drives. In their sense of humor, they put up their own posters also in the shop. The posters included one word, "GOYA," which all knew sent the message "Get off your - - -."

We developed similar compensation plans for the sales department, but based on sales, and for top management, at the end of the year, based on the general success of the year just ending.

So far as management, in general, was concerned, we established a firm policy that no persons would be brought in from outside to fill management positions. All such jobs would be filled by promotion from within the ranks.

As I write these lines I realize that this is my autobiography and not a company history, and I must somewhat confine myself to anecdotes that tell something significant about my history. But, I want to say, in a summary before the fact, that I could set goals and enjoy accomplishment because of the cooperation of the great number of capable loyal people that made up the organization, each of whose career could make an interesting story.

R.L.Puette our head application engineer became V. P. of Manufacturing as Mr. Claflin, the older head retired. After some in-between reorganization steps, Ed Jung, regional manager in the New York-Philadelphia area became V. P. of sales with Robert Whitehill as Sales Manager. John Cortelli, one of our outstanding engineers became Chief Engineer. These were all men who could take a full delegation of authority and run their departments without supervision.

This was not yet the day of the personal computer. However we had installed, as rentals from the I B M. Company, some main frame computers that had capacity for all our accounting and payroll calculations and distributions. In those days these were machines to talk about with pride. We were looking especially upon their ability to handle inventory against the backlog of orders, and assure that each large part, or tiny bolt or screw, was on hand to complete the backlog. The kingdom would not be lost for the want of a horseshoe. You call that merging the backlog into the inventory, with the computers knowledge of all the parts available. It worked beautifully and kept production flowing without the interruptions of waiting for parts.

And the time had come to do just that. The war was drawing to a close and we had on hand an enormous backlog of "post war orders," a designation that was heard frequently about the plant, and industry for that matter. They represented the domestic needs of industry that were accepted as orders to be held until the military demands and regulations ended. We were preparing to, yes, get the jump on competition by clearing up the backlog fast and getting back to normal procedures.

One procedure we utilized was far from normal: Selling was not the current need, production was. We brought our sales force into Cleveland in relays, residing in good hotels, and put them to work in the shop on their own customer's orders- -doing the actual work as well as expediting. This was not an arbitrary program, it was worked out with the application engineers in the districts and with the union leaders at the factory. It was explained over the address system to all employees,

Our district men were all engineers who had had factory training in producing electric control, and the Union leaders at the factory understood, helped by our explanations, the advantage to all in getting the backlog out of the pipeline of production. As the plan developed the enthusiasm soared; it became a team work that was spiritually satisfying as well as financially rewarding. As I look back on this I can feel again the warmth of satisfaction that comes from an undertaking in which all the parties are really working together on a common goal.

One situation that I recall, with abiding pleasure, was the years of working with our Canadian subsidiary. There was a fine gentleman named Walter Foreman about whom, for the want of better words, we would say was a "member of the old school." I remember that his social drink at a party was orange juice with a bit of bourbon. Some years before I came with the company he had come to Cleveland and arranged with P. C. Clark to take some of our designs to Canada and produce the Clark products for the Canadian market. He had arranged with another U.S.electric company to produce some of their specialty products also.

He founded on the premises of the Railway power and Engineering Co., in one of their large buildings, a company known as the Canadian Controllers. For years the company had three owners, Clark, Railway Power, and the other American Electric Co, which shall remain unnamed. It immediately became my purpose from previous thinking, to change this setup. I wanted there to be only Clark products and two owners, Clark with a controlling interest, and Railway Power with a substantial interest to make it a real Canadian organization, managed an operated by Canadians, and for the national sales organization of Railway Power to be the sales organization of Canadian Controllers also.

This was accomplished. I asked Our Treasurer, Carl Wendt, to go with me to Boston, and bring his check book. We met with the other electric Co. officials, and after much careful explaining of our program that could not include them, and some pretty rough bargaining, we arrived at a meeting of the minds and acquired their interest. We had been right to believe that the company had a poor cash flow, and that Carl's checkbook, money on the barrel head, would look good to them. Also they had little interest in a growth program for Canadian Controllers. We wanted to expand the show across the border.

We immediately went to Toronto, and put our plan before the Railway Power and Engineering. We absorbed their inventory into the company as a part payment, which was increased by cash, on a ratio, that left Railway owning forty percent of the company, instead of thirty three and a third. In the enthusiasm of the meeting, at an initial proposal by the Canadians, we decided to build Canadian Controllers a new plant, and start without delay putting into action the many plans for growth that we held in common with the Canadians.

We left the meeting feeling the show was already on the road; time proved the authenticity of that feeling.

Walter Foreman had already passed the retirement age. He announced that he wished to retire. I appointed Bill Turner, Walter Foremen's general manager, President, and continued myself as Chairman of the Board. In a short time we had reorganized the company with a full staff, and, when the new factory was finished, we offered a full line of Clark products made in Canada, by Canadians, managed by Canadians. The business grew beyond our expectations.

But I must divert from business While writing about the Canadians. They were a hospitable bunch. Bill Turner was of Scotch decent, six feet five inches tall. In addition to being an excellent engineer and business man, he could play jazz music on the piano by ear. He knew many good jokes which he had difficulty telling: as he got near the point of a joke he would begin to laugh so vigorously that he had a hard time finishing the punch line of his story. He would have to reach for his handkerchief to wipe away the tears of laughter.

A great institution for which Bill Turner was responsible was an annual fishing trip to North Bay and lake Nipissing, about two hundred miles North of Toronto. The trip was manned by several of us from Clark Controller, several from Canadian controller and 5 or 6 key men from the Canadian Steel Co., The latter all good customers. A fact we were not unmindful of, but we all had a wonderful time.

Bill used to chuckle in the morning as he fixed the orange juice, fixed it with a little bourbon. And he fixed the boats with a bottle in each that could only be used within the ground rules which stated: you could have one drink for catching the first fish, one for catching the most fish, and one for catching the biggest. There was one exception: your companions in the boat felt obligated to keep you company--too bad if you should become a lone drinker. That generous impulse meant that all in the boat had a drink when any had one.

We took with us in the boats only bread and oil, we had to catch our lunch, and cook it on the shore. We caught the big Northern Pike and Walleyes, and often had Indian guides to fillet and cook the fish.

There were three full days of horse play and foolish things said and done to amuse, but all enjoyed the good clean fun, and went back to their jobs refreshed. And, we hoped, with our customers inclined in our direction.

Back in Ohio there was another company that should be explained in its relationship to Clark to complete the physical picture of our total organization. Our electric control panels were mounted in steel Cabinets. The larger panels took cabinets ninety inches high and several feet wide. We bought the cabinets from cabinet manufacturers. I wanted to make our own. Such steel work was a specialty requiring a lot of heavy duty, single purpose, machine tools, and a certain breed of men called steel workers. To develop our own steel shop would take time.

As though a message from fate, the president of the Good Roads Machinery Corp., at Minerva Ohio called me, and suggested that we meet and talk about the possibility of our acquiring his principal company, and with it, the American Electric Switch co., his subsidiary. I was immediately interested: The road machinery company had the steel workers and the tools to make our cabinets, and the American Electric switch company made manually operated wall switches that would fill out a notch in our electric control line.

There are interesting stories about the negotiations, if only we had the space and time to tell them! Suffice it to say that the president was his own man: He had a lodge built on the company grounds, with a room full of exotic wines and liquors. He had in the kitchen of the lodge a restaurant size refrigerator and freezer. He bought his meat a whole steer at a time. You may guess from these items that he loved to entertain his dealers and customers at the factory. He did.

After three negotiation sessions we acquired the business at a fair price, and sent in one of our young men with a business degree to be General Manager. He went with orders to go for a profit in the businesses per se, and to build a wing on the factory in which to manufacture our cabinets.

Back at the main plant we were fortunate that a factory on each side of our plant became vacant and we bought the properties. One gave us much needed additional office space in front, and more research and development area in the center and rear. The building on the other side afforded a substantial increase in manufacturing room.

The pressure taken off our main plant enabled us to remodel our reception facilities and sales offices in the main building there. For awhile remodelling was the order of the day, but it expressed the growth that was taking place in the company, and probably had a psychological feedback that contributed to the expansion mood that was underway.

Chapter XV

Gates Mills and Cleveland

Gates Mills was and is a horsy town. They would, in our day, ride to the hounds in season, and be properly dressed to chase the illusive fox. A large part of the abundant charm of the village was the social affairs at the hunt club and the horse shows that had national, and some international, appeal.

Consistent with this characteristic of the community, there was an old stable on the property of the home we bought. The people, who preceded us in the premises, left us with a building suitable for several horses, the accouterments and apparatus required. But we were not yet concerned with horses. That came some years later in the wholehearted interests of Margo, our youngest. For other purposes, we converted the building into work areas.

I loved that edifice. As time went by, it was transformed into a series of well equipped studios. There was a dark room for photographic work, a pottery workshop for Marge's ceramics, and a painting studio for doing graphic art in any medium. A sculpture studio occupied a large space, in the building's center, for modelling, mold building, and carving. A separate room became a foundry for the casting of bronze sculptures. Incidentally, the extensive tooling, essential to supporting the studios, made the ensemble a place where almost anything could be created or repaired.

When we moved into the home in Gates Mills our children had already picked up a few years: Margo was 7, Renon 12 and Coliver 15. They had already demonstrated to their parents that they were very unusually wonderful (no prejudice involved).

The moves we made during the year had required the kids to adjust to several new school arrangements, to suit our temporary locations, which they did most graciously. Margo illustrates the point: At the end of kindergarten in Nyack, when she was six years old, she did not follow the custom of entering first grade. Her teachers had considered her quite precocious and eligible for second grade, which she entered. We, of course, were proud of the appraisal.

Our first home in Cleveland was in the Mayfield school district; Margo entered the second grade there. As explained in chapter fourteen we sold our home in Mayfield, and rented a place in Willoughby while we searched for a home In Gates Mills. She transferred schools again still in the second grade. And then, when we moved to Gates Mills she had become seven years old, and, on the record, ready for the third grade.

For most grammar school grades, Gates Mills was also in the Mayfield school district. The exception was for kindergarten and a few beginning school grades. There was a very special small school in the town designed upon high educational standards for the early years, and convenience for the mothers. The Superintendent of the school thought that Margo should not enter third grade, but should drop back and take second grade again, so that she could receive their unusual brand of education, and be with the seven-year-old kids.

One day, after Margo had been for awhile in the school, we asked her how she liked the Gates Mills school. With considerable enthusiasm she replied, "It's the best second grade I've ever been in."

Gates Mills was a village of winding roads and gently rolling hills among tall trees that continue a part of the old Western Reserve forest. Home lots were measured in acres, not square feet. There were minimum limits on the acreage upon which one could build, and architectural approval required of what was to be built. The results were charming. The village might remind one of a traditional New England town, but still possessed of its own unique quality of beauty.

Our house was Greek revival with genuine Corinthian columns. As we remodeled, we removed a large wooden porch from among the columns, and replaced it with a flagstone court from which rose stone steps to a iron railed landing at the front door. I was required to demonstrate my sculptural prowess by hand carving flutes in extensions to those large diameter columns. The extensions were needed to bring the columns down to the stone court.

When we bought the house we had plans for remodeling which plans grew. We were several years executing our designs. We left few things unchanged on the property, or the property itself. The land and the house received the magic touch of the Hoges, mother, father and the three kids. The latter contributed expert boy and girl power to the accomplishment. The place came to be very much our own. We all loved it.

Here I wish to ignore chronological order, and relate some anecdotes which give glimpses of occurrences that were intimate parts of our lives, both parents and children, and show the course we were steering, and the set of the wind in our sails.

Coliver, a naturally gregarious and friendly person, soon found her place in Mayfield High School. She was a good student and an enthusiastic participant in the school's extracurricular activities, particularly drama. Within the scope of her opportunities she promptly became famous, a star. I am not disposed to ingratiate, she was especially good and recognized as such. She graduated from Mayfield, and entered Hollins College in Roanoke, Va.

Her first date was a blind date with a cadet from VPI in Blacksburg, Va. That cadet, named Brooks Parker, was the man she married a few years later. And upon that sentence there hangs a story of love triumphant.

Collie, her nickname, finished two years at Hollins, and transferred to Colorado College at Colorado Springs for two final years to her graduation. Her major was psychology. But it was not as smooth as that sounds. Brooks was waiting in the wings for her, and the Army was waiting for him.

He was one year ahead of her in school. The ROTC training at VPI made him a lieutenant after graduation. They could see ahead some camp training in the U.S., and then many months in Germany in the army of occupation. That came to mean one thing to them: get married now! Their determination meant that collie would drop out of Colorado at the end of one year, marry, and be with the Brooks at his camp assignment in the U.S. and return to Colorado College for her final year while Brooks was in Germany.

It made good sense to them, supported by good strong emotions. But it collided with our insistence that nothing be allowed to interrupt an educational program until at least the four year college course was completed.

Another family practice was involved in a positive way: we actively taught our kids to be independent and responsible. Collie said of our objections, "You taught me to be independent, and now, when in this very important matter, I am sure I love the right man, and it's the right time, you object to my independence."

Rest assured, our objections were only temporary: We saw real love shining through, and our hearts went out to them. We approved and supported their move. Brooks was very much the right man: Collie flew to Fort Leonard Wood and married him there.

After a sojourn at Camp Belvoir in Virginia, while Brooks was in Germany with the Army of occupation, she went back to Colorado College and graduated.

The years have proved that this was a marriage made in Heaven.

We were already living in a real learning period where we were discovering our good fortune in having children who could demonstrate vigorous personalities and strength of spirit at critical points in their lives, and make courageous decisions.

Several years after we settled in Gates Mills, our son Renon had become locally famous for his football and basket ball prowess. He was indeed a star player at the Mayfield Highschool where he had been playing for two years. Where decisions come from is not always explainable, but he decided he wanted to upgrade himself in General. He wished to transfer to the Western Reserve Academy, a preparatory junior college in Hudson, Ohio.

He took entrance examinations and was informed by letter that he did not qualify. His past grades also were not helpful. The rejection was pretty all inclusive. He read the letter with tears in his eyes but refused to take it as final. I agreed and responded that it was an opportunity, "Here you have been told that you cannot do a worthwhile thing that you want to do. Make it your business to prove that you can. You will grow with the effort."

And he did it. On his own initiative he inquired at school, and found an independent academic coach. He asked his mother and me to approve, which we, of course, did, and he was soon on a regular schedule of being drilled in important subjects.

From his coach he found out about a school in Tarrytown, New York that specialized in training students to be super qualified, if they would take a concentrated and strenuous course for some eight or ten weeks. He came to us for immediate approval, got it, and was off for Tarrytown. He wrote home regularly about his progress, and also corresponded with the Head Master at the Western Reserve Academy.

To make a long story shorter, he finished the course, came back to Cleveland, took the Academy entrance test over, passed it with high grades, and was admitted to the school without question. This must have been a turning point in his life.

At the Academy, he finished the two years left of high school with good grades in all courses. He still was a football star but gave his studies more or equal time. When he graduated and went to V.P.I., as his chosen college, they put him on the Varsity team in his freshman year.

Here again he reached a studied decision and came home to review it. He wished to end his football days, resign from the team, and concentrate on the serious business of living, and the practical matter of learning. Through college, he sought the technical aspects of his primary course, Engineering, and the general education of Liberal Arts subjects in the school's academic environment.

He had thought we might not like losing the honor of having a football-star son. We were proud of his athletic ability, but we were delighted with the promise of his newly chosen life style which has stayed with him through his entire career.

Margo our youngest had no school adjustments to make after the second grade experience. We have told how she had been ahead of herself in Nyack. Seven years later, when she was ready for high school, the whole family was wiser about schools. Margo knew where she wished to go, Laurel, a private preparatory school for girls. During her four years there we received only good reports on her performance, with special notes about her excellence in art.

The university of Colorado, at Boulder was her choice for her college degree.

But the year before her high school career, when she was thirteen, her interest in nature and the Western life style, as portrayed during the early days of television, through Hop-along Cassidy and his horses, had reached a blooming point in her life: she wanted a horse of her own.

That desire was genuine to her nature. She had a very active sense of wonder about all creatures which included not only horses, but dogs, squirrels, lambs, roosters, and even giant frogs. All of these animals were, at one time or another, entertained by her as residents on the premises. A horse would give her another very concrete expression of her natural interest. This became obvious: she drew or doodled horses on our telephone books, or any other available paper about the house.

But, Alas, her family were not sold immediately on acquiring a horse. Ignorance was their trouble; probably mostly her father's. Stables to clean and horses to groom was not on his program. She said she would do all the work, and in time he learned how right she was.

To make her point of buying a horse she performed a unique war of nerves: She remained perfectly friendly, said no more about horses, but in some subtle way you knew she was obsessed with wanting, and wanting you to know it. I thought she was gaining weight because of compensatory eating. Either a lot was going on or my conscience was putting the bite on me.

One day, out of a blue sky, I heard myself say at breakfast, "Why don't you and mother go out and look at horses." In my great wisdom, I added the admonition, "Don't buy the first horse you see, there are a lot of horses in the neighborhood. Let's get a good one." They looked for days, and the first one they had looked at turned out to be the best.

We let Margo buy the horse and ride him home, a trip of several miles. Unknown to her, we were maneuvering back roads, and taking up, ever so often, positions on side roads that crossed her route, waiting for her to ride by. We wanted to see her on her new horse, and we were anxious for her safety. We were not yet aware that she was already an expert rider. The horse was a colorful palomino, warm light brown with a lighter main and tail, truly beautiful. Margo named him Pegus with a subtitle of "Pal-O-Mine."

We had acquired from our next door neighbors a one horse stable, and moved it to the back of our property. We fenced in an area around the stable that made a good paddock, When Pegus came home he just moved into his own quarters. There was hay and oats on hand for supper.

To repeat myself, these stories illustrate how, in family conference, our children had convictions that led quietly to their prevailing when their cause was right, and the issue was essential to the expression of their true selves.

Parents are lucky who have such kids.

To bring this story back to the Clark Controller plant, I was primarily concerned with the human equation. I endeavored to remember that every employee was an individual. Philosophically, an individual is a scenario taking place on an extended scale. He is responsible for his spiritual and physical welfare, and with his or her home situation that he wishes to support. What he realizes in his private goals is the measure of his growth in life. He reaches out for opportunities. As an employee, he relates to company Goals and his part in them as they pertain to his own progress.

The two things do not always coincide: There come times when the national economy is in recession, and an industrial plant may have to do, what we call today "downsize," which is a euphemism for layoff or fire. From my days as a railroad blacksmith I remembered the pain and suffering of persons furloughed, which was the euphemism of that day for a company layoff.

My ideal as CEO was to build a company in which its employees could grow, through the education of the workplace and school, to the limits of their capability. We had

ongoing arrangements with colleges in Cleveland where
cooperative courses enabled any of our employees to work for
a degree or just advanced training. There were many
employees who became engineers, or business managers through
the aid of these courses. As a company we established a
policy of paying all tuition for any one who would take any
course and maintain a degree of C or better. To emphasize
that we really meant any course, we said, "yes, tap dancing
included." We believed in the general power of education and
the advantage of letting the student choose his course.

When one is working with people, and considering their
personal interest along with goals of the company,
downsizing is a tragic contradiction that enters the picture
when the general economy shrinks. It is a happy time when
the economy expands and jobs are created by company growth.
The situation is much more stable when the company
advancement is steady as the result of creation of new
products and markets.

The negative economic necessities, for the security of the
company, that affected personnel in depressed times, were
intellectually acceptable but emotionally repulsive. It
became a central element, in our established company policy,
to strive to maintain a general rate of growth in the
population of our employees by continuous progress of the
company through the development of new products and skillful
marketing.

We increased our budgets for research and development, and
emphasized sales training. Some of our district office
application engineers caught the fever of, what we called,
"imagineering," focusing more creative thinking on the daily
job. The word itself was invented for the program by Pete
Williams.

Very soon we had in development a, new-to-the-market,
across-the-line starter, a central element of standard
electrical control equipment. The basic idea, too technical
for this writing, came from a district engineer. It was
unique in design, real high tech for the product. In time it
opened, for us, substantial new markets.

From several other district men, in collaboration, there
came preliminary designs and a drive to develop, a line of
compact relays especially for the machine tool industry.
These relays eventually put us up front in that lucrative
field, where heretofore, we had been practically an
outsider.

All the while, our research and development department was
at work on a comprehensive program that was continuous and
fruitful for the steady progress of company, and job
security.

Even I personally got back into design, and developed a pneumatic device called a safety air valve. In fact it was a couple of one and one half inch valves in tandem, under control of a number of, built-in, quarter inch ball valves, that told the big ones what to do, and when to do it. We had been, for years, the leading company in safety electrical control for large presses that formed body parts in the automotive industry. Yet, found ourselves defending some product liability suits because of air valve failure, valves we did not make but bought to complete the press operation.

For those who might be interested, press operators who start and stop the cycle of a huge forming press, by pressing and releasing electric push buttons, are not, in the cycle, controlling the driving motor of the press. The motors are 150 horse power, they run continuously through working periods.

Between the motor and the press there is a large air operated clutch which is actuated by an one-and-a-half-inch electrically controlled air valve. When the clutch closes the press comes down and forms the body part, and then returns to the up position where the valve closes, and shuts off the air pressure, and releases the clutch. If the air valve sticks, and does not discharge the air pressure from the clutch, the press will repeat its operation. And, sad to say, may do so with the workers hands between its jaws.

Good standard valves, available in the market were used, but after some years of operation and maintenance they proved not to be up to the standards for safety on presses. I insisted that Clark Controller step over into the pneumatic field and develop an air valve built integral with other air devices that were all single purpose, safety press control. After getting for a long time no response, I stuck my neck out at a brain storming meeting and declared, "If some of you geniuses don't develop one I shall do so myself." As time went on that is what I had to do.

With two fine men, Harold Cotshott and Ben Carlisle, helping we tested and retested designs and redesigns, often late into the night. It's too long a story and too technical to tell here, but my wife said, for months she became a valve widow.

With one hundred and fifty pounds of air pressure being instantly discharged at frequent intervals the laboratory sounded like an artillery dual at the front. Ben declared, one evening, that if the valve tripped open again, he was going to do some fine screaming. But let it be noted that finally we got it.

At the patent office I was given a basic patent and several
design patents, all of which I signed over to the company.
We were bringing to the automotive industry market a very
real increase in safety for press operations. The use of our
special valve was made legally mandatory in certain areas.

Companies are like people: when they grow up they have
acquired a distinct personality. A company's personality is
a product of experience influenced by the employees and the
management. The Clark Controller Co.'s personality was a
compliment to both, back through its history. My job was
made easier by the fraternal spirit already established in
the company, and a tradition of mutual cooperation.

As I write this I can read a silver plaque all neatly
mounted on a wooden base hanging on the wall of my studio.
"Pure corn," you might say: The plaque thanks me for able
leadership, and pledges complete support and cooperation to
me and my programs. It was presented at an Old Timers
Dinner, and dated March 31, 1951.

I found out, as time went on, that if this ornate instrument
was corn, it was a very wholesome grade: Support and
cooperation is exactly what I received throughout all the
years of my administration. I feel today gratitude to the
employees and their leaders of the times proceeding mine in
the company management.

In a biography it is customary to mention such things as
honorary memberships. During the full term of my presidency,
I was a member of several of the different Who's Who in's,
principal of which is Who's Who in America, and listed, with
some biographical notes, in their annual volumes. The
regular business societies and associations I will omit for
brevity.

As the company grew and prospered, it made an attractive
target for raiders, and we had experiences of attempted
hostile mergers. On one occasion, I was advised by an
investment banker, on our board, that a certain electrical
company was buying heavily in our stock on the exchange. I
immediately contacted the company to discover their purpose
in the buying, and a meeting was arranged with their
investment banker.

At the meeting, in his New York office, their head broker
came across to me as oily: He rose from his desk to his
feet, and walked like a prowler, saying nothing as he
circled his large office, appearing in deep thought. Then he
stopped and turned toward me, and broke his silence saying,
"Mr. Hoge, so often in acquisitions we have to hurt
somebody. I am happy here because I can be the instrument of
merging your company, and doing only good for you. I can
greatly increase your salary, and see that you have many

shares of the new stock we will issue. And what is more, we can assure you a place in the management, second only to my client who would own the controlling interest in the new combination."

Their plans were well laid, and the above was obviously an offer to buy from me a positive recommendation to Clark Controller share holders that they tender their shares, at a price to be offered. This procedure would save the buyers millions of dollars compared to leaving the stock price to market action.

This was not a merger we wished even to consider. In my opinion, it would not be in the best interest of our shareholders. I stalled for time and a way to temporarily stop the buying of our stock. I simply said, "You've got it all figured out; maybe you see something we don't. Give me time to consult and think it over."

I believed that, if they thought I might eventually agree, they would immediately stop buying in the open market. They would look forward to later making an offer directly to our shareholders, at a firm price. I presumed that they thought they had made me an offer I couldn't refuse. I had expected something of the kind beforehand, and had developed a plan.

We had been advised by our investment banker that the owners of company buying would be close to their limit of cash and leverage if they completed the deal. Could we make the transaction too expensive for them?

There was a way. Our product development program needed a large influx of cash to exploit the products created. We were going to the market for equity capital, selling an issue of convertible preferred stock that could bring in several million dollars. The plans for this issue of stock were already well matured, and we could complete the procedures within days.

The stock would be a preferred without voting rights, but convertible to common, with one vote per share, when the common stock market price reached thirty dollars per share. The common was already about twenty two dollars per share. If we accelerated the issuing of the preferred it would hang like a sword of Damocles over the heads of our would be entrepreneurs: If it got out they were buying for a hostile merger the common stock would go to thirty, and beyond, over night, and millions of dollars more would be needed to buy the convertible stock as it became common through conversion.

And that is what we did. As soon as the convertible hit the market, I had a call from our erstwhile pursuers asking if our company would buy the block of Clark stock they had bought. We did buy it at a good price with some loss to the raider, and the raid was over.

Competition was keen in the Electrical Control Industry. The price for custom designed control for some manufacturing processes could run into multi-millions of dollars per order. They were prizes worth the extra effort to obtain. Some devices or circuits were covered by patents, but most of the equipment and the designs for its use were naked in the market. Nevertheless, mutual respect was characteristic among the leaders of the competing companies.

As I write this, I cannot recall a CEO or official of an electrical control competitor I didn't like as a business contemporary. They were men of high ethical standards, creativity and sociability. Much joint effort went into what was good for society and the electrical industry. As companies we were members of the National Electric Manufacturers Association (NEMA), and, through its good offices, continuously carried on studies and activities of mutual interest, such as the standardization of products, that has made the efficient application of electricity universal.

The Control Division of NEMA would meet in the Springtime. I do not remember the dates but it was always when the dogwood was in bloom in Cleveland, Ohio. I noted this as a fact as I drove my car out of the driveway, and pointed it toward Hot Springs, Va. A tradition of generations was continued down there, each year, by our springtime meetings at the Homestead Hotel. There were many committees, and much real hard work was done for over a week at the Homestead. But also, many good golf games were played during the occasion. Business was forgotten on the golf course, and we learned that our competitors were also just ordinary men working for a living, and trying to make a contribution to the general welfare.

I have always been grateful for having been in those acts for many years. I wouldn't go so far as to say with the Negro Spiritual, "In those numbers, when the Saints came marching in." They were not Saints--just good guys.

However, the Justice Department looked at the whole Electrical Control industry, and thought the divisions of the principal companies were operating too close for competition. The department declared that these companies, and the leaders of their sales divisions personally, were in violation of certain antitrust laws, such as being in a conspiracy to control prices.

The government indited sales executives, not for agreeing to prices with competitors, but for being present at meetings where, it was charged, some agreements had been attempted or consummated. Regardless of whether or not those particular individuals participated, it was asserted, they were guilty of conspiracy by the act of being present.

Even if one was not indited, the long periods of Grand Jury investigation, and eventual trials, were time consuming, and the ambience was stressful. Congressman Kefaufer undertook congressional investigation. It will not be my intention to go into the details of these periods. There may have been technical violation of the law. The courts found that there had been. In the Control Industry, at least, we felt there had been no moral violation.

And so we move on with our story. "It is a small world," we are often advised, and that is usually a pleasant scenario of meeting people in far away places that were important to you or some of your friends back home. One exclaims, "You really knew the Jones; they were our dear friends too." We could reply here, "No not the Jones, but we knew the Stanleys. They were our next-door neighbors in Cleveland, Ohio in 1945 and have been dear friends for fifty years." With no mutual plans or common reason, we found ourselves neighbors in California after 1965; not next door, but within a short drive for many reciprocal visits and friendship enhancements. We had California, Tom and Milley too. Our reasons for being residents in California are later in this story.

But back to work, my twenty years in the Cleveland picture, and my business and personal association with the heads of some of America's largest corporations, were tremendously educational. As was my participation in the many organizations essential to the coordination of the diverse establishments that made up the industrial picture of the times. There were trade associations, there was the national Chamber of Commerce in Washington, and the National Manufacturers Association which always held its annual meeting, in banquet style, in the ball room of the Waldorf Astoria Hotel in New York.

One would have had to be insensitive not to have felt a glow from the importance of being a part of what was happening, being asked to speak at meetings, and, better still, listening to the wisdom of others. I attended, enjoyed, and was impressed, as any small town kid would be to find himself playing baseball in the big league. And I learned.

Big business has wrung up some bad marks, particularly to many good people, with good causes. But to know representative leaders as human beings with real problems and real interests, one learns that there is greatness at the heart of American free enterprise. It is daily expressed in the simple act of just doing business, and doing an abundance of it well. I felt like a better man for having been a part of that picture in many joint actions with my contemporaries.

To break these activities down into a recitation of individual instances over twenty years is not the purpose of this writing. Over these years the contacts were almost daily. It seems, in looking back, that it was a process of learning about people and liking most of what I learned.

Making that statement lets me turn my attention away from the fine offices, hotels, and the Fortune 500 type of companies, and into our own shops in intimate contact with the very real people who worked there.

That experience often made for ambivalence. My early days in the railroad shops gave me understanding for the working person's point of view, and a desire to voluntarily support high grade working conditions and the maximum compensation that the economics of our business could afford. The union representing our employees did not always agree with our idea of what that was. We had some tough contract negotiations that forced me, at times, to the side of protecting the corporation for survival and fulfillment of its other many plans an obligations. I had to learn to say no at the right time and place, and hold the line. That was and is a large part of the story of collective bargaining, as seen from the management point of view.

Our union leaders and shop committee did their duty and sought what they believed to be fair. They were mostly reasonable men, some outstandingly wise and constructive. Working with them was personally satisfying as well as being organizationally methodical and rewarding. we never had a strike during the twenty years of my administration.

I testify to having had real affection for the shop people in general, upon whose skill and loyalty all else in company welfare depended.

We worked three shifts during the war, and for a long while after, and I visited each shift as an interested individual walking about the place. I became personally acquainted with our shop employees from tool makers to floor sweepers, and the same for office personnel supporting their activities.

It was during the years in Cleveland that our children finished their school days and married. Renon graduated from Virginia Polytechnic Institute, and, very soon afterward, Married Joanne Wright, his sweetheart of many years.

Margo came along a few years later, graduated from the University of Colorado, and married Paul Gathers who lived in Boulder. He finished his chosen education by graduating from Colorado State in Fort Collins.

We have recorded earlier the details of Coliver's education program, her graduation from Colorado College, and marriage to Brooks Parker her dear friend throughout the entire period.

My wife and I commented over the years How fortunate we considered ourselves to find that we had two in-law sons and a daughter all of whom we could sincerely love as our own. I still am happy to record such a pleasant fact.

And one by one they came, the grandchildren. We had never been grandparents before, and each new child was a miracle, a joy and a projection farther into the future. I will not attempt to give the details here but there were years of visiting our children's homes, and seeing their children grow from babies into men and women, a new generation on the way. They brought new love and life into our old house by their visits home. There will be more on this long after we leave Cleveland for a new career in California.

This seems to be the place to begin drawing to a close my career as an engineer and a business person. If we were writing a history of the company, or of the family, we could fill books about the eventful years in Cleveland, all of which influenced the development of our subject, but I have made it my task to pick representative episodes, and leave it to the readers imagination to complete the picture.

The war ended in 1945, but, as stated earlier, our company did not shrink, it expanded in all departments. Here in the early 1960's our research and development program had given us shining new products that shone with state of the art technology, and cried out for more capital to build new facilities, and automate manufacturing procedures. We raised working capital in the equities market by our convertible stock issue, but much, much more was needed. We had outgrown our physical size and capital. A merger seemed in our near future. The company was without debt, and there were markets waiting for its products and services. We had conversations with appropriate companies and had many opportunities.

However, some other people saw Clark Controller as a prize package if it could be bought in the market. For example there was a second entrepreneur who started buying our common stock. He had already merged several companies. We feared he wished to bleed the company's resources, and reduce its research and development expenditures to increase cash flow, which was not the direction we wished to see the company move.

Simultaneously we had an offer to open discussions with a national company whose business and Clark's business would reciprocally complement. The logic of working together, expanding Clark's facilities, and automating the manufacturing of its standard products lines, was clearly in the picture. A merger by stock tender made sense in our discussions. Also it would be protective against those who might wish to get Clark in the market place, and exploit its resources by downsizing its activities. There was agreement on both sides of the table.

I have said little about any art activities in Cleveland but there was plenty. The stable studio served its purposes, as partially explained at the beginning of this chapter. I was able in it to establish the photographic equipment, and develop the methods of enlarging and printing mural size pictures in black and white or color; some as large as four by five feet.

In sculpture, the procedures and tooling were put in place, and exercised to produce all manner of stone carvings, including marble and granite, that were exhibited at such prestigious places as the annual Cleveland Art Museum May show.

The intricacies of mold building were mastered and many enjoyable castings from my own clay modelings were produced and exhibited. Cold castings were made in hydrocal or calcium aluminate. And, yes, we produced, in our fully equipped foundry, high grade bronze sculpture that won prizes in art shows and acclaim among a circle of artist friends.

For ceramic work, potter's wheels and kilns were installed, and Marge did outstanding work winning prizes, selling, and giving fine pottery to her friends and admirers.

I painted in oils and water colors, and had, in the converted stable, an efficient studio that patiently waited between sessions. It was ready for use on a moments notice which was an essential feature for spare time service. I was able, for relaxation and stimulation, to do many paintings that were exhibited with honors. I was a member, exhibitor, and, for a term, president of the Chagrin Falls Art Association.

Our interest in the arts and the pursuit of our hobbies was a mighty force in where we went and what we did on our vacations. I never traveled without water color paper, brushes and colors. Marge loved to especially visit world famous potters in their studios, and I the celebrated sculptors and the art foundries that enlarged and cast their works.

The art galleries of Munich, Florence, Rome, and Tokyo became as familiar as those in New York. Robert Tratzel, Curator of The Haus de Kunst, Munich Germany's main art museum, from photographs, invited me for several years to show in their annual international. Even with my vanity, I was always lazy enough to overcome the impulse to crate and ship large sculptors to remote destinations.

I had planned for years to retire at fifty five, and have a third career in art, but, at that age, I found myself too busy, and engrossed in the creative art of building companies, to even consider retiring. At fifty nine the picture had changed: the creative part of one plan had reached fruition. It was a good time for me to step aside because it coincided with the company's merging into the really big league to allow its expertise to leap forward in that frame of reference.

It was agreed that I could be released, remaining for a year Chairman of the Board of the Clark wing, not present for operations, but available for consultation during the transition.

I was now free to put my art work to the test of the market place and competitive art shows. The place where we were to settle was to be determined by its suitability to that purpose. We had for some years thought of Munich Germany or Florence or Rome Italy as the place. We now wished to test them in the order shown. We arranged a trip to spend an extended period in each place, living in an apartment, working with the arts, and showing in some galleries, pretending to ourselves we were residents of the city.

The test was a great experience: we spent months among some really great artists, and learned how they conducted the business part of their profession, and enjoyed the purely art part for its own sake. Rome almost got us, we stayed over a month on the Via Venito, and almost cried when we left, but we had decided that being an expatriate was not for us. We returned to the U.S., and headed for Carmel California for a test visit there.

In Carmel we rented a small house and became acquainted with the artists, art galleries and museums. We soon understood we were in one of the most active fine art communities in the world, this was it. Buying a place to live and work at our arts was not easy. I happened to be one of few sculptors who cast his own bronze. Carmel was zoned for studios but not for bronze foundries.

We found our ideal place atop a small mountain among the hills of Carmel Valley, a village located eleven miles from the town of Carmel by the Sea. For scenery of the ocean we had a short drive. For scenery of hills, valleys and mountains we had to look out of any window or glass door, or walk out on a patio. An eternal inspiration to express in the arts. We bought the place.

Upon our return to Cleveland, we faced the job of extracting ourselves from a house we had lived in for twenty years. Attics were full of abandoned property, and the garage was loaded. And we had to sell the property. To save the reader the tedious detail, let it be said simply that, in time, all was accomplished, and we pointed our automobile toward California.

Yes, of course, we sang a few bars of "California here we come."

Chapter XVI

Carmel Valley, California

As I find myself, in writing this autobiography, addressing the point where I publicly start a new career I recall an important bit of personal philosophy that has repeated itself throughout my life. I am aware of it now. I find myself saying, "I am a human being with a right of entry to life that is as fresh as it was 91 years ago. I seek to see more of this relationship in the maturity of the years." In 1965 when I came to California to seek recognition as an artist I was thinking the same thing from the perspective of 61 years.

The soul is a real thing, an entity that stands apart from and acts through the body. I remember myself at three years old, and find that I am remembering the same person that I am now, and can reflect upon today. The awareness of the sameness of myself then and now is sure and profound.

The person I recall in that three year old period is not remembered as a small body with small hands, feet or what not; he is remembered as a complete personality, in a spiritual sense, independent of physical ties. The person I am conscious of now as I write these lines can be similarly described, and so could it be in 1965.

The handicaps of age and the alterations of the body with time are not in the equation. I am still that person I have always known. And so through life the same person has always been there using tools, like the body, and contrivances and facilities like this computer at which I am writing. In recall, all tools and contrivances fall away and are unnecessary to sensing the whole person.

And, to not let the rhythm of that thought go unattended, it is that whole person that is "one with God." It is that spirit, that soul, who was made and is made in the likeness of God. God is not a physical body. Someone has said, "Not an Englishman 12 feet tall." He, She, or It is a spirit at home in an infinite universe that He (for the want of a better word) created, and so can human attention be engaged with the inexhaustible phenomena of the boundless and the everlasting, jump light years in the blink of an eye. Truly was "he made in the image of God."

And so we came here like any young couple eager to begin their careers, but this time probably closer to the spirit and its desire for expression. I never felt the pangs or the elation of retirement. I considered the move a natural step within the larger parameters of a comprehensive life. We moved our studio equipment into studios prepared, or being prepared, in our new home.

With suitable help I dug large rocks out of an unfinished basement, and then dug long and deep pits for foundry work. The pits were 42 inches deep with sand floors to protect against dripping molten metal. They were arranged so that covers of one inch thick plywood fit into place and gave us a level floor when foundry work was not in progress. In the pits, gas fired bronze furnaces were built underground. Also built in the pits were two large electric kilns for curing molds. In a surprisingly short time we had the shop and foundry part of the studio finished and all equipment in place for production.

In a joining basement section we installed two potter's wheels an two kilns and built the shelving and tables that completed a ceramic studio for Marge.

The fact that we had accumulated or built all of our equipment over the years enabled us to be in business even before it was all neatly placed in studio areas.

I went from the basement studio to down town Carmel interested in finding associates in art and places to exhibit. The Carmel Art Association and Zantman Private Galleries were obviously prestigious, maybe the most so. I soon was showing my sculpture in both places but not without some waiting and adjustment to the the climate of the local art field. I was, on first try, rejected as a member of the Association.

Quite naturally, being a retired engineer and business man did not seem, to the powers that were, ample qualifications for an art career. Something more convincing concerning my credentials was needed, and it came along:

Several of my large bronze sculptures taken into the Carmel Art Association gallery and exhibited on a table for the board of directors to view for approval were lying exposed the day after the board meeting at which they were rejected. The work generated interest in Gallery visitors, the interested parties were referred directly to me. Two couples came to my studio and bought all that was exhibited for a total of several thousand dollars.

Urban Renewal in Monterey was in progress. The committee on monuments commissioned me to make a portraiture monument, for The Custom House area near Monterey's Fisherman's wharf, in bronze mounted on a shaft of granite, to Pietro Ferranti, one of the founders of the fishing and canning industry, so important to the growth of the city.

The Monterey county fair came along with its competitive art show. I won first prize in sculpture.

I did not apply again for membership in the Association, The board of directors of the association voted, to request a visit to my studios. In several visits all the members inspected my collection of my own work. We had enjoyable conferences, and I had a chance to explain the years I had worked at art as an avocation. These meetings were not only clarifying they were the beginning of some friendships that have lasted.

No one advised me of the purpose of these visits. That became clear when Sophie Harpe, the secretary of the board called: I was not at home, she left word with Marge, "Tell Bob he is now one of us." I was a member by invitation and not application.

I greatly appreciated that they had reconsidered their rejection, and always felt it to be an honor to be a member of this prestigious organization of fine artists. Several years later I had the honor of being president of the association, and the pleasure of working with a strong board to advance the interests of the organization and the welfare of its members. One just had to grow in such an ambience which, I believe, I did along with the organization under our guidance.

For three years in a row I won first prize in sculpture in the county fair competitive shows. I also exhibited paintings in these shows receiving honorable mention for the works. For one year I was the chairman of the art branch of the fair. I also served on the board of directors of the Art Coordinating Council of Monterey County.

At the Monterey fair, where I won the prize on the first occasion, Fred Maxwell, owner of Maxwell Galleries of San Francisco, was the invited judge. Following the show he invited me to lunch with him in the city, and proposed that I show on a regular basis in his main gallery which I, of course, did. I would drive to San Francisco, double park on Sutter Street in the middle of town, and unload heavy bronzes for the gallery. The work was difficult but the recognition welcome and the sales immediate. I did a lot of hauling.

The monumental bust of Ferranti presented some interesting production problems. This is as good as any place to give some detail of the lost wax process at the time this commission was executed. First I modeled the bust in Italian plastilina which is a clay mixed with oils, including lanolin, instead of water. The clay is everlasting without ever drying. The same clay is used over and over again.

When the clay model was complete in every detail I built a multiple-piece mold of synthetic rubber with a plaster of Paris backing. From this mold I cast, by the slosh method, a hollow wax duplicate of the clay likeness. With the slosh method one pours melted wax into the mold, sloshes it around by manipulating the mold, and pours the excess back into the melting pot. This leaves a thin coat of wax over the inside of the mold. After a short cooling period the pouring and sloshing is repeated. The same steps are taken again and again until a light quarter of an inch of wax is built up. The mold was removable piece by piece. When removed I had a hollow one quarter of an inch thick wax copy of my clay model. This wax copy was to be duplicated in Bronze.

I attached, by using a hot knife, wax runners welded, on one end, to the inside of the wax bust, and joined on the other to a large, one inch diameter, vertical runner surmounted with a sprue, which looked like a large ice cream cone. My plan was to have no sprue attachments to the outside of the bronze, requiring cleanup and grinding in the bronze. It was also in the plan to use the one inch vertical runner, when cast in bronze with the sprue cut off, to firmly anchor the bust to the granite pedestal. It was required that I make some special tools to work down inside of the bust. I was enabled to make the connections, through the lower open end of the bust, and proceed.

I filled the inside of the bust with the investment mold mixture of water with silica flour, plaster of Paris and fire clay, burying the runners out of sight, and establishing the core of the investment mold for the bronze casting. The mold material sets normally like cement or plaster and forms a refractory material that can take the heat of the molten metal. Using the same mixture I built up layers of refractory on the outside of the wax. After a couple of thick layers I wrapped the mold in chicken wire, and applied two more thick coats of my mold mixture. The chicken wire was for mechanical strength and to assure that the mold did not break open from expansion under 2150 degrees of melted bronze,

So far we have a great big mold enclosing a wax sculpture. Normally I would have set a mold up in a fifty gallon steel drum, put some water in the drum, turned on the gas heat, and steamed the mold until the wax drained out. For this mold I had a steel working company in Salinas make a special tank over four times the size of the regular drum. I had piped the mold with quarter inch copper tubing. The tubing was connected to a drain through the side of the tank. Using steam heat I drained the mold of all wax.

Following the above the mold had to be dried and cured for five to six hours at twelve hundred degrees temperature. In anticipation I had already built an extra large electric kiln below the floor level of the studio.

The operation was scheduled so that the mold was cured during the time required to melt the bronze. I had provided two overhead electric cranes in the installation. With one crane the hot dry mold was removed from the electric kiln, and set up on the sand floor of the pouring pit. With the other crane the crucible filled with one hundred pounds of molten bronze was removed from the gas fired furnace and placed in a pouring shank.

The pouring shank was a heavy duty steel contraption built to accept and clamp the hot crucible. It was swung on a crane hook, and provided the operator, who was me, two convenient handles for pouring the bronze into the sprue of the mold. In this case the bronze flowed smoothly in and drew down into the sprue as it cooled. It was time to be elated that the deed was done with success. With the relax of tension, Marge joined me in a suitable dance on the studio floor.

The following day when the mold had cooled and cracked with cooling I broke it in pieces away from the bronze within. I was elated as I uncovered the shining metal and saw come into view the permanent features of a man important to many living contemporaries and to the history of the California coast. I dug the mold material from the inside of the bust and sand blasted the outside until it shown like gold in the studio light.

I meditated as I worked on how form is a fundamental concept. Materials including living tissue have little meaning until they take on meaningful form. In its relationship to human life form expresses the spirit within. I was glad that my work as a sculptor was to sit in a public park, and speak of a man that was a leader on the spiritual side of building a human community, speak to his old friends and generations to come. I handled the bust with affection as I cleaned it up and gave it a patina, using suitable acids, mixed in water, brushed on and manipulated in the flame of a torch.

After I cut away the sprue I had a bust ready for mounting on the granite pedestal. I had provided the Raymond quarries in the High Sierra mountains the monument dimensions, and arranged for them to supply two slabs of black granite, each weighing approximately a thousand pounds. One slab, a square, was to lay flat in a concrete bed, the other was to stand vertically anchored to it with stainless steel pins set in matching cement-grouted holes in both pieces.

In the top of the vertical slab of granite we drilled a deep two inch hole to receive the one inch square vertical runner, as described above, attached to the inside of the bust. At the time of the on-site assembly, which I personally handled, the large hole in the granite was filled with cement grout. The bust was placed in position with its long stem, vertical runner, buried in the grout, to hold the bust in position forever?.

As I was working on this installation of stone and metal a construction watcher, probably fifty years old himself, spoke up and said, "When you gonna unveil it dad?" I thought I was pretty young to be called dad by this character.

However, it was a good question. In due time the committee responsible arranged an unveiling ceremony: I untied the cords, dropped the curtains and behold! Pietro Ferranti belonged to the ages. Appropriate speeches were delivered to applauding people of the waterfront and, following that, those of us on the inside of the proceedings retired to a testimonial lunch.

And then there was Pelican Joe: When I lived in Gates Mills I had some winter vacations in Florida and I fished and fished. There was a pelican that showed up more than one year with an obvious liking for me or my boat. He would join me daily and go where my boat went. I really think it was the food that attracted him.

He was not like other pelicans. His feet were stubs without the flexible material between his toes. Marge and I concluded that he had gone north in the winter and stayed too long, and got his feet frozen. He could not fish so easily with his pals. He sat on my boat as I cut up bait fish and gave him pieces. On one occasion I was sitting on the middle seat of my boat, intent on fishing, when I felt something from behind come over my shoulder, and as I turned my head I was looking into a pelican's eye. His beak was over my shoulder and lying against my chest looking me in the eye saying," Please, some fish."

I witnessed changes in that pelican, an increasing trust in Marge and me, probably some affection. In time he made himself at home, and during that time Marge and I named him pelican Joe. We acquired an affection for him, and, at last, in Carmel Valley, from old photographs, I made an over-life-seize bronze of him that won first prize at the fair. Later I modeled him with his beak up with a fish in his mouth, and I made him again half life size. Many people loved Pelican Joe, and expressed their sentiments by buying copies at, I hope, reasonable prices.

Living creatures, of course, were to be a large part of my stock in trade. Dolphins, hippos, owls, eagles, horses, dogs, and cats were added to my repertoire of human figures torsos , ballerinas, portraits, etc. Studying the animals

always caused me to wonder what they were thinking as they
posed for me. Particularly looking into their eyes. Pelican
Joe did not have the equipment to make a bronze of me, but I
wonder if he missed me after I went to California. They too
have an intelligence and feelings.

There was a sculpture portrait of a particular dog that I
did on commission. The dog posed for me like a human. she
did drool for the dog biscuits I kept on the modelling
stand. Her name was Gretchen. I became so convinced of the
dogs humanness that I made a bronze copy for my own
collection and did the head in Marble also. I affixed my
sentiments in Japanese haiku as follows;

> Looking, the dog asks,
> Are you living in my house,
> Or am I in yours.

Becoming known, and forming Friendships, took place rapidly
through a common interest with collectors of sculpture and
painting and the abundance of artists, craftsmen and gallery
owners. My studio, for its unusual facilities became a
curiosity that many called on the telephone and asked to
see. I was always glad to accommodate and explain the
processes and display my sometimes unique equipment. I
confess to liking to talk about what I considered my
creation.

The Monterey Museum of Art had my place on a list of studios
to visit for a price on visiting day. The museum supplied
the docents. On one occasion there were eight hundred and
fifty visitors on a single day. I want to say for the
visitors who came, not a single thing was damaged or
trampled by the stream of people. They came and went with
sincere and respectful interest.

It was easy to become known with such exposure, and
rewarding to make friends with the type of people that came.
Over the years coming to my studios, the painting and
modelling one and the bronze art foundry and workshop, has
been called a field trip by some of the local educational
organizations. I have enjoyed talking to the visitors. Also
I have been on the local lecture circuit and have given
slide lecture talks to all the various clubs, the Rotaries
for example, and retirement community meetings on the
peninsula. Due to a large telescope these talks have
included astronomy as a companion of the arts.

Not too much can be said about the friendships formed
through art work. The common interest in such a rewarding
subject creates a warmth back and forth between the artist
and his client that grows and widens beyond the narrowness
of a single subject that originated it. The empathic

relationships that have grown over the years here in
California are the best part of the whole procession.

The foreign travel that we began from Cleveland we continued
and repeated after moving to Carmel. I never took a vacation
trip without carrying along water colors, paper and brushes.
We also practiced language to improve our contacts with the
people of other cultures. We took a trip around the world
immediately after retiring from engineering and business
management. Nearly all our trips from Carmel Valley took us
back into old friendship situations in other countries. In
1992 I wrote an essay entitled "Speak and Be Heard." to
illustrate how speaking the language can open doors that
stay open for years to come.

That essay bridges the gap between time before our arrival
in Carmel Valley and five years after. Over many years we
visited Japan numerous times; Egypt, Greece, Iran, Burma,
India, Syria, and all the European and Scandinavian
countries more than once, and then to China. And, of course,
painting trips in our contiguous United States and Hawaii
many times. Instead of detailing these trips I shall let
that essay give the flavor of our approach to travel, and
our good fortune with favorable response in foreign
countries. Following is the essay.

SPEAK AND BE HEARD

As I entered the Board Room, I was astonished to see twelve
men sitting around the long mahogany table with wires
apparently coming out of their ears. Each man was connected
from his right ear by wire to the right ear of the man next
in line from chair to chair around the table.

In the seat nearest the head of the table was one man not
wired by his ear. He held a microphone in his hand to which
the wire connecting the dozen ears was attached. All were
Japanese visitors; the man nearest the head of the table
with the microphone was their interpreter. I was there as
president of the company to extend a welcome to this
delegation of corporation executives, that had come over
from Japan to observe and record any technical or
organization knowhow they encountered in several Cleveland
electrical manufacturing companies, which information they
thought might be applicable in their own companies.

All the men looked tired or bored, but I only had to start
my talk with "Nippon no tomadachi" (Japanese friends) and
their faces brightened. After a few more words in Japanese,
they removed the ear pieces, and smiled with delight. Such
is the power of hearing one's own language spoken when one
is abroad in a foreign country.

But such also can be a power for the speaker of a foreign tongue when he is abroad in that land. Knowing even a small vocabulary of foreign words, and only a bit of skill with the grammar, can change one's status from just a tourist, who meets only hotel clerks, taxi drivers, busboys, and other professionals in their line of duties, into a welcomed guest in the lives and homes of ordinary citizens, and can lead to warm and lasting friendships.

I recall once in Syria, I had learned by rote to say in their language "Good morning , it's a nice day, and thank you very much," I spoke these words to a Syrian taking his son for a visit to a classical ruin. He responded by introducing his son and inviting my wife and me to his home for homemade yogurt. The yogurt was curing in an enormous bowl sitting in the sun out-of-doors in a courtyard. Except possibly for a fly here and there, it was very special yogurt that could have persuaded me to regularly indulge. The members of his family were numerous: his wife, her parents, and other people. Having no further knowledge of the language, we did not learn their relationship to the family, but all made us warmly welcome. The few words we had learned paid big dividends.

My wife and I knew many more than a few words of Japanese, and our reward in Japan was greater than a dish of yogurt and an hour of pleasant visiting. The better we did our homework on the language of any prospective country, the more numerous and deeper were our intimate contacts with representative people of the land.

Early on in the days of our traveling we decided to know some words or phrases in the current languages of any projected itinerary. "Living Language" tapes and their language guide books were the means to accomplish this end. We used a tape recorder that had the advantage that it could be stopped at any point and reversed for instant replay.

Native speakers clearly pronounced what we were reading in the instruction books; we repeated after them, stopped and reversed the tape, and did the act over and over until we retained most of what we practiced.

As an additional learning tool, we prepared white cardboard signs exhibiting boldly lettered phrases that we displayed at strategic locations in our house, including, of course, the bathrooms and even the garage. These signs were valuable reinforcements in our attack on the language of the day. Almost unconsciously, we found ourselves reading aloud these signs as we passed them in our normal movement about the premises.

This system of home education did not make us fluent in all the languages we studied, but we learned a number of useful

phrases and a limited ability to create and understand
simple sentences needed in travel situations.

The charm of things Oriental, and the unique interpretation
put upon these things in Japan caused us to extend and
repeat our visits there, and learn the language better,
including colloquialisms which bring out especially the
style of Japanese thinking and feeling. For example, when a
Japanese says, "Arigato gozaimasu" he is thanking you, but
the literal translation of the two words is, "It is
difficult." He is recognizing the enormity of what you are
doing for him. When he wishes to express his pleasure at
having met you he uses words from his language which
literally say, "For the first time I hang upon your
honorable eyes."

We became, for a period, quite proficient in Japanese, and
that, among other related cultural exchanges, led to
friendships that forty years later are warm and sincere and
have been extended to a second generation. Several of the
children of our old friends in Japan have visited me here in
Carmel Valley, California. Others now live in this country
and come by with greater frequency. We also learned to
communicate quite well in German, and have had the same
experience of developing lasting friendships in Germany and
Switzerland.

It had been seven years since our last trip to Japan;
Expo70, the Japanese world's fair in Kita Osaka, was in the
news. We decided it would be a good time to see some old
friends with a good show thrown in. Hotel reservations were
becoming scarce. I wrote to Mr. Mogi in Tokyo and Mr Nabari
in Suita City, near Osaka, and asked them to help with
accommodations. I was not prepared for what happened.

The manner of our reunion was divided into two parts: first
a reception in Osaka by Mr. Nabari, and entertainment and
assistance there, and, after a few days of Expo70, our
movement to Kyoto and three days of fun and games with a
host of new and old friends.

Takanori Nabari was one of the twelve that were mentioned in
the first paragraph of this article. Now in his home, and as
CEO of an electric manufacturing company, he radiated
hospitality as he performed all the actions of a gracious
host.

For several days Nabari loaned his secretary to be our
special guide at the Expo70. She was most helpful and
charming; over our protests that it was not necessary, she
came to our hotel room each morning with the day's
activities all planned. Her name was Etsuko. It is
interesting that Etsu means joy and rapture in Japanese. The
"ko" is on the end of nearly all girl names in Japan; it is

a diminutive, an endearment. Her name would translate as Joy, with endearment in the mind of the translator, and that was appropriate: she cared for our every need with manifest joy.

We were entertained for cocktails and dinner at the Nabari home among several Japanese couples invited to meet their honored guests. All the ladies were in their beautiful kimonos, and we ate at tables on the floor in traditional Japanese style. The word perfection comes to mind. Friendships seem to be a natural byproduct of an interest one shows in the culture and language of the host country.

The Expo70 Fair was magnificent and, in looking back upon its demonstration of Japanese genius and determination reflected in it, was a harbinger of the industrial expansion to come and the miracle growth of their economy.

My time was up in Osaka, I called Mr. Kusai in Kyoto to ask about a reservation he had made for me, and mentioned that I was coming to Kyoto the next day. He said, "No you are not. Please stay at your hotel; we wish to pick you up there." The following morning six men in two cars drove over from Kyoto to Osaka and accomplished that purpose.

We arrived in Kyoto around noon, and went directly to a restaurant which boasted of having a couple of "world famous" tempura and sushi "masters;" Masters or no, the sushi and tempura were delightful.

Following lunch, we attended the afternoon performance of the Miyako Odori, which translates literally the Capital Dance, but is spoken of colloquially as the Spring dance, or, when it's not spring, as the Dance of the Four Seasons. The dance is performed at the Gion Corner theater which belongs to the training school for professional geisha girls. One must be a junior or senior in the school to perform.

The dance is extravagant in the number of dancers, the costuming, stage settings, and choreography. Words like fantastic, exquisite, and even incredible, would be needed in comments as one observes the perfect display of dignified but captivating sensuality of these dancers.

During the dance Mr. Kusai, with whispers close to my ear, commented on the dancing; I responded a few times by directing his attention to some particular dancers. To my surprise, My references influenced Mr. Kusai,s selection of entertainers at dinner that same evening.

Dinner was at the Doi Inn in Kyoto. The Inn was a charming expression of Japanese style, with several connected buildings wandering up a hillside in an extensive garden. In the inn, the principle customs of living, eating and sleeping, were accomplished sitting or lying on the floor.

The establishment was private; nonmembers were welcome only as guests of members. Their Japanese gardens were artistic creations, expertly planned and attended. The buildings gave off the impression of having been carved in mahogany and cedar and kept well polished over the years to produce an at home feeling loved by the Japanese. Feeling at home proved to be easy in their well appointed guest quarters.

After a couple hours rest, there was a knock on our door. Our personal maid was there to guide us to dinner and what proved to be a celebration. The room we entered was suitable for a banquet, but practically empty of furniture except for three large floor tables. We were arriving after all the other guests had been seated; the tables were full except for two seats open at the head table for "Mr. Hoge" and "Mrs. Hoge", it said on the place cards.

An exciting and pleasant surprise at our table was the smiling faces of the twelve men that I had encountered years before, wired for sound in my board room, in Cleveland, Ohio. The impact of deja vu was terrific; there was an element of family reunion, planned to be that way. We welcomed each other with repeated bows that evolved eventually into American style handshaking and a few hugs.

The party beginning was the first of two earnest large ones to be held in this room on consecutive nights. The sponsors from around Tokyo wished to host one and those in the Kyoto area the other. Some of each group had been to Cleveland and others I had met in diverse situations in Japan. There appeared to be a friendly competition as to which group might entertain best the guests they seemed determined to celebrate. They gave us two hospitable evenings of special entertainment.

Japanese are notably serious workers, but the men play with almost the eagerness of children. It is well known that their parties are stag; Marge, my wife, was the only woman guest at the celebration. Geisha girls were hired for entertainment. The girls are educated and specially trained to entertain. They recite long classical stories, they play their samasens and kotos, they dance, smile, sing and keep your sake cup filled to the brim. They definitely are not, what might be referred to euphemistically in Paris as, ladies of the evening.

The gentlemen had spared no cost; the geishas come at a high price. That the girls looked familiar was a real surprise. When one took up her position at my right elbow, and commenced to fill my cup with the warm rice wine, I recognized her. She was a girl that I had pointed out to Mr.

Kusai at the Miyako Odori that very same afternoon. This was
when I realized that they had hired a portion of the girls
from the Miyako Odori; with musical instruments and all
their talent they came to entertain us in style.

I shall pass up telling of the wonderful food we had with
Kobe beef and much much more, and get on with some mention
of the amusements including games in which the guests
participated. Someone had been tipped off that I had
memorized the "Oboro Ni" which is a Kabuki song that tells
of the young Samurai warrior who is away in a distant land,
sorrowfully dreaming of his geisha girl in the Higashi Yama
(Eastern Mountains) district of Kyoto, and much about the
moon coming up over the mountains, and how beautiful was his
kimono clad girl in the moonlight .

They had brought in a Samurai dress uniform, including the
sword. I was required to step into a side room and dress as
Samurai. I was then escorted to the stage where two girls
stood beside me playing small stringed instruments. A girl
sat on the floor playing a koto (Japanese harp that needs to
lie down) and the music of the "Oboro Ni" began. I attempted
to sing in the kabuki style of distorting one's voice, and
being very throaty. I will not comment on how well I did;
that didn't matter. There was much applause and calls for an
encore, but what else could they do?--we accommodated--what
else should we do?

To suitable music we marched single file through the lovely
Japanese Garden and through the hotel. Probably the rice
wine made a contribution, songs were sung and some rather
silly games were played, but it was all good clean fun.

Art brushes were provided, and black ink was ground and
mixed, by a couple of Geishas, on the little sloping stones.
It was surprising how many of these business men were
proficient in Sumi E painting. I had practiced quite a lot
in my studio, and got by rather well when it was my turn
before the audience.

I also did a quick portrait of my beautiful geisha helper,
and gave it to her. She gave it back to me and said "Give it
to me again and say, "keep this always."--and that I did.

The evening went on into the night where we finally finished
by singing (what else?) Auld Lang Syne.

During free hours of the day there were Ofuros, (honorable
hot baths) that were almost rituals, walks in small groups
through the gardens, and afternoon visits with refreshments.

Eventually it was time to leave. I went to the cashier's
desk to pay my bill, and was informed that it had been paid,
and that tipping was not allowed. As we left the hotel by

taxi, some of our friends were there to see us off. Joined by some of the hotel personnel, they moved into the driveway as we pulled out, and waved goodbye to us until we were out of sight. Marge remarked, "They are just like us sending the kids back to college after a visit home." At the railroad station I could not pay the driver; he too had been prepaid.

This entire visit was an experience to remember. Not all, but I believe much of what developed then and over the years had its roots in our determination to speak the language. Sayonara, Oyasumi nasai. (Goodbye, and have a good rest.) End of essay.

On this trip I only found time to do a water color of a very old banyan tree which I have the pleasure of looking at as I write this. So with many of my paintings, I, according to plan, still have them. For painting sales I kept only one outlet in Carmel, Beach's Gallery, and a fine small Gallery in Carmel Valley Known as Mrs. Wilson's. The world famous Donald Teague would annually win the gold at the American Water Color Society Show in New York, and give its first post New York showing at Mrs. Wilson's. I felt honored to be in such company showing and selling for me. Most of my paintings I did not want to sell they became and remain memorabilia.

From the time we arrived in our Southwestern home until Marge's health problems slowed us down in the late nineteen eighties we traveled the scenic highways of California and visited its wonderful state parks and resorts. As though it were our own grand pass, we would, in season, head for Tioga Pass in Yosemite, and drive over into the High Sierra country, and go south to Death Valley or North to Lake Tahoe and on up to fish the feather River country. There was so much to see in our new home from the Lassen Volcanic National Park to sequoia National to Kings Canyon and on south to the Salton Sea and over to Borrego Springs. We lived not in Carmel Valley but in California. The whole state was our front yard.

I painted pictures of the deserts, the mountains, the ocean and the country in between. I also painted the live oaks of the coastal areas, and was careful not to sell what was wanted for our collection. To this day the pictures I kept in a personal collection, with sculptures, are comforting voices from the past that seem perfectly at home in the present.

I have a strange feeling that I am moving up on myself today, and I wonder at what point will the writing, take its own head and become current events. The loss of Marge is very much on my mind as I write these lines. Marge was an expert potter, a gourmet cook, a person who loved people and whom people loved. Our social and personal life was fun, but it was serious with a host of warm and sincere friends, some with whom I now feel like family in their presence, where reciprocal love is strongly felt. At our fiftieth wedding anniversary there were at least one hundred close friends in addition to family present. Invitations were not sent to just acquaintances. That was a high point of significance in our life. We were grateful that coming to California with such high hopes had been and was a success beyond our fondest dreams. The modest party was a grand symbol of what life is all about.

During 1980 Marge's Asthma began slowly to restrict our actions but we kept up a satisfying life style with wheel chairs in airports, a few simple medications and some personal care. On a trip to China during 1980 we noticed the restraints. I had to carry Marge up steps in airports and she had a few acute attacks of her ailment. I will not detail this period we were happy living together and with our many friends. It did come, a period of crisis where I was a care taker and Marge a patient. It was a serious period of two years where emergencies succeeded emergencies. Wasn't it a terrible time? No. It could have been but not with Marge. I never saw a tear or heard a complaint; As the emergencies passed she was happy for having had such a good life, such a "wonderful" family and so many loving friends. She insisted it was time to rejoice in looking back upon the life that was ending as she knew it would.

I had lived with the lady for nearly sixty years and still I had to learn of the really wonderful person she was as I saw her "approach her grave as one who wraps the draperies of his couch about him and lies down to pleasant dreams." Our love transcended what had gone before. I do not look back upon this two year care taking period as a hardship. I consider it a privilege to have seen Marge so close up and realize the reality of the spirit and the presence of God within. It was a season of the sincerest love of our lives. In addition she made me proud of her and of humanity in crisis. I want to end this paragraph with the last stanza of a poem I wrote for "This and That"
"Miss you? yes dear, I'm sure I do
But I have an antidote for sadness:
The legacy I got from you,
Your love, your joy,your gladness."

On one occasion when Marge had a crisis, and we had rushed her by ambulance to the hospital, her condition was diagnosed as immediately terminal. With special treatment she revived and was discharged several days later. The morning after her return home I was fixing her breakfast and she sat smiling almost as if she were laughing at all the excitement we had just been through. She looked at me and gave me a special sweet smile that I can see as write. Then her expression changed, her eyes flashed, not in fear, but with complete surprise. She said, "I can't breathe." I caught her as she collapsed at the kitchen table. That was the end and those were her last words. I even recall that finality, always in memory of that heart felt smile on her face just minutes before.

I have spoken in this autobiography about three careers. The manuscript has brought me up against the near termination of the third one of these. It was a "we" program. On December the second nineteen eighty eight a significant part of the meaning went out of it.

It was almost like beginning a fourth career as an individual. In that career I have been writing, painting and living life somewhat as an extension of what was manifest before. This came out as my "Thoughts on This and That," sent in the form of essays and poetry, at intervals, to a mailing list of friends. Some of these writings were published by Alta Vista Magazine. And now this autobiography, I am writing close to current events, which are not usually the subject material for autobiography.

I feel with Tennyson's Ulysses,
"I am a part of all I have met;
Yet all experience is an arch wherethro'
Gleams the untraveled world..."
"Though much is taken, much abides; and though
We are not now that strength which in old days
Moved earth and Heaven, that which we are, we are;
One equal temper of heroic hearts,
Made weak by time and fate, but strong in will
To strive, to seek, to find, and not to yield."
But "...To ,follow knowledge like a sinking star,
Beyond the utmost bound of human thought."

BELLE-HAMPTON

All proceeds go towards preserving the art of Robert H. Hoge.

To learn more about the rich history of Belle-Hampton and the founder's ancestors, contact the owners through social media or our contact page.

www.ingramcontent.com/pod-product-compliance
Lightning Source LLC
Chambersburg PA
CBHW051827160426
43209CB00033B/1941/J